The Stone of the Plough

Ann Walker is a practising clairvoyant and medium and, even though she describes herself as an 'ordinary housewife and mother', she has been described by the *Daily Mirror* as the 'next Doris Stokes'. She lives near London with her husband and family.

by the same author

Little One – Message from Planet Heaven
Heaven Can Come Later

The Stone of the
· Plough ·

THE SEARCH FOR THE SECRET OF GIZA

Ann Walker

ELEMENT
Shaftesbury, Dorset ● Rockport, Massachusetts
Brisbane, Queensland

First published in Great Britain in 1997 by
Element Books Limited
Shaftesbury, Dorset SP7 8BP

Published in the USA in 1997 by
Element Books, Inc.
PO Box 830, Rockport, MA 01966

Published in Australia in 1997 by
Element Books Limited
for Jacaranda Wiley Limited
33 Park Road, Milton, Brisbane 4064

Cover illustration by Paul Allen
Cover design by Bridgewater Book Company
Design by Roger Lightfoot
Typeset by WestKey Limited, Falmouth, Cornwall

Printed and bound in Great Britain by
Hartnalls, Bodmin, Cornwall

British Library Cataloguing in Publication
data available
Library of Congress Cataloging in Publication
data available

Hardback ISBN 1–86204–082–6
Paperback ISBN 1–85230–937–7

· Contents ·

Part Three

Preface

To those who believe in God, no explanation is necessary.
To those who do not believe, no explanation is possible.

A Message to the World

I was so taken aback with all the miracles on this journey that, initially, I had to blank them out. That is, to accept them at face value, then put them to the back of my mind and get on with White Arrow's work. This was the only way I could deal with the full enormity of all that I was experiencing. Miracles operate beyond our normal understanding, and I have witnessed an ongoing stream of them!

Please do not think that I am ungrateful or blasé about the wonders and the holy Presence I have been privileged to witness. I will never be able to thank God, White Arrow and the aliens enough for the wondrous gifts they have lovingly bestowed. The whole reason for these writings is to bring their message to the world.

I am solely their voice and witness, and my first duty is to tell the world of their coming. God's love is coming to our tortured, sick world. This is the greatest love and the greatest gift humanity has ever known.

I give thanks every day for the blessings I have been shown. That makes me sound a bit religious, though it is actually an expression of simple human awe and rapture. I have never been a religious person and know little about organized systems of worship. White Arrow says all worship is good. Religion is humanity's word, faith is God's word.

White Arrow has always been a kind, gentle and good being. He is a Native American of the Spirit, full of warmth and compassion – and a sense of humour. On this journey, I have been gently shown who White Arrow truly is, and what his mission is on Earth. I already instinctively trusted him with my life, before I knew who he was. He has always honoured my free will to choose – to choose to accept or to deny him. Choice has always been offered to me every step of the way. These choices have not actually been difficult, for I simply held by my choice to trust rather than to doubt.

Never have White Arrow or the aliens *demanded* anything of me. I have had my struggles, yet I have followed this journey wholeheartedly. There are not enough words to describe the feeling-tones involved when I fully came to realize who I was working for – when I allowed it finally to sink in! I may never know why I was chosen for this, but, by the same token, that is not for me to question.

I must keep to my task, which is to prove to you, to mankind, that White Arrow speaks truth only – and he gives proof and verification too. That is my work. What you make of this miraculous journey is your choice.

White Arrow has been here to help us on Earth many times before. He now comes again. He and the aliens come from the Highest. They come in boundless love, for the sole purpose of helping us. Everything I tell of and reveal is carried out in compassion, goodness and in the knowledge of God.

So please, no matter how unusual the events unfolding in these pages may seem, do give them full consideration. Look and learn: without this knowledge there is no help for us. We humans have shown that we cannot help ourselves.

I, Ann Walker, am a relatively ordinary woman who also works clairvoyantly with the Spirit. I have been chosen to pass the message of White Arrow and his friends to the world. Be sceptical if you wish, but these words are true. They will be verified and proven. Please listen. It might be that you find yourself in a position to help White Arrow to help us, humanity. May we all live to see a better Earth. May we deserve it!

QRESTUAE PQULLE
In the knowledge of God

Ann Walker

Please note: certain pieces of information and drawings have by necessity been excluded from the book. This is because we wish to respect the rights of the Egyptian government, guardians of the pyramids, and to prevent investigators engaging in a potentially destructive get-there-first onslaught on the pyramids and their environs. As White Arrow points out later in the book, release of the full information and evidence awaits the correct time. Apologies for this; it is a wise and necessary step in current conditions.

Acknowledgements

The following people have played an invaluable role in helping me with my Egypt journeys.

Hala Askar: My eternal gratitude and love for her devotion to helping me on my road and for her devotion to White Arrow. She is an expert in her field and an expert guide. And to her family for their help and understanding.

Abdel Hakim Awayan: Many thanks and gratitude for his knowledge and guidance in the translations of the drawings and for his devotion to White Arrow. He is a man with great wisdom and knowledge who is known worldwide.

Fergany al Komaty: My eternal gratitude for his help at the Great Pyramid of Giza. Again, he is an expert in his field. Without such help the journey would have been more difficult.

Sheban Helmi Mohamed Serug: The holy man of Saqqara, whose faith and devotion has gone beyond humankind, for his help in helping White Arrow.

Valerie Smith: For her support on my journeys. Also, gratitude to her family for the faith they have shown in allowing her to be with me during these journeys.

François Dumonteil-Lagreze: François has always been there to help with the languages. Without him, my journey would have been impossible.

James Stephenson-Ward – artist: My eternal gratitude for his faith and devotion to White Arrow.

Adrian Gilbert: For his information, interpretations of star-patterns and encouragement.

Palden Jenkins: To whom I owe thanks for his fine work in editing this book and in giving support.

Francine Prince: My eternal thanks to her for her support and knowledge of Egypt which encouraged me greatly.

To all these people I offer my eternal thanks.

My eternal love and gratitude to **my husband and children** for their faith in White Arrow, for without their support this journey would not be possible.

Part One

· 1 ·

Indians and Aliens

'I helped to build the pyramids! I helped to build the pyramids!' The chant seemed to draw me back from the incredible visions I was experiencing during my fast inside the tipi. I was undergoing a 'test of worth' for the Indian spiritual elders.

'I helped build the pyramids!' the voice exclaimed again. My eyes started to focus on the shape speaking in front of me. It was Bear, one of the aliens who had become my friends since I had started this incredible journey. I listened quietly while he spoke. 'I built the pyramids,' I heard him say. I looked at him. 'I was there when they were being built. I helped.'

How old is he? I wondered. I did not doubt him – how could I? It was just that it sounded like something beyond the limits of credibility. White Arrow then spoke. 'While you slept, Little One, we came. You died and became alive again. You were reborn. We returned your gifts. Use them wisely! I will show you how to use them as you go forth into the future. Bear will be with you on your journey to Egypt. Go to him, for he will take you forward.'

Then Bear said, 'I will show you the keys to open the pyramid doors. That is why I have been chosen for this journey, to show you the secrets of the pyramids, for the sake of the world. For through God I left many secrets, to be given at the right time. That time is now near. I have much to show and teach you before we enter the Pyramid of Giza.'

It seemed as if I had been talking to them for hours before the light of day appeared. Bear's revealing messages and guidelines would help me on the next part of my journey. This journey had so far taken me to meet the Assiniboine Indians in Montana and the Mandan Hidatsa Arikara Indians in North Dakota, USA, far from my home in England. The next phase would be in Egypt.

White Arrow and his father were also present in the medicine wheel. I had been left there to fast. However, this was no ordinary Red Indian and his father. They were of the Spirit – and of the Highest. They were here in answer to the prayers of a world in torment, and its people of all nations. Through their holy love and with our faith they are here to help save it.

I am no Red Indian warrior undergoing this test of Spirit. I am Ann Walker, on the face of it an ordinary woman – a rather ordinary person in a very extraordinary situation. All this may seem bizarre, and it is. Yet, here I was, on sacred Native American ground, in the company of the most Holy and High in the Universe, and White Arrow. They have heard Earth's cry for help and have come here once more, in answer to our prayers. They have brought help from other galaxies – help in the form of aliens who have also heard of our plight and have travelled light-years to help us, when it seems we either cannot or will not help ourselves. They all come with love and compassion.

I will tell you their names, since you will be hearing quite a bit about them in this book. Zipper, Alien Girl (real name Joyzet) and Michael are all from the same planet. Bear (also known as Akas), from further away, has travelled the furthest. Then there is Eagle (Zupuital). All of these I came to know, trust and love over a period of three years.

However, if you are to understand anything of this, I must take you back to the beginning. I am a practising clairvoyant. For the past 16 years I have been honoured to know White Arrow, a Red Indian of the Spirit, whose unconditional love, guidance, patience and wisdom has helped me and thousands of others with their problems. In 1980, White Arrow showed me seven very simple symbols (*see* figure 1.1) which he told me were very important. They held the keys to the start of a great journey which he wanted me to undertake, to help him help humanity.

White Arrow told me to send the symbols to the spiritual elders of a Native American tribe in Montana, which I did. In 1991, at the invitation of the elders, I travelled to Montana to meet them. They told me that the symbols White Arrow had given me were sacred. The symbols held messages for the world, known only to the spiritual elders of their tribe. Before they could give me any more information on the symbols I would have to prove to them that I was with White Arrow the Spirit and not one of many others who

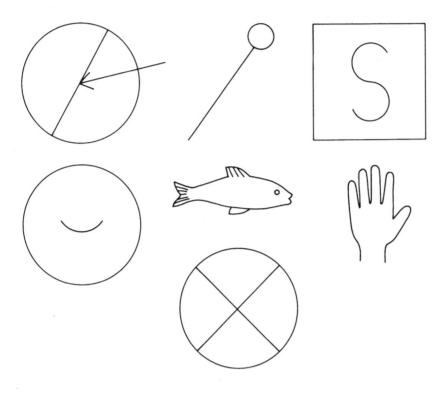

Figure 1.1 White Arrow's seven symbols

have misled and mistreated this noble race of people. So there was I, a London housewife, undergoing their sacred fast.

At that time I had no idea just how important the journey was to be. I was taking the first steps on an incredible journey of trials, revelations, tests and discoveries which would reveal White Arrow's true identity, his purpose on Earth. His purpose is to help humanity unlock great mysteries hidden for centuries from human eyes – hidden until the time was right. He is to give proof of the truth he speaks. According to White Arrow, the time is coming very soon for these mysteries to be revealed. The people of Earth need to know, for in knowing the mysteries we can truly listen and act on his words.

Why should *I* have been chosen to carry his message? I have no idea. Only God knows the reason. The fact remains that, knowing White Arrow as I do, and trusting him implicitly, I accepted gladly and without hesitation when he asked me to undertake this journey to help him help us. I knew his purpose was loving. He sought to forewarn us of the dire consequences to mankind if we do not heed the warning he brings. If we listen we can avoid a global disaster and the impact of a lethal cometary fragment due in the year 2042. If we do not listen, I shudder to think of the result.

The full story of the American journey and the predictions he and the aliens have revealed for our future are fully catalogued in my previous book *Little One – Message from Planet Heaven* (Century/Arrow, 1994). White Arrow speaks only truth. I assert this from my own experience, and my books offer you the option to judge for yourselves. He will give irrefutable proof of his existence and his message to the world. Indeed, if I had known of the magnitude and consequence of my part in this whole thing I would have asked for somebody else to be given the job! But White Arrow already knew the magnitude of the journey and kindly revealed only as much as he thought I could bear at any time – not that I was exactly underworked!

I mean no disrespect by making light of things – it is just that if I were to try to bear the enormous burden of the information unfolding to me without releasing my apprehension through laughter, I would surely falter or go insane! There may be some of you out there who are already treating this whole thing as very far-fetched. I do not blame you! That is your choice, and free will is our divine gift.

However, do read these words with an open mind. For I believe you will come to see, slowly and surely, that the words I speak for White Arrow are true. What you think of me does not really matter: if any of you were yourselves telling me this story, I too would probably find it hard to credit! Yet I can only repeat what I have witnessed. I pray that you take heed of the warnings and give consideration to the proof that White Arrow gives you, through me.

Now, let me return to my story. The first part of the journey, to America, was complete. White Arrow then instructed me to go to Egypt. Apparently there were things there of great importance which he was to show me – things which would further demonstrate the urgency of his message.

So we begin. White Arrow and the aliens had told me that the time for them and their message to the world would be coming soon. My work, should I accept the journey, would be to gather concrete proof of the truth of their message and to establish beyond all doubt that they are who they say they are – of God and from God, with love and concern in their hearts for us, the human race. God has heard the Earth's prayers and has sent help – though perhaps not the help that we, in our vanity, might expect! No, something far greater than we could expect. Looking round at our treatment of our own planetary home, this is something more than we perhaps deserve.

White Arrow's and the aliens' Report on the World Condition (given in *Little One*) was astounding enough. Now, Bear was here in the medicine wheel, telling me that he had helped to build the pyramids! This, just as I was trying to get used to all the events happening in America! How can *anyone* get used to *this*? Sometimes, when it was all getting a bit overwhelming, I tried to step back from it, to get back to 'reality' – shopping, family meetings, everyday things. I found that when my trepidation got too great, humour, family and friends comforted me and gave me renewed courage. How else would I deal with the huge adventure ahead?

I can now tell you that the aliens, Bear and Eagle, were present in Egypt when the pyramids were erected. The parts they played in this elaborate mystery will unfold as all the pieces of the journey come together into a bigger, rather awesome elucidation of White Arrow's work. This clarifies who he is and outlines the watchful presence of our alien friends.

But for now, back to the journey – the second phase of it. So we begin . . .

· 2 ·

A Meeting Out in Space

Back from America, at home in London, it was good to be with my husband Tony and our family again. The feeling of having my feet back on the ground was a great relief. America went well, but the work over here would have to continue. I had to chronicle the events I had experienced with White Arrow and the aliens.

It was 7 January 1993. White Arrow wanted me to return to the spacecraft – the aliens' operations base in their interactions with us on Earth. They took me there occasionally for discussions and experiences. This was a form of travel which seemed to render space shuttles cumbersomely obsolete. As I sat and waited for them I wondered if this visit to their craft had anything to do with Egypt. Perhaps this time they might show me around the inside of the ship – so far, I had only seen certain parts of the interior. I would have to wait and see.

Suddenly, I was on board the ship. There was no journey involved, just a kind of translocation. I was in a room in darkness, yet I felt White Arrow's presence around me. I knew he was there. There were three bay windows at the far end of the room, running from floor to ceiling. It was the room where White Arrow's father sits. I could see the heavens clearly through the windows. I decided to walk past the table and chairs towards the windows, almost scared of what I might see. From where I usually sat at the table the windows were clearly visible.

As I looked out I saw the most amazing sight. It was our Earth, just the edge of it. It was so moving, I felt like crying. I understand now how the astronauts who went to the moon must have felt when they saw our Earth from space. It was the most beautiful sight I had ever seen. The ship appeared to be stationary, in geosyncronous orbit, because the view of Earth did not change. I felt delirious with excitement and joy, privileged to be one of the few people to have this rare view of our planet. What an experience!

Earth's sky was a bluish-black, and lights glimmered in the distance down there. I was trying to make out if they were stars or lights when I felt something pulling me back. I stopped gazing. White Arrow was here. I turned and saw him standing by the wall of the ship. I glanced over to the chair where I usually sit at these meetings. It was lit up. This usually meant that it was all right to sit on it – if the chair was not lit up it meant I could fall straight through it. Once lit it was solid to sit on, but I checked first anyway. As I sat down I was thinking about the mist I had remembered seeing around the world.

My attention was then drawn to White Arrow. He had something in his hand. It looked like a sheaf of papers. I was trying to see what they were when, in a flash, the room was lit up in colour. A door opened and Bear entered – this time he was in the form of an alien. I was surprised, since I usually see him in a bear form. Then Eagle, her hair as golden as ever, Michael, Zipper and Alien Girl followed, one by one taking their places round the table. White Arrow remained standing – he rarely sat down unless it was to show me something.

From where I was sitting, Michael was to my left, Alien Girl next to him, and Zipper was seated furthest to my left. On my right sat Bear and next to him Eagle. I felt a tightness in my stomach, the queasy feeling of apprehension one gets before a big occasion. Although it was not as severe as the pain I had once experienced on my first visit to the ship, the nervous anticipation gripping me was real enough.

White Arrow was now walking towards me. He was dressed in a blue-silver spacesuit. His red-toned skin made a powerful contrast against the blue of the suit – it was the same man inside the suit though. I thought how nice he looked. This was the first time White Arrow had appeared to me without being dressed as an Indian, and it startled me a bit. I felt that he might spontaneously change into the 'real' him and I was not ready for that. It flashed through my mind that there must be a meaning to it. I panicked. Please don't change, White Arrow, I heard myself say to myself. He came and stood behind me.

The chair at the head of the table started to light up. I knew

White Arrow's father was here. As before, a ball of nerves hit my stomach. The chair swivelled slowly round and I saw the cloak and the crown. 'You have done well, Ann Walker,' I heard him say. 'Our journey is far from over, but you have served well, and I too have been observing the oil.'

I nearly fell off my chair. I had grasped that he knew everything, but I was not prepared for *this*. I had been watching the news on TV about an oil slick off the Shetland coast in Scotland shortly before I was taken to the ship. He spoke again: 'You, the people of Earth, have still not learned how important your planet is to you all. Mistakes are still being made. My children – the animal kingdom, the plants and the sea – are being killed. It pains me as much as it would if it happened to humans. You humans have interfered with Mother Earth, with the animals, insects and plant life. All life-forms look upon you to take care of them, but this is not done.'

As a human I felt I had let him down, but I could not speak for the whole of humanity. I could not ask him what I could do about it. Humanity has known for some time what has to be done – we have known of our responsibility to take care of our planet. But we have not done it. For the first time, I felt unhappy on board the ship. I felt his sadness and disappointment in humankind.

White Arrow laid his hand on my shoulder. As he did so, his father was leaving. His chair started to spin, the lights went out, and then he was gone. White Arrow was now at the top of the table, standing by the chair. He still carried the papers with him. He discussed something with Zipper. Microphone-like objects appeared round the table and Zipper spoke to Eagle through his. I did not understand their language, so I looked around. I was curious and fascinated by White Arrow's suit and sudden change of appearance.

Zipper pointed to me as he was talking to Eagle. White Arrow shook his head as if disagreeing. Then he started walking towards me, and as he did this he passed X-ray-like pictures to everyone at the table. Zipper leaned forward and placed his picture in front of me. Having been through this procedure before when compiling the report in *Little One*, I presumed that I was here this time because of Egypt. I had already received some information from Bear's pictures, so what was this?

I straightened the picture in front of me. It looked like an X-ray with red markings, drawings and words which made no sense (*see* figure 2.1). I knew it would not make sense – I had to absorb it

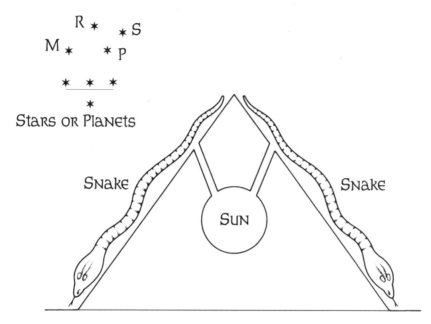

Figure 2.1 Zipper's picture

mentally, and then somehow it would be translated into my language. I do not know how they do that, but it does happen like that. As I focused on the picture something silver flashed past the corner of my sight. When I looked up to see what it was, it was gone. So once again I focused on the picture.

My intuition was that I had to wait until the stars in the picture were in position – the date would not become clear until then. It had something to do with astronomy (*see* Appendix). I reckoned that this had something to do with the date when I would have to visit Egypt, and what I was to look for when there. Was it light of some sort? I reflected on things for a while.

Bear passed his picture to me next. As I looked at it, he pulled it away and Alien Girl gave me her picture. Bear then spoke to her in his native tongue – I noticed he did not need to use his microphone. So why were the microphones there? I was not sure, but then I was not even sure why *I* was there yet! So I decided not to worry about the microphones.

My attention went back to the picture Alien Girl had given me (*see* figure 2.2). I sat in silence studying the picture, trying to absorb it in my mind. So far none of it was making sense, but I remembered that when I had received the last five pictures for the report

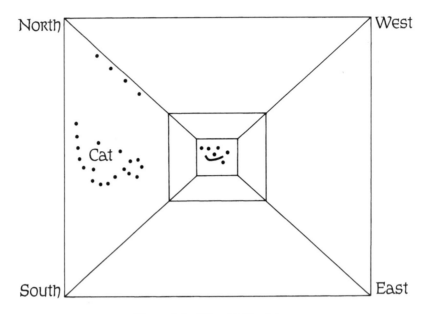

Figure 2.2 Alien Girl's picture

a few months before, none of them had made sense immediately. Slowly, many things had come forward from them and I had made sense of it all. So I knew that the same would probably happen this time.

I shifted my focus back to the ship. Bear now put his picture in front of me (*see* figure 2.3). He gently put his hand on mine. It was only the second time he had shown himself as an alien. His hand felt strange: he had no fingers at all. His hand was flat, its texture smooth and hard to describe – I had nothing to compare it with. Yet the gesture was of love and it reassured me. I found myself wondering how they lived on his world and how they used their hands. I secretly hoped one day he might show me his world. I looked again at the picture placed in front of me. 'When the two are in line, we will be ready,' said Bear.

At this point I should explain some of the events which occurred during these meetings. The aliens had given me a special medallion. The principal purpose of this was for us to keep in touch. It was a sort of intergalactic mobile phone, but that was only one of its uses. The other main use was mind-boggling. For the moment, though, suffice to say it could help me travel in another dimension in the same way the aliens could, to meet them as they met me. Going between the two realities was thus just as easy as going next

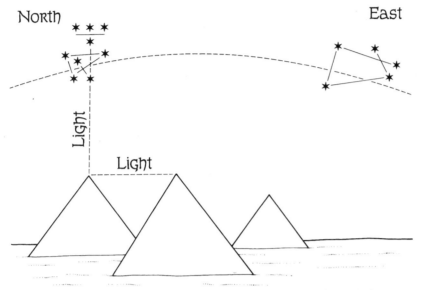

North   * * *   East
          *
      * _|_ *
       \ * \ _
        * *
Light

Light

When the Two are in line we will be READY

Figure 2.3 Bear's picture

door. The concept took a bit of getting used to; you might imagine
how hectic the reality was!

Going back to the drawings I had been given, I realized I would
have to go back to them repeatedly to understand their meaning.
I had hoped that the preparation for the Egypt journey might have
been easier – but I should have known better! After all, we humans
have tried for years to unlock the mysteries of the pyramids, so
why should it now be easy for me?

Next, Eagle pushed her picture towards me (*see* figure 2.4). She
and Zipper talked briefly, then she turned and looked at me. Her
eyes were fascinating – they seemed mirror-like. Looking into
them for too long made me a bit nervous, though I knew Eagle was
a good being. Nevertheless, it did take a bit of getting used to. I
turned my gaze back to the picture. I was curious as to what was
so important about the pyramids, and how this related to the
matter of saving the world.

Michael was just about to hand me his picture when I suddenly
found myself looking at the three large windows. Instantly, I had
left the room and felt I was floating outside the spacecraft, gazing
around. It was breathtaking. I was seeing hundreds and thousands
of stars. We were now not where we previously were. These stars

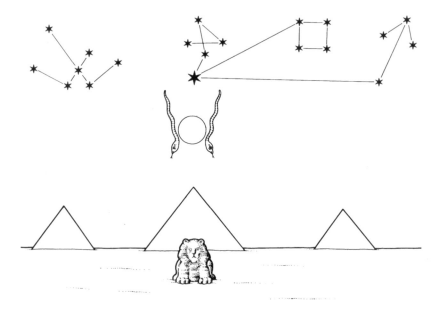

Figure 2.4 Eagle's picture

were much closer, and Earth was nowhere to be seen. I felt both fright and excitement, trying to take in the magnificent view. I turned and looked towards the ship's window. Looking through, I saw the room. White Arrow was still inside the room – then suddenly he was there with me outside the ship.

'White Arrow,' I said, looking at the beauty of the stars, 'what more could mankind want?'

White Arrow asked me, 'Are you happy?' I looked at him and then back to the beauty of the galaxies and stars. There were so many . . . how could I *not* be happy seeing this? It was so over-whelming!

'Why have you chosen *me*?' I asked him. I did not listen to his answer. At that time I did not actually care why he had chosen me – I was just so glad he had. I felt as if I could happily stay out here for ever. However, I knew there was much still to be done, and this short glimpse was but a taste, a taste of the infinite heart of God.

No sooner had I thought this than I was taken back to the chair, with Michael handing me his picture (*see* figure 2.5). For a brief instant my eyes strayed longingly to the window. The beauty and peace of it all had been indescribable.

Looking at the picture, the impression I got was that I should

SPHINX

I believe that the Pyramids were constructed and patterned after the Stars, the Secret of unlocking them is in the Stars. They used the Patterns of the Stars to keep their Secrets safe in the Pyramids.

Figure 2.5 Michael's picture – the Sphinx

look for the pattern of the Lion (Leo) in the sky. I was to draw the constellation on top of a picture of the Sphinx, to look at the Sphinx from the side elevation, then to look at the markings on the Sphinx. I understood that the pyramids emulated or mirrored the stars – the secret of unlocking them was in the stars. The pyramid-builders used the patterns of the stars to keep their secrets safe in the pyramids. I wondered whether the reason White Arrow had taken me outside the ship was to show me the connection between the stars and the pyramids.

Later on, I received help in interpreting these stellar patterns. In October 1994 I received a phone call from my previous publisher at Century/Arrow, saying he had found an expert called Adrian Gilbert, who had recently co-authored a book with Robert Bauval called *The Orion Mystery*. Upon meeting Adrian I found out that he is one of only a few people who can interpret such star-patterns. Later I sent him the five drawings. He then phoned me to say we could have a meeting, not knowing that I had one more star-pattern yet to show him. Unbeknown to me, this drawing was to indicate, in a pattern showing various planets in line, the date of the meeting when he was to give me an explanation of the five drawings. These explanations are in the Appendix at the end of this book.

The FULL CIRCLE of the KING'S ROOM

King in the centre – covered in gold – on each
side is an important person from his government
– one could see the future –

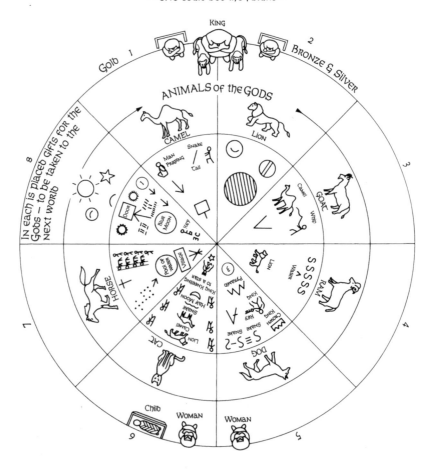

The Floor of the King's Room

Figure 2.6

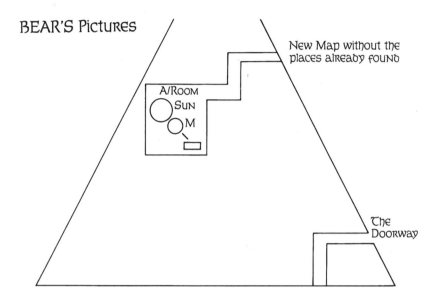

Figure 2.7

Bear gave me more drawings (*see* figures 2.6–2.19). I knew when I had completed them that I would find the proof of these when I found a hidden chamber buried somewhere in Egypt, and only White Arrow could show me the way to it. After receiving the last drawing, I looked at them all, hoping I had drawn the pictures correctly on board the ship. The aliens all seemed happy enough. They were talking amongst themselves, and Zipper got up from his seat. White Arrow walked towards me. I sensed that he was

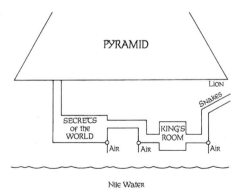

Figure 2.8

This is A/Room – Symbols to open door
(given by Bear)

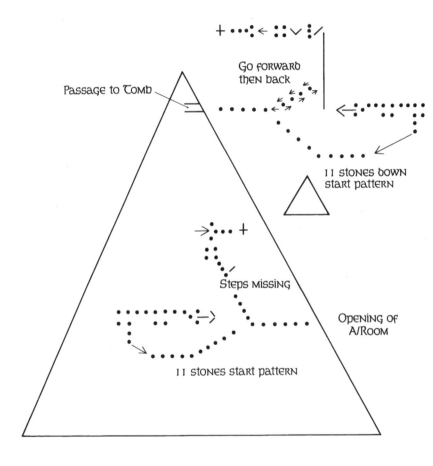

Check if the light I see marks the Cross
Also check if this belongs to Pyramid or Lion

Figure 2.9

going to say we were returning home. As I thought this, I was back
in my front room!

This is to open the KING'S ROOM

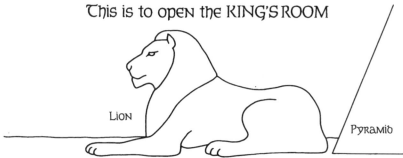

Lion

Pyramid

To the East of the LEFT PAW where the SUN is most hidden – go to it and sit with your back to the paw. Move your RIGHT HAND to the LEFT side of you. Keeping your hand there, get up and face where your hand is. Now follow the pattern.

> Left – Down Forward – then Up
> Follow it back again. Sit and then put your left
> hand to the right – Follow the same numbers

Figure 2.10

The BEGINNING of the TOMB

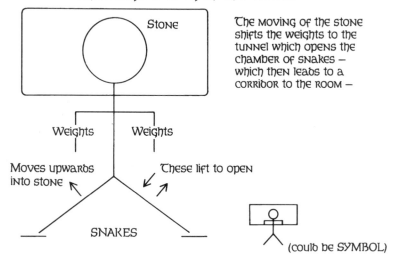

Stone

The moving of the stone shifts the weights to the tunnel which opens the chamber of snakes – which then leads to a corridor to the room –

Weights   Weights

Moves upwards into stone

These lift to open

SNAKES

(could be SYMBOL)

Figure 2.11

Go to the Place that Light is Least
– There is only heat from light
and force moves the stone

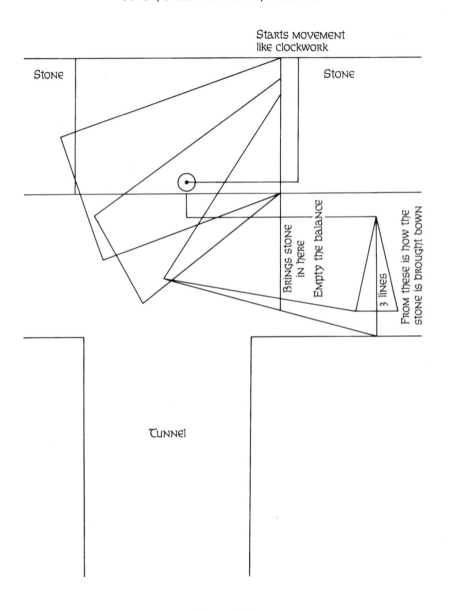

Figure 2.12

ON THE SAID NIGHT

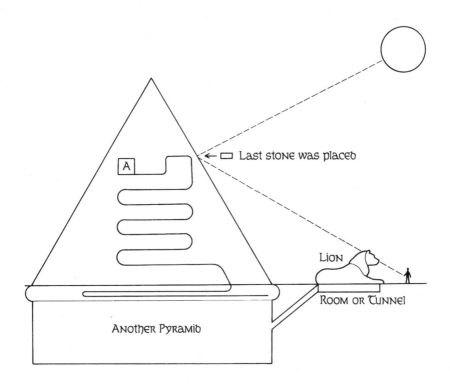

IN the hidden Pyramid below Giza lies the
WEALTH of MANKIND –
There are many keys to open this

The water from the Nile made it possible
to build deep before the Top Pyramid was laid

Figure 2.13

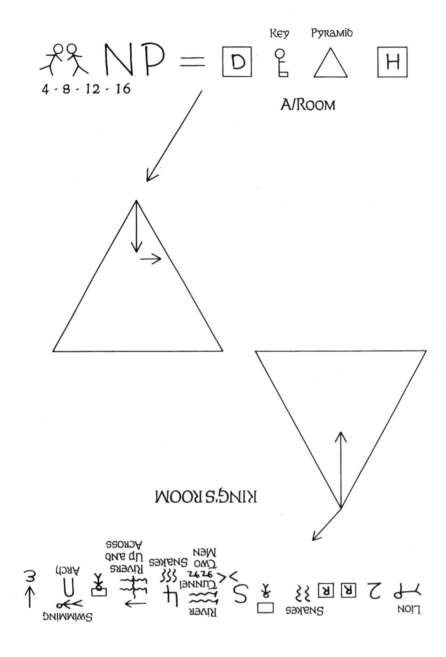

Figure 2.14

A/ROOM DOOR

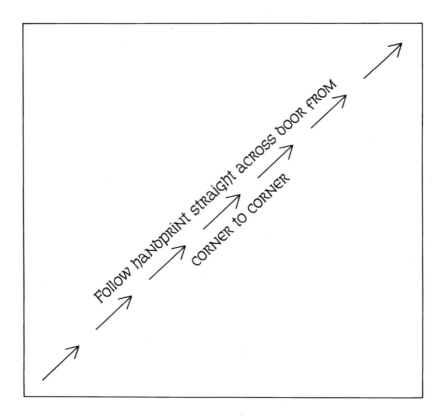

The WEIGHT behind the Door will be released by your Hand movements – as soon as you reach the last handprint remove self from door a few feet away

Figure 2.15

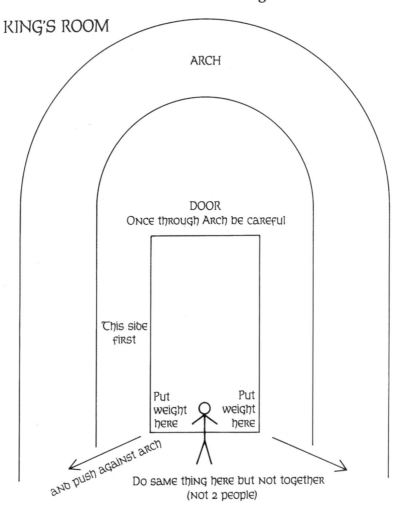

KING'S ROOM

ARCH

DOOR
Once through Arch be careful

This side
first

Put
weight
here

Put
weight
here

and push against arch

Do same thing here but not together
(not 2 people)

Before you go through ARCH put a stick, big and long enough to touch door. The door is designed to cock when a certain weight is there, so it will be O.K. for door, but what is before door can be unlocked with stick. Do this before entering Arch. When you walk through Arch it will set something off to hold door more firmly. Crawl through. It is the height that sets the door. Remember, crawl ONLY one at a time and it is important that you crawl through the centre, not the sides.

Figure 2.16

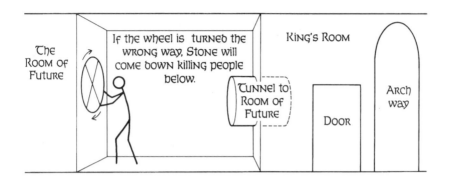

Figure 2.17

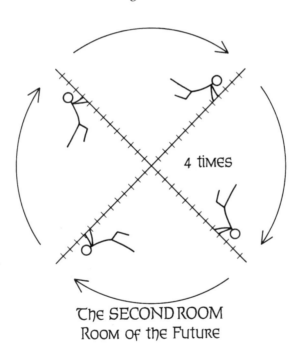

4 times

The SECOND ROOM
Room of the Future

Figure 2.18

BE CAREFUL, there is a Stone above the Door which is set to fall as soon as the door is opened. Be prepared for that.

DOOR

King's Room

Figure 2.19

· 3 ·

Demotic Clues

For nearly a year I had been trying to decipher the meaning of some Egyptian demotic symbols White Arrow had given me (*see* figures 3.1–3.4). No words from White Arrow and the aliens were given

DEMOTIC WRITING

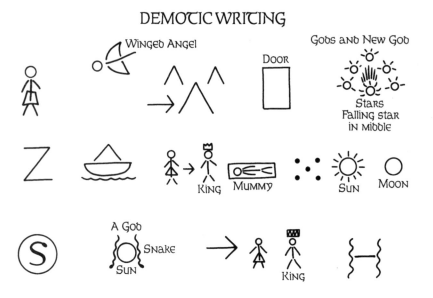

Signs connected by the unusual movements universally shows the coming change of the Angel or Messenger or the King or the Snake that the cycle is symbol of where it ends it begins.
Translated into English, 25 July 1994, by Abdel Hakim Awayan

Figure 3.1 Demotic symbols (1)

Three PYRAMIDS. IN ONE OF THEM IS AN ANSWER
to a question in the form of a symbol SSS.
Plus 5 stars – the SYMBOL of FIVE STAGES
Translated into English, 25 July 1994, by Abdel Hakim Awayan

Figure 3.2 Demotic symbols (2)

at the time I received them: I was given just the drawings, to be
kept until later. Two contacts of mine, Mrs Prince and François,
were helping me with research into them, but we had all drawn a
blank.

Then White Arrow himself came to me one day during Christmas 1992. He told me the symbols were not to be found in books
– I would have to go and visit villages around the pyramids in
Egypt, and he would lead me to someone who could tell me their
meaning. I should have known: this was the same as with the

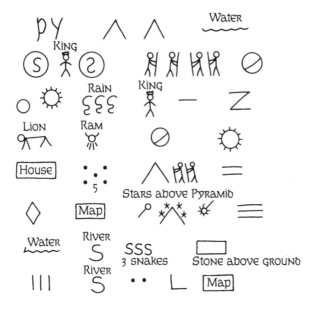

Double Pyramid — A couple facing, dividing two powers struggling — and as stubborn as a Ram.
Translated into English, 25 July 1994, by Abdel Hakim Awayan

Figure 3.3 Demotic symbols (3)

Indian symbols I had been given before. Trust White Arrow. There were to be no short cuts on this journey!

Some days after my visit to the spacecraft, on 11 January, François came to see me. Before Christmas, he had said he would get in touch with an Egyptian lady who was an expert on Egyptian symbols. To be honest, I had all but forgotten about it, until he mentioned it again. He had sent her the symbols and had phoned her to see how she was getting on with them. She apologized for not getting back to him sooner, but she had found out something very interesting.

The symbols were in fact not to do with the pyramids. They were Egyptian symbols that ancient local villagers used among themselves. The word she gave for the symbols was 'demotic'. This was the legal-administrative, simplified form of ancient Egyptian script – as distinct from hieratic or formal script, as used by the initiated priesthood, and hieroglyphic, which was confined to carvings on stone. Demotic was introduced from around 600BC and was the only widespread writing form in general use for 1,000 years after that.

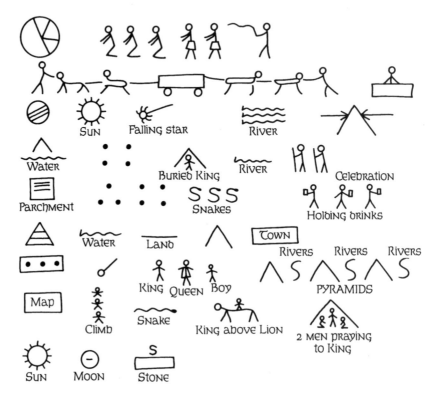

The WHITE ARROW is equal as the Shepherd is Shepherdding the five stages by force (whip). The Shepherd is expecting struggle. The Shepherd is the SON, the KING, and the QUEEN and the TRIAD.
The Shepherd is the SNAKE and the Lioness.
Translated into English, 25 July 1994, by Abdel Hakim Awayan

Figure 3.4 Demotic symbols (4)

She also told him that she had given the symbols to a university professor in Egypt, who was going to try and find out what they meant. I was greatly relieved to find that the symbols, though not found in books, were indeed true symbols. This would prove they were authentic, so they might be taken seriously. François also told me that the lady was a tourist guide and that he would ask her if she might be my guide when I visited Egypt. Things were slowly starting to come together. White Arrow was showing me proof of the influence of Spirit.

DIPÎNOÂ

HERE lives aN old maN. He kNows what it meaNs.
The book it came from is a Bible that was writteN
thousaNds of years ago.

Figure 3.5 DIPÎNOÂ

There would be a lot more work ahead before all the pieces fitted into place. I hoped to go to Egypt in May 1993 to meet people from the villages to ask them about the messages, then to visit the pyramids. Hopefully I should by then have more information to help me on my journey. So far Bear had given me 20 pictures for Egypt, plus five from my visit to the ship, and the demotic symbols.

Four days later, I received good news. François told me the lady in Egypt had agreed to be my guide. He also mentioned that she had shown my drawings to her professor and that he had asked her to ask me to redraw them for him. This was a relief, because I had accidentally sent *all* of the pictures to Egypt, and White Arrow had not wanted that. Now I would redraw them and send only half of them this time. White Arrow likes to protect his work from getting into the wrong hands!

White Arrow and the aliens gave me another piece of the puzzle during one of our meetings: the word DIPÎNOÂ. Zipper drew a picture (*see* figure 3.5).

I intuitively knew that something was hidden between the pyramids, at a place hidden from the world. I was to look towards the north when standing in front of the Lion (Sphinx) at Giza – it was in that direction. Zipper wrote: 'Here lives an old man. He knows what it means. The book the words and drawings come from is a Bible that was written thousands of years ago.'

By 18 January we had discovered what language the word DIPÎNOÂ came from. We had wondered whether it could be pharaonic, from the high language used by the kings of the time of the pyramids. It seemed to be the name of a place. But François phoned back to say the word came from ancient Greek and that it meant 'double temple'.

Zipper informed me that the name was given to a village by the pyramids. After more searching by François we found there was a place called Ma'Badain – meaning 'two temples'. When he asked where he could find this place he was told it was at Mabao el Wadi, meaning 'Valley of the Temple'. He was also given the name Nazlet el Simman. For now, I had found the answer to DIPÎNOÂ. Whether Nazlet el Simman played a part in all this I would have to wait and see. François was going to get a map, to see if we could find the Valley of the Temple.

Lots of clues. At least I knew the word given to me by White Arrow was a place name, and we had found the place. Later we hoped to find out more about it from the Egyptian lady guide and her professor. I hoped they could help, but it was in White Arrow's hands. During this time I had also discovered that when the medallion I had been given was red or blue I could call on Zipper and the aliens – but it would have to be for help with something important, not just for everyday trivia. If they needed me for something they would contact me through the same colour signals.

On 25 January the medallion was showing red. I turned to White Arrow and he explained that the aliens needed to talk to me about Egypt, so I was to go to the back room and talk to them. I could talk to White Arrow every day, but at the time the aliens were only in touch when there was something specific to be done.

François had also been in touch that day. He had found out that Nazlet el Simman was to the north of the Sphinx. I was almost certain this was the village I would have to visit, but I would have to be sure. The journey looked set for May – if by then I had gathered enough evidence to go ahead.

Later I went into the back room to talk to Zipper and the others. Bear was there first, then Zipper appeared on the chair with Alien Girl next to him.

White Arrow was the first to speak. 'Listen. Bear will be with you on this important journey. I have brought the book back, and I want you to look at it.' Zipper proceeded to take something from Alien Girl. It was the old Bible from which the word they had given me had come. Then he showed it to me. He flicked through the pages, showing me page after page of writings and pictures. In some of the pictures I could just about make out what looked like people building the pyramids. It was all very quick – as soon as I looked he turned the page. It was not written in my language.

Suddenly, he shut the book and showed me the cover. He wiped the dust away and I saw the name ZIP̂ZENTLÊŶ VIII. Then I was shown a fish. I had a feeling this had to do with the feeding of the 5,000. This was all so strange. What was the connection between Egypt and the feeding of the 5,000?

Zipper was about to leave when I asked him about Eagle. 'Yes,' he replied, 'she is helping Bear. Bear is helping you. The journey is of great importance.' With that, he vanished. Bear was still there. He used his own language and gently growled, then he put his hand on mine. Before he left he spoke in my language. 'Do you know how lucky you are to have Zipper help us on this journey?'

'Yes – I'm lucky to have you all!' I meant it. Zipper was someone very important to them and very highly regarded where they come from.

I later learned something else: in Roman times, when early Christians wanted to meet and talk about Jesus, they had used the sign of the fish. François phoned me; from information found so far it seemed that the language they had shown me was thousands of years old, a form of Greek. I still did not know the connection between this and the Egyptian symbols, but there must presumably be one. As far as the 'VIII' (eight) was concerned, we had a few ideas, but we would have to be exact. This would mean going back to Zipper and cross-checking with him – and a lot more hard work! Still, I was grateful to White Arrow for bringing in the right people to help on the journey. François was French, born in Egypt, a language expert who knew many other experts in many other subjects.

On 26 January François brought me some maps of Egypt, to see if we could find the village that related to DIPÎNOÂ. As we looked at the map, right next to the Great Pyramid was the Valley Temple and next to that was Nazlet el Simman. I thus found where the word DIPÎNOÂ belonged and was happy – at least I knew where I was to go.

I hoped this part of the journey would get easier, but there was still so much to do, on top of sorting out the meaning of the words and pictures. I also had to research the stars. It was not going to be an easy journey, but I felt driven to do it – I just could not let them down. Suddenly I had the feeling that the first word, meaning 'two temples', could hold the key to the second word, ZIP̂ZENTLÊŶ VIII: would someone at DIPÎNOÂ know the meaning of the second word?

That afternoon I asked White Arrow to send Zipper to speak to me. Later my medallion started to flash red, so I knew he was around. When I entered the back room he was already there, sitting on the chair waiting for me. He told me to keep my eyes wide open. He had his eyes wide open too, and he looked intently into mine. I knew why: he was healing me. Zipper had done this once before, and it had really helped me. Then Bear arrived.

'I need to see the Bible again, Zipper,' I said. As I was saying this, Alien Girl appeared by his side and handed him the book. He held it out for me to see. It was the writing on the cover I needed to check – I looked at it again to see if I had missed anything.

The book was written in one language, the aliens spoke their own different language, and they were trying to tell me how to spell it all in my language – so the process was, as you can imagine, not without its problems! I knew that we would eventually have everything spelled right. I looked over to Zipper. He must, I surmised, be really fed up with me today; all the time I kept asking to have another look at the book. As we worked, Zipper told me to concentrate on the spelling. I became so deeply involved in this that I almost got up to leave without saying thank you and good-bye to everyone! Zipper smiled. 'Before the end of the week you will have some help, so do not worry, Little One.' Bless him, I thought. I pray I don't let them down.

By 27 January I had confirmed that the word DIPÎNOÂ means 'two temples'. I intuited I would have to go there, to find a man living there near water (possibly the Nile). The sign of the fish would be something I would have to show him. This would be a clue for something he would tell me. We were still not sure what ZIP̂ZENTL̂EŶ VIII referred to. The name of the language used is koine, a form of Greek script, which was the common language of the Greek cultural sphere from the close of the classical period, a century or two before the time of Christ. The second 'Z' in ZIP̂ZENTL̂EŶ was a Greek 'E' or Σ – hence the confusion.

I needed to talk to White Arrow. Since I had started on this journey we had not had much time together. As soon as I started waiting he was there before me. He spoke. 'I understand your anxiety, Little One, and how heavy the work is, but you have done well. I am proud of you. Egypt is urgently important to the world. Otherwise I would not put such a burden on you. In Egypt lie secrets to help my father's people and your world too. Your life will never be the same, and I will protect you. We will be having many meetings with the aliens concerning Egypt, but you have now been shown how the medallion works. Remember: when it goes red or blue Zipper will want to speak to you. Talk to him as soon as you can, for while he will wait, he has other things to do, so you must not ignore the calling.'

'I understand, White Arrow.'

White Arrow spoke again, this time referring to the two words given: 'You have the message. When the time is right, I will tell you when to go to Egypt. Meticulous attention must be given to this journey so that when you arrive everything is prepared.' White Arrow hated to waste time, so he would be precise about what would be needed on my journey. I knew I was not yet ready to know what would happen in Egypt, on this first journey.

I was lost in thought when, suddenly, White Arrow's father spoke. 'This journey holds many keys to the future. It is important that my people are shown them. They are secrets that people have tried to open for many centuries, to no avail. It is only now that these secrets will be given. I've sent White Arrow and the aliens to you to give these secrets to the world. Secrets that, if mankind had given more attention to the planet Earth, would not now need to be told. I come to help this world and its people, and I have chosen you, Ann Walker, to help me. I have chosen you for your faith. Mankind must remember that there will be no more secrets next time, and that the responsibility for losing mankind is on man's own shoulders.'

I thought for a moment – mainly about the part concerning humanity. I had earlier been watching television and had heard that yet another species had become extinct – yet do we worry about it? A few of us do, but how much importance do we attach to it? If we can drive an animal to extinction we can surely do the same to our own species. When will we ever take the warnings seriously? Animals and insects have lived on Earth longer than we, yet it is we who are causing their extinction. How easy it would be for humanity to destroy itself! How many warnings do we need? If we do not learn now, how will we be able to learn tomorrow?

Have we lost our love and faith so much that we want to destroy ourselves? It would seem so. And yet God has not lost his faith in us. If we refuse to listen and pay heed to his words, then God has the right to forsake us. The responsibility rests on our shoulders – a terrifying thought when one considers the destruction and decay we have already brought on ourselves and our planet. I am no one special, yet I can see it. Every day, every one of us can see the destruction we are causing. Why are we hell-bent on destroying the most beautiful thing we know, the thing which cradles all life in her arms, Mother Earth? What people forget is that we are all part of her. Our souls came from God, but our bodies need the Earth. We did not just *appear* here at the beginning of time.

White Arrow's father left and I looked up at White Arrow. He spoke again. 'There will be plenty of time for us to talk more, Little One, but for now we must return to the journey to Egypt.' I understood his concern.

Two days later, on 29 January, while I was in the hairdressers, White Arrow suddenly appeared. He said Zipper wanted to see me because there was another message. There was presumably a good reason why White Arrow could not just tell me what it was himself. I knew I would have to wait for the medallion to light up before Zipper was ready to see me. Bear had been around that morning, but he had not stayed long. At 4.30pm the medallion turned a red colour, so I went to the back room and sat down. Zipper appeared on the chair in front of me.

The letters 'ZIP' came into my mind straight away. Zipper said nothing, but he was smiling. I was used to his smile now – he was always loving, and more so when he smiled. At first, his smile had triggered nervous laughter in me – laughter was one of the first emotions we shared together. It helped overcome my fear of the aliens and break down the barriers of suspicion we humans have towards the unknown. It felt good to know that laughter is universal in God's worlds.

Zipper had brought the archaic Bible with him. Instantly, 'VIII' came into my mind. Bear and Alien Girl were there also. Now Zipper was showing a page from the book. It was a picture of the stars. I did not understand what the connection was. 'Go back to "ZIP",' Zipper said. Now he was handing me a picture.

Zipper showed me the 'VIII'. 'When you are in Egypt, I will lead you to the Eight. Until then, no one must know, for your sake.' On the book's cover was '1487' – was it BC or AD? Then I saw a man on stilts. This was mystifying. As I looked again the word 'juggler' formed. Is the man on stilts a juggler? Then I was shown another word from the book: SÛILTÛEA.

Zipper was writing again. He would write with his finger, and for the first time I could clearly see the 'paper' he was using. It was similar to what they used on the ship – what I regard as X-ray paper – but they wrote with their fingers without using pens or similar implements. How easy it was for them to do this! But of course, they were another breed of person, far more accomplished than we, living in another reality.

Bear had been so quiet I had almost forgotten he was there. The medallion started to darken, the red fading. They would be going soon. Bear and Zipper both put their hands on mine as a farewell gesture. Then they were gone.

On Sunday, 31 January, in the afternoon, the medallion started to glow red about 20 minutes before I was due to see Harry, an old friend of Tony's, for a meeting. I was starting to worry if I had time to go into the back room before Harry came. Then I heard Zipper's voice: 'Get the pen and paper, Little One.' He then communicated six more words for my Egyptian journey.

It was then I realized that I would not have to go into the back room all the time for messages. White Arrow and Zipper had already shown me the book where the words came from, so now all they had to do was give me words and I would know what they related to. Thank goodness! The words they gave me were: SALEŶFRIEN, CŶTĤFRAYSCH, P̂UUALẐETTŶ, K̂HATYEŜTLEY, CUP̂SLUEP̂ and DÛELLP̂HEE – all for Egypt.

· 4 ·

Zipper's Riddles

It was Monday, 1 February 1993. François was still waiting to hear from the Egyptian lady – she was supposed to be seeing her professor that week. He said only scholars would know about this writing, so it was lucky he knew a few. It was actually more than luck: White Arrow was helping put it all together, bringing in the right people at the right time.

People were trying to warn me that what I was in the process of showing the world was dangerous and was going to be hard on me. I had not really given much thought to what might lie ahead. But now, yes, I did feel a bit scared, though my faith in White Arrow was greater than my fear. While I had life in me, I felt committed to helping him. It did not matter what people thought, though it was important that they read the report and thought about the dangers it referred to.

White Arrow came. 'White Arrow, I hope you know what you're doing,' I said.

'Yes, Little One.'

'White Arrow, we don't seem to have time to talk much nowadays,' I added.

'Little One, there is much to do, and, yes, our time together is less now. But remember, I will be with you always, by your side.'

'Thanks, White Arrow. That's all I need to know.'

Recently, I had fully informed François who White Arrow was. I asked him to go away and decide whether or not he wanted to follow the journey. François had given it some thought and said, yes, he did want to help.

He phoned back about the six new words I had given him to investigate. He needed to know if they were separate or together.

KOINE GREEK

	Meaning	Greek
1. ZIPZENCLEŶ	(Animals Plough)	ZιIIZEΞΨMEY
2. SÛILCÛEA	(Isis, Goddess)	TΦIΘΨΦEA
3. SALEŶFRIEN̂	(To save)	TAMEYZΣIEΞ
4. CŶCHF̂YRAӮSCĤ	(The Living Earth)	YΨΘ2YΣAYTΓΘ
5. P̂UUALẐECĈỲ	(To take care of the suffering)	IIΘΘAMZEΨΨY
6. R̂HACYEŜCLEY	(To seek the Stone of the Plough)	ΦAΨYETΨMEY
7. CÛP̂SLUEP̂	(I was created)	ΓΦIITMΦEII
8. DÛELL̂PHEE	(ALMIGHTY GOD)	ΔΦEMMIIΘEE

Figure 4.1 The koine Greek words

I called on Zipper for feedback. As I did so the medallion glowed red, so he must have known. He appeared, with Alien Girl carrying the book. The answer to the six words appeared straight away.

Zipper explained that the first two words joined the six next words, and that they were koine Greek (*see* figure 4.1), a language thousands of years old. They all formed one sentence. I looked at the words again. Zipper smiled at me. He was a lovely person. Alien Girl gestured to me in acknowledgement – I smiled back. Then Bear arrived. Now we were ready to begin with the words in detail. Zipper opened the book and spoke. 'This is a message for the world. You will understand that when we have finished.' François had found out what the words meant in English.

I looked at the message. I had worked out 'Animals under the plough' – they were the stars of the zodiacal constellation Leo. The Plough is a constellation (the Great Bear, Ursa Major), and so the message was presumably coming from there. My next question had to be, 'Why is Isis linked with us?'

'She is Eagle, Little One,' replied White Arrow.

I took a deep breath. I had just got used to working for the aliens, and now I was being told that Eagle had once been a goddess, a long time ago on Earth. I would have to ask François or Mrs Prince to tell me about Isis, but for now I had to work out the reason why the message was important. Isis had been sent from the stars to help save the living Earth, to take care of the suffering and to help us seek the Stone of the Plough. She was created by Almighty God.

The Stone of the Plough. The Stone of the Plough. The rest of the message was clear, but what and where was the Stone of the Plough? My mind kept turning the words over and over. I knew White Arrow would help me find the answer, but would he do so now? Was the Stone *from* the Plough? My stomach turned. Yes, I had got it! Somewhere in Egypt there was a stone that came from the stars. It was somehow connected to the Great Pyramid of Giza. I suddenly understood that I had to help them find the Stone of the Plough.

But how? I turned to White Arrow. 'I will show you, Little One,' he said. 'With your faith we will find the Stone of the Plough.' He left. God willing, the stone would be located on my journey to Egypt.

I saw the medallion glowing blue and red. Zipper was needed somewhere else. He showed me what to do with the words, and said he had to leave, but Alien Girl would help me finish them off. With that, he just vanished in front of me.

Bear then spoke. He would wait, to help get things finished later, since I had to go back to my clients, themselves waiting to talk to White Arrow. These aliens were so patient and understanding! Despite my limited human capacity to understand things, they never got annoyed or impatient with me. I do love them all.

By 3 February, I had found out that not all the given words could be translated. Only in Egypt would I find a person who could interpret them. I asked White Arrow about them. 'I have shown you what is important for you to know, Little One. You can leave the other words, for I will show you what they mean through another person. It is enough for now.'

White Arrow said no more about it. Whenever I worked on something for him he would give me some sort of verification of what I was working on, so I did not worry too much. I knew I could put everything away till he wanted to attend to it. Also, the Egyptian lady had rung François, saying her professor had said that the beginning and the end of the drawing were missing. Yet he gave confirmation that the symbols were indeed in demotic writing, thousands of years old – factual proof of the correctness of the Spirit!

François asked me to ask White Arrow for the beginning of the demotic drawings. We discovered that some of the other words, like ZIPZENTLEŶ, came from a time when Greek was a common language used by the people of Egypt, when Egypt had been absorbed into the Greek cultural sphere. That was why I was getting Greek words. It was all making sense.

I found it all very hard going. The previous year had been challenging enough, but I could see this journey being much harder. I wished I could rest, but I did not dare walk away from it all. It was so important to White Arrow and ourselves. I looked at White Arrow. 'Do not worry, Little One, I will be your strength. Your rest will come, I promise, but we must think of the world.'

'I know,' I said. I trusted his word, but this was nevertheless not easy going!

The following day I gave François some more demotic drawings. They were some of the initial ones. He was going to send them off to Egypt. White Arrow would not let me send all of the material until he was sure I was in touch with the right person. By 7 February, we had word back from Egypt that the demotic symbols did make sense. They asked for more drawings, but I felt that I should wait. They had mentioned that some of the symbols were missing. I was not surprised, since White Arrow would leave out key pieces until the right time. The Egyptian lady was keen to know more; that gave me an indication that she knew White Arrow's message was important.

Another fact I had discovered was that the fish, one of the words given, is important in Egypt. The term given is OXYR HYNCHUS, the name of a specific fish. The same word in English means sharp-snouted fish, as in the case of a river pike. In Arabic it is translated as EL KARAKI, but it can also mean a kind of *papari*, a papyrus or ancient paper-scroll.

The connection between Greece and Egypt was also making sense. Alexander the Great and Cleopatra, both Greek, had each ended up ruling Egypt. Another word given was also linked: APOCRYPHA – it means 'hidden writings', connected with the Nile, Moses. We also found that the first Bible ever written, the oldest one known of, written before the birth of Christ, is called the *Septuagint*, the old Greek Bible.

It is told that 72 scholars went to an island on the Nile in ancient times. Could it be that there were hidden writings inside the pyramids not yet found by man? The puzzle was slowly coming together, but many pieces were yet to fit into place. It would take some time to connect all the clues from this vast historical picture. At least I sensed we were on the right road. Whatever lay ahead was something very big and important.

I was nervous about showing something this important to the wrong people. I knew I was about to find out secrets kept for thousands of years. The thought of sacred knowledge in the wrong hands sent chills through me. I could not let White Arrow down. I needed to deserve his trust and faith in me. Out of the blue, I wondered whether we had the facts right about when Jesus Christ was born. Why that should come into my head at the time, I didn't know.

Things were getting so hectic! The medallion started to glow red – Zipper and the aliens wanted a word with me. Zipper was already in the back room when I went through. Bear and Alien Girl were also waiting. She brought the archaic Bible with her again – I had thought I had finished with that for a while! So many things were going on at once, I did not know how to keep up with it all. I felt totally exhausted. I had been working solidly for the previous two months, with very little rest. It had not stopped all through January, and it looked like carrying on all through February. I looked at Zipper. 'Sorry, I don't mean to moan, but I just feel so tired. I'm sure I'll be all right later.'

He smiled empathically and took the book from Alien Girl. Back to work! Zipper opened the book. Inside was a picture of a place, but I could not make it out very well. Zipper got up and walked over to me. With his finger he started drawing, showing me something (*see* figure 4.2).

Zipper said the words 'juggler' and 'man on stilts', and then the words XERMENTS SAGRETES. François later translated them into the correct Egyptian spelling, since I was spelling phonetically: CHEI-ROMENTES – GONIA PENTOS. After that, 'North, RENTES (corner)' and the number five. The translation seemed to mean a sensitive person who works with the Spirit, then north, corner, number five. Seemingly I had to find a juggler, a man on stilts, five corners, and a person who worked for or believed in the Spirit, who was connected with the north of Giza.

I looked at White Arrow. Who and where would I find this person? Did the juggler imply a circus? Did I have to find a circus

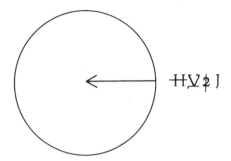

This is a major hall of records site, primary time capsule for the present soul influx's history & initiations. Keeper of the Beacon has the emerald jade gemstone temple.

Translated into English, February 1996, by Abdel Hakim Awayan

Figure 4.2

in Egypt? 'Patience, Little One. Later you will understand. It is only in Egypt you will find the answer.' I prayed it would become easier to understand when I got there. For the life of me, I could not understand the message.

In the book I saw a house, and 'VIII' appeared again, and a man whose name began with PZ came too. 'PZ' means 'God'. Did he work for God? Was I looking for a holy man? Did the house belong to this man? Would this be a house in the village I was supposed to visit? Was this the right village? Would he know what 'VIII' meant, or was it the number of his house? So many questions running through my mind!

Zipper shut the book. It was very old. I immediately realized how stupid my questions were – Zipper always knew what he was doing. 'Little One, we have been watching you. Please do not worry.' Bear growled sedately in agreement. Eagle and Michael had just turned up. 'You will be protected,' said Zipper.

'I know, Zipper, but every now and then I get scared of people who might try to use White Arrow and yourselves, through me.'

'Have no fear. Everything is taken care of, I promise. We will bring you more pictures, but we will leave the last of the messages until it is safe to give you them.' I knew what he meant. 'There is no more from the Bible today. I must leave now.'

'Thanks, Zipper.'

We all exchanged goodbyes and they vanished. Suddenly, I thought of Bethlehem, but I could not think why.

The next day, 8 February, I had a surprise. For the first time Zipper came into the back room while I was in the middle of one of my regular clairvoyance sessions for a client. He told me he needed to talk to me that afternoon. Later, Zipper was there with Michael. I said 'Hi', and Zipper smiled back. 'You worry too much,' he said. 'Everything is planned. It will be all right.'

'I hope so, Zipper!'

'First, we must get on with the work in hand. It is important for the world.' With that, he gave me a picture of a circle with a new life in it. Albert Einstein (with whom I had earlier had clairvoyant discussions) had shown me that before, but I still did not know what it meant.

'This is different to then,' said Zipper. 'This is a new life for you.'

'It's certainly that, Zipper,' I said, referring to events of the previous 18 months.

'You will understand later,' he said quietly.

Alien Girl appeared with the book. She passed it to Zipper, but instead of just showing me a word or a page as before, he was looking through it as if searching for something. I looked around for White Arrow. 'It's all right, I'm here,' I heard him answer.

Meanwhile, Zipper was talking to Michael about the book. I sat and watched for a few moments. It was obvious that they had an intellect far superior to ours. Looking at Zipper, I could actually tell that he had great knowledge – wisdom was so natural to him. He looked up at me briefly, as if acknowledging my compliment, then busied himself with the book again.

We all seemed to be waiting for something to happen. Suddenly, a white light appeared in the room, instantly, with no sound or movement. I found myself wishing all of this could be a lot simpler! Bear and Eagle joined the assembly. Finally White Arrow's father appeared in the form of a lion.

'We want you back on the ship,' he said. I knew this was a command, but not an immediate one. I would be able to go the following day – at least that was the feeling I was given. I felt the reason for all this waiting was to hear what White Arrow's father had to tell me. White Arrow's father changed from the lion form into the man in the golden cloak with the dazzling crown. He handed me a staff and spoke once more. 'Lean on it, Ann Walker, for I am the staff.'

The importance of the situation overwhelmed me. I felt nauseous at the thought of the Most Holy in the Universe addressing me. I was trembling with fear and worry, totally overawed by the situation. He spoke again. 'Have no fear, Ann Walker, I walk with you.'

For the first time I knelt down. With every nerve in my body and mind I said, 'Forgive me, if I have ever sinned.'

Gently, he said, 'Get up, Ann Walker. I come with great news. Soon, the arrival of my people will come, and I know you will take the news to the world. My people on Earth will believe I am here in answer to their prayers. I will talk more tomorrow.' With that he left.

Zipper then said, 'It is not pictures I bring you today'. The meeting today had been for White Arrow's father to come.

On Tuesday, 9 February, I waited to go back to the ship. I was overtired. Although I felt exhausted, my mind was racing, mulling over the possible consequences of this whole journey. How long would it take? Months? Years? The rest of my life? The work never seemed to stop! Would it always be so demanding? If it were not so important I would have walked away from it ages ago. But I could not, and I had to accept that . . .

Suddenly, I was on board the ship. The room we used for the meetings was in darkness. I walked to the window and looked out at the heavens. It looked so peaceful and beautiful. Gazing at the stars from the ship was a rare and special experience. It made me realize that, no matter how tiring the work was, I was very lucky to be here and have such a privilege. I felt White Arrow's presence and turned around. He was there, standing by the top end of the table. As I looked towards him I could feel my tiredness once again bearing down on me. 'White Arrow, you have to send me help. I really don't think I can do it all on my own.'

White Arrow beckoned me to the chair where I usually sat. As I walked towards him the room lit up. My chair lit up too – it was all right to sit on it. I had the feeling that this room was provided for my benefit. The furniture seemed to be only partially solid, like a hologram. I was a bit wary of that: the table could bend and one could fall through the chair if it was not lit up. I sat down in the chair and immediately felt like resting my head on the table. I had the feeling one gets when one is totally exhausted, but I snapped myself out of it. I had to forget how tired I felt.

I looked up at White Arrow and smiled. 'So much is happening, White Arrow, that it's hard for me to keep up with it all,' I said.

He put his hand on my head and said 'Little One, I promise help is at hand.'

Just then, I looked around and saw Zipper sitting at the end of the table, Alien Girl next to him, then Michael opposite Bear and Eagle. Eagle was seated next to me. I had been so tired I had not heard them come in. We all sat quietly and I sensed that we were waiting for White Arrow's father to arrive. The chair at the head of the table was still empty. White Arrow walked over and stood by the chair, looking out of the window, with his back to me.

As he turned back round to face me, a staff suddenly appeared in the centre of the table. It came from nowhere. It just seemed to materialize from the table. It was an old wooden stick. It just lay there on the table. I looked round. Everyone was quiet. Then suddenly, without a word, everybody touched it, one by one, including White Arrow. Although the room was still lit up, it seemed to darken a little.

I heard movement. It came from the chair at the top of the table. I watched as it lit up in all the colours of the rainbow. It was truly a miraculous sight. I had seen it light up before, but not in these colours. White Arrow's father was here. I watched, amazed, as the chair turned round. There, in front of me, was the most beautiful coat and crown, of every conceivable colour. For a moment, it blinded me. Slowly, the colours started to shimmer less and I could see quite clearly – not seeing the father, just the coat and the crown.

'Ann Walker, touch the staff,' he said quietly. 'Today, I give you the staff. It is in your guardianship. Use it wisely. This is the help you have asked White Arrow for. This will give you power and strength. I am the staff – remember that. With this you will go forward and show me to my people. Teach them of White Arrow, tell them of his coming. The staff will protect you on your journey.'

I know I should not have, but I had to say something at that stage. 'How will I use the staff? How will I know it works?' I blurted out. I was sorry I had to ask this and said so.

'I understand, Ann Walker, and White Arrow will teach you. Go to him tomorrow and he will show you. We put much trust in you. There will be many times when you do not understand, but we will show you everything. All in good time.'

Just then, the Earth appeared in the middle of the table. I watched the globe of the world light up as the staff disappeared in front of my eyes. Then White Arrow's father looked at White Arrow and spoke again. 'Take my son to your world. Help them to know that I have heard their prayers. Show them, Ann Walker, of his existence.'

· 5 ·

Jesus, Mary and Isis

It was 10 February 1993, and the research was still going on. Mrs Prince knew of the village to the north of Giza – it was the village Nazlet el Simman. She also told me that large snakes were very important to the Egyptians – I had had two strange dreams the previous year, both about large snakes. In one, the snake was about a mile long, and in the other one I saw a drain in a stream that suddenly changed into a huge snake, of fantastic size.

Also, that night, sitting out with the aliens, I saw another one. Mrs Prince went on to tell me that large snakes played an important religious role for ancient Egyptians and that there were drawings of them in some of the tombs there. The link between snakes and Egyptian tombs comes from the fact that the pyramids are full of hidden winding tunnels, guarding their secrets, suggesting a similarity with snakes – secretive, winding, mysterious creatures. The obvious similarity between them alludes to the underworld, to hidden worlds resembling the tunnels of the pyramids.

White Arrow showed me a snake and staff entwined together. This puzzled me. The next day, I found out that the snake and the staff were very important to ancient Egyptians. It made sense now that White Arrow had brought the snake and then changed it into a staff: it symbolized hidden sacred knowledge.

On 16 February an Indian friend who is a barrister came to see me. He told me he had to give me a name he had been given by the Spirit, although he didn't know the meaning of it. The word he gave me was SCHROZ, which I guessed to be Greek. At my request, François checked and phoned back shortly afterwards: 'Yes, it is Greek. It means "fish".' Again, the fish! I was puzzled as to why a fish was important, but I knew that White Arrow, by giving it to Chris to pass on to me, was doing so to prove I was on the right track and was making progress.

Someone else had told me that it was but a few days' walking from the place where Jesus was crucified to the pyramids. I had not checked this yet, but it felt right: there was a link between Jesus and the pyramids. I did not yet know what the link was, but I was sure I would find out . . . in time.

On 19 February I was feeling exhausted by all the pressure of work – it had been non-stop. For some unknown reason I had asked François to find out where Jesus had gone after his birth in Bethlehem. I found out that he was two years old when he went to Egypt. The British Museum stated that he went to Matariyah and Heliopolis, a place near Cairo. Why we were following the road of Jesus I had no idea, but in my heart it did not really surprise me. I knew that, somewhere in the hidden tomb, we would find evidence of Jesus and of the Second Coming. Which of the villages was I supposed to visit first, when I arrived in Egypt?

Later, I received the following information from Adrian Gilbert, which is relevant to quote here.

Heliopolis

Heliopolis is the Greek name for the very ancient Egyptian city of Annu, called On in the Bible. It was sacred to the high father of the gods, whom they called Atum. He was the invisible god who they believed created the universe. The hill of Annu was identified with the primal creation of land emerging out of the water. It was therefore sacred to Atum. There were a number of temples built here and many priests, but the most important was the temple of Atum. This had a holy pillar standing in it – the first obelisk. It probably represented the phallus of Atum, symbolic of his creative power. There was also a temple (perhaps the same one) sacred to the phoenix or bennu, a mythological bird depicted as a grey heron. It was thought that every so often it would come to visit the temple of Annu, where it would deposit a ball of myrrh containing the body of its dead parent. The appearances of the phoenix were infrequent: maybe once every 1,460 years or even longer. When it came it was the herald of a new age.

Also at Annu was a special stone called the benben. This seems to have been shaped either like a cone or a small pyramid, and it may have stood on top of the pillar of Atum. In *The Orion Mystery*, Robert Bauval and I suggested it might have been a meteorite, but it may also have been metal or, who knows, even part of a spaceship. There is a prayer in the Pyramid Texts which brings all of these legends together. It goes:

> *O Atum! When you came into being you rose up as a high hill,*
> *You shone as the benben stone in the Temple of the Phoenix in Heliopolis.*

The benben stone seems to have disappeared at about the time the pyramids were built. I imagine it is the same object that White Arrow calls the Stone of the Plough. Whatever it is, it is obviously of vital importance, as the Egyptians used to put replicas of the benben on top of their pyramids. These replica benbens are black stones which look like little pyramids. There are a couple of them in the Cairo Museum.

On 23 February 1993, Zipper gave me eight more words (*see* figure 5.1). At this stage I knew he was giving me sacred words that could be given only to the right people. These words were Coptic.

The visit to Egypt was drawing nearer. Although things were getting sorted out slowly, I had to be absolutely sure of my facts. I still had not sorted out the stars, but I was now getting the feeling that I could leave that until later. François had said he would go to the British Museum to see if he could find anyone who could read Coptic. I sent a silent prayer to White Arrow to help – I already knew that very few people knew the Coptic language.

What François found was that we had been given the names of places where Jesus had rested when he and his parents fled from Israel. Jesus had been to four places in Egypt. Interestingly enough a priest at a church François visited told him one place was in Cairo, mentioning that there was a tree at that place, in the middle of an open circus. My mind immediately went back to the man on stilts – the juggler. Was this what White Arrow had meant? I decided to go there first when I arrived in Cairo.

I also asked White Arrow and the aliens for more help with the words. On 24 February my medallion started to change colour. Zipper and White Arrow came. Zipper took the old Bible from Alien Girl, who had just arrived. White Arrow said, 'Listen and look.' They gave me one word (*see* figure 5.2).

I had not seen this word before. It looked as if it might be Greek. I looked up at Zipper and thanked him. With that he and Alien Girl waved goodbye and left. After I had faxed him, François phoned me. The word meant 'born to Mary', in koine Greek. I felt the whole message had something to do with an Egyptian church near a tree in the circus (or yard) in Matariyah, and I knew it was connected with the Virgin Mary – but that was all.

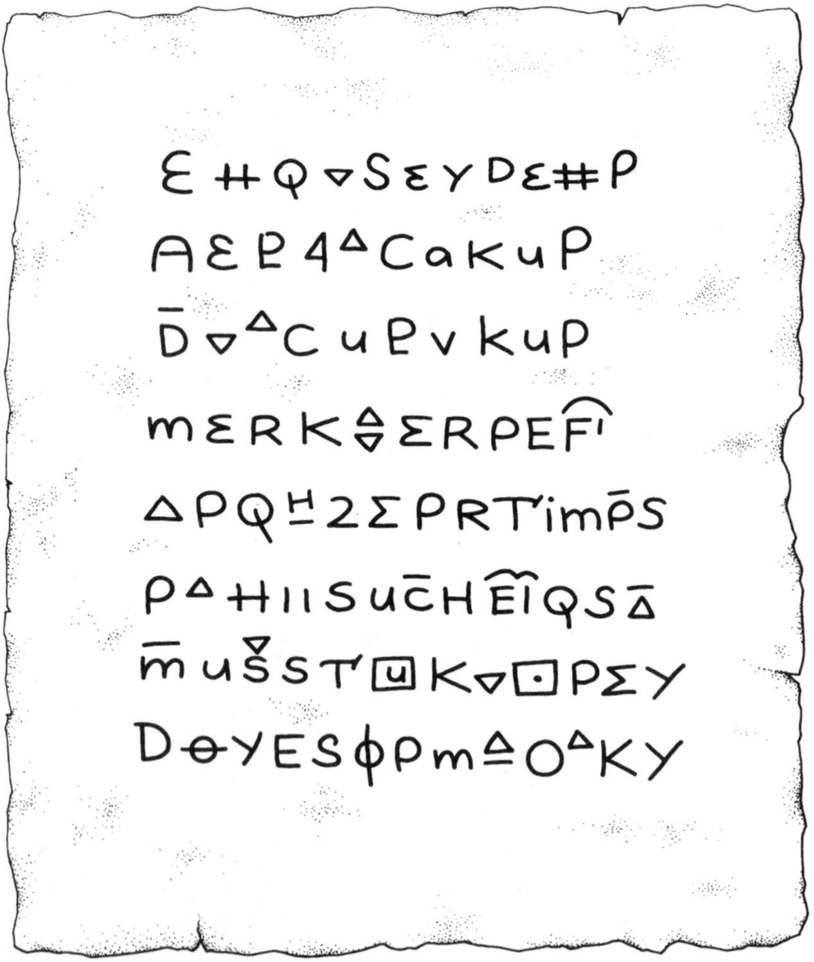

Names all of eight Goddesses who Created the Egg where the Universe is. The Gods are known by name: Co-Cokit, Ho-Hohit, Amun-Amunet, Sho-Shet.
Translated into English by Abdel Hakim Awayan

Figure 5.1 The Coptic words

ΣΤΚṼΗΘΜΡΣΥ
(Maꝛy Boꝛn)

Figure 5.2

'It's been hard work trying to figure everything out, but it is all so exciting as well.' This was my diary entry for 27 February. I was thinking how lucky I was to work for White Arrow. The words had given me my first clue as to where to start, although there was a lot more to do before I could open the tomb for White Arrow. Working with these old languages can be very difficult, but considering what White Arrow was about to reveal, I was not surprised that he would choose a cryptic, step-by-step method, so that only the people he guided to me could help me discover their meaning.

Jesus had been to four different places in Egypt, but my thoughts started wandering to the place where the tree was. White Arrow was taking me to the place with the tree. Much of the report in *Little One* had been about the rainforests and the importance of trees to the health of all life on Earth. There was a connection – the Tree of Life. Slowly but surely it was all making sense.

Meanwhile, Mrs Prince believed that the only people able to translate the Coptic words must be in Egypt. Coptic is not widely known, and there are very few experts in this field. She suggested it would probably be a local priest in Egypt who knew. Isis the Goddess also seemed to be playing a big part in deciding where I was to go in Egypt. Adrian Gilbert wrote some notes for me.

Isis and Horus

The ancient Egyptians believed that civilization had been brought to their land by the gods. According to a collection of texts known as the Thermotica, the souls of mankind had originally been sent down to Earth by God as a punishment for a transgression. They were clothed in human form like Adam and Eve, and forgot, whilst in the body, where they had come from. Unfortunately they began to destroy the Earth and one another with their wars and misdeeds. The Earth cried out to heaven for help and God sent a retinue of anthropomorphic 'gods' to teach man the right ways. The leader of this party was called Osiris, and he was married to his sister Isis. They also had another sister, Nephthys, and a brother, Set. Osiris was a good king, teaching respect for the law. However, his brother Set became jealous and plotted against Osiris and murdered him. Set then chopped up the body into 14 pieces and scattered them around Egypt.

The grieving widow, Isis, secretly collected up all the pieces of her husband's corpse and stitched them back together again to make the first mummy. Using magic and calling on the sun god, Ra, for help, she managed to resurrect Osiris long enough to have intercourse, and she became pregnant. Osiris, his work on Earth complete, ascended to the heavens (Duat in Egyptian) where he became the judge of the dead. Isis, meanwhile, hid herself amongst the papyrus groves of the Nile delta marshes and gave birth to a son called Horus. When he reached manhood, Horus challenged his uncle Set to a duel, to see who should rightfully inherit the kingdom. After a long, drawn-out battle, during which Horus lost an eye and Set his testicles, the gods decided in favour of Horus. He reinstituted the rule of law, called Maat, and put things to rights.

Thereafter, all Egyptian pharaohs were considered to be incarnations of Horus whilst they were alive. After death they were expected to be transformed into Osiris so that they could join him in the heavenly Duat. To do this they had to go through the same processes as Osiris: mummification, symbolic resurrection (the 'opening of the mouth' ceremony) and finally ascension. I believe that what they meant by saying pharaohs were an 'incarnation' of Horus was that they were mediums or channels through which Horus, symbolized by a hawk, could communicate with mankind. The 'gods' were undoubtedly extraterrestrial entities. I suspect they were physical and arrived in some sort of spacecraft. Presumably it was only the soul of Osiris that went back to their heaven, which seems to have been understood by the Egyptians as being the Belt of Orion. Personally, I think Isis and Horus did not leave the Earth but are still here as spirits.

Isis is also associated with the star Sirius, called Sothis by the Greeks and Spdt by the Egyptians. The Egyptian calendar was based on the cycles of Sirius – its dawn or heliacal rising in summer-time heralded the flooding of the Nile. Sirius is not only the brightest star in our sky (not counting the planets) but it is also a very close stellar neighbour, only 8.4 light-years away from us. It has been suggested by Robert Temple in *The Sirius Mystery* that extraterrestrials came from a planet that circles Sirius. Temple also believed that they came on a craft which splashed down in the Persian Gulf, and that they instructed the people of Babylonia in their religion. In Mesopotamian mythology there was a being called Oannes (the same as Johannes or John) who was half-fish and who emerged from the Persian Gulf. He taught them their arts and sciences just as the Egyptians were taught by Osiris. The connection between Mesopotamian and Egyptian religions is not fully understood, but there are many parallels.

I was so fortunate to have Adrian, François and Mrs Prince to help me on this. Although François had not visited Cairo since he was a child, he was very up-to-date with everything. Mrs Prince had been to Egypt many times and knew much about the gods and kings. Their combined help was immeasurable, and without them my journey would have been much harder and longer.

I am not surprised that White Arrow found them, for timing was so important in giving his message to the world. I reminded myself that I would have to look into the Eye. This had to do with Isis' son, Horus.

· 6 ·

Horus the Bear

It was 1 March 1993. White Arrow said I had to see Zipper every day of that week – it was important. Zipper appeared. Alien Girl appeared next to him, with Michael, Eagle and Bear. We were all present. Zipper smiled at me. He was showing me a picture.

The picture was of an eye. Then the word 'Egypt', then a fish. Then I thought of the temples belonging to DIPÎNOÂ; but what had the temples to do with the pyramids and the Sphinx? I then knew I was to look for the eye and the fish when I got to Egypt, but I did not know the connection between them. I resolved to remember this for the journey.

Bear had come forward. He has but one eye, and he said he would use that when we were out there to show me. I would come to understand his strength only when I was in Egypt.

I asked Zipper about the last eight words on the picture. We had found out that some of the letters in the words given might be mathematical. I asked Zipper about this and he explained, 'Yes, they are part of the key to open the pyramid. We will show you when you go to Egypt, I promise.'

'Will I meet the right person to show me the key?' I asked.

'Yes, we will take you to that person's very door. You now have your credentials – the people you meet will know what they mean.'

'Have patience, Little One,' said White Arrow quietly. Patience is something I still have to learn!

White Arrow's father was with us. He spoke. 'The time is coming when we have to take you to Egypt. It is important to my people. The staff will help you outside the pyramid. You will hold the staff and call on me. It will help your search, for the divine spirit is with you. The walls of Jericho will come down. I wish you to return to the ship. I have much to tell you. Listen to White Arrow, Zipper and the others carefully. What they have brought you many would fight for, but it is for mankind. Ann Walker, you must take it to mankind.'

White Arrow's father then left. Before he did so, the snake appeared and once again gave me the staff.

'Are there any more words today, Zipper?' I asked.

'No, the ones you have are all you need for now,' he replied.

I realized that from now on the road ahead would be much harder. White Arrow and I would not have the time together that we used to have. Selfishly, I would miss this. Yet what about the other aliens? Had they not also made great sacrifices, and left behind loved ones on their planets to answer White Arrow's call? I felt myself blush at my own self-importance and apologized to them.

I was beginning to learn a lesson they already knew. They had already given up much of their lives to come and help humanity – and they were not even from our planet! Everyone seemed to understand my struggle. I was very moved. Then Zipper got up. This meeting had ended. 'I'll see you tomorrow,' he said and gave me a smile. They all disappeared.

Two days passed. I found it all so incredible. I sat thinking about how far-fetched the whole situation seemed. Yet I reminded myself that everything White Arrow or the aliens had given me had proved in the end to be 100 per cent accurate. Yet it was frightening, too much, and I wondered, why me? Why would White Arrow choose someone like me to help? It was no use worrying about it – there were far more important things to worry about! White Arrow had never let me down, so it would be crazy if I let him down. I owed my life to White Arrow and his father. So I chose to carry on, for everybody's sake.

They wanted me to return to the ship today. Suddenly I was on board. There was no warning! This time I arrived in their medical room. Then before I knew it, I was back in the meeting room. Why the medical room first, I do not know. Once again, the room was in darkness. White Arrow was standing near the window, so I walked over to him.

I followed his gaze. I could see the Earth in its full glory, so beautiful and majestic from our view in space. It was truly an awe-inspiring sight. I turned to White Arrow and saw a tear fall slowly down his cheek. It was overwhelming. I felt choked with emotion, angry, so angry at myself and humanity. White Arrow was crying for *us*, mankind and Mother Earth, for all our pain and suffering. It was a cry of love. I felt ashamed for mankind – and for myself, habitually complaining as I do about my own problems.

Whatever doubts I had suddenly left me. There was no way I would turn my back on White Arrow's journey to help save our living planet. I looked back at the Earth, to respect White Arrow's privacy during this very personal moment. Suddenly, I felt his presence go. The room was still in darkness. I watched the Earth for a few moments more, then turned around. White Arrow was now standing a few feet behind me, back to his normal self.

He smiled and beckoned me to come and sit down. I took my place at the table. As I looked again at White Arrow I was astonished to see that he was encircled in a blue light. I wiped my eyes and looked again. The blue had now gone. I marvelled, thinking how lucky the world was to have this alien, White Arrow. His father had sent him to help us. It made me feel very humble in his presence.

I was wondering why I had been brought up to the ship today, when suddenly the room and the chairs began to light up. The room filled with a wonderful perfume. I relaxed into my chair. White Arrow walked towards the window once again. I felt he might be waiting for something out there. Suddenly, something flew past the window. It was so fast, I could not make out what it was – it was the first time I had seen activity outside the ship.

Then I was back in the medical room, then I was going to and from my chair to the medical room in short, quick visits. It was making no sense – it had not happened before. I felt apprehensive but I knew I would not come to any harm. Then I was back in the meeting room. The door opened and Zipper, Alien Girl, Bear, Eagle then Michael came in to take their seats at the table. We all acknowledged one another.

For the first time, White Arrow sat in his father's chair, although it was not lit up as it usually was when his father came. To see White Arrow sit there made me wary, because I knew now he must be even more important than anyone could have realized. God had sent us help before, but I wondered if the prophets, adepts and teachers of history had been as close to God as he.

White Arrow was speaking to the others in a language I could not understand. In the meantime I occupied myself testing whether or not the table would take my weight, should I want to lean on it; it did, and that made me happy. It is a strange human characteristic, reaching for the tangible in the midst of the unknowable!

There were still conversations going on round the table as Zipper spoke some words to me: SUNQUED TES'HPEQE. I did not know the meaning, but I knew I would find out in time. Meanwhile Alien Girl came over to me and put a paper in front of me. It was the X-ray-type picture again. Before I looked at it White Arrow spoke to me: 'Do not worry, Little One, I will show you it later.' I was still thinking about the words they had given me before the picture.

Alien Girl returned to her chair. I liked her. Just then, White Arrow gazed at me, his bright blue eyes seeing through me. I felt transparent. Then he said, 'On your journey to Egypt I will be with you. We will be as one. Bear and Eagle will also be with us. I want you to follow us and listen to us. When you are there you will be protected, so do not fear.' I had been a bit worried, because there had been reports of tourists in Egypt being threatened and killed by fundamentalists. Now I knew I would be safe.

He spoke again. 'In the coming months before you go, and when you return, there will be many meetings that will take place. I will give you the necessary strength, for this journey will require a lot of concentration from you. I will be by your side to help you understand. I know it is hard, and you have done well, but it is going to get harder. I know you realize this, but remember I will be at your side. Soon the door will be opening for people to know of my coming. You will be out there on your own, but remember, you will have me at your side always.'

He turned to the others, then back to me. 'My father has sent these people to help. Call on their help at all times, for they are your friends as well as mine. I have spoken this way today because of the tide of events that are to take place soon. I want you to have no fear of me leaving your side.'

Suddenly, all of them put their hands on the table and laid them on each other, one by one, in the middle of the table. White Arrow came towards me. 'Stretch out your hand, Little One. Lay it on top of theirs.' As I did so, White Arrow placed his on top of mine. 'Now we are one,' he said.

We all sat back. It felt solemn and quiet. The other aliens then left silently, one by one. The room darkened again until only White Arrow and I remained. Once again he beckoned me towards the window, pointing towards the Earth. 'This is my work, to save and help your world. It must be done soon, before all perish. Come.'

As he turned, I was back home. 'Do you want me to see Zipper tonight?' I asked. 'Yes,' he replied, and was gone.

That day I also had more verification of the words given. The British Library had replied about the second set of eight words (I had given them only four of the second set of eight words for security reasons). They confirmed that they were Coptic. I was pleased. They had also been in touch with a professor who knew the language, who had asked to see some more. François and I sent him four more words to decipher. I decided at this stage that I could send no more. All White Arrow wanted me to do was to find verification of these Coptic writings, so I would know that what I wrote was genuine, but that was all – I was not to give out the secrets until the right time.

I somehow knew that these and drawings still to come held secrets people had searched after for centuries and I had to be careful by keeping them safe. I hoped the professor could decipher them, but something told me they were not yet for my knowledge. In the meantime I was overjoyed that they were indeed verified to be Coptic – only White Arrow could have given me words that came from the time of Jesus Christ and I could not have known anything about such a language, let alone written it.

Zipper later arrived with Bear. White Arrow was also there. So much was happening that it was difficult to keep up. Alien Girl was here now with the old book. Zipper spoke. 'We will show you more writings later, but I want you to concentrate on the first eight words. During these meetings I will show you where you are to go in Egypt. When in Egypt, keep in contact with the medallion. It will help. I will want to see you tomorrow. It is important these meetings take place this week.'

With that, Zipper stood up. I promised him I would make time for the meetings. Zipper smiled and said he would see me the following day. Bear growled his farewell, Alien Girl bade me adieu and I said goodnight to all of them.

On 3 March I saw François. He brought me a copy of a letter from the British Library, verifying that the four words of the eight that were sent were Coptic. I was over the moon. Proof at long last! The other words, SUNQUED TES'HPEQE, which I had received the day before were easier to translate, since they were in Arabic. I had been told that they derive from the pharaohs. The pharaonic words mean 'Keeper of the Shapka (token)'. The set of eight words were Coptic and the last three words pharaonic, thousands of years older.

The next day, Zipper was there, waiting. When I came into the back room I was asking White Arrow a few questions to do with other things, and Zipper was not amused. I apologized, for I knew his time was important and not to be wasted. Incidentally, that morning, when I had been out, I had seen Zipper quite clearly in the medallion – it was the first time he had communicated that way. He never spoke, but just looked around.

Bear was there, and Alien Girl had appeared with the book. She and Zipper conversed for a minute, then he spoke to me. 'Soon you will be going to Egypt. We must help you on this journey. I will be giving you certain words that hold keys to where to go – not all, for you will be *led* out there as well. We will start with the next words: SYRETQETE FUH MORQHSET SHURMETTE PUSHQTE DESHUQE. You will find these words.'

I knew that these words were not Coptic but pharaonic, like the previous three. Zipper's feet suddenly changed colour – red, then green. I did not know why. I hoped that, when this was all finished, I might learn more of the aliens' ways.

I asked Bear and Eagle about the writing I had done on Isis (researched by Adrian Gilbert), hoping it was all right. Their answer was a revelation. 'Eagle was Isis the Goddess,' said Bear. 'I was Horus.' I was stunned. I had not realized that both had been gods to the Egyptians. I decided to do research on Horus.

Horus

There were two gods who bore the name Horus: the first was a solar deity and brother of Set, the second the child of Osiris and Isis. In later times the Egyptians appeared to have been either unable or unwilling to distinguish between the two. The offspring of Osiris and Isis was also considered to be a sun god, and thus the two gods became one.

The name Horus is a latinized form of the Greek Hores, which in turn is derived from the Egyptian Hor. This name may come from the same root as the Egyptian word for 'high' or 'far away'. Horus was represented as either a falcon or a falcon-headed man. His two eyes symbolized two heavenly bodies: the right eye was the sun and the left the moon. However, the phrase 'the Eye of Horus' usually referred to the moon. It was this eye that was lost to Set, and later, after being recovered, was presented to Osiris to aid him in his resurrection. The four sons of Horus, Imset, Qebehsenuf, Duamuttef and Hapi, acted as guides to the dead.

The falcon was sacred to Horus from the earliest times, and the image of a falcon on its perch became the hieroglyphic symbol representing the word 'god'. Many sanctuaries were dedicated to him. In each one, his priests appear to have developed their own collection of myths associated with the god. So varied did these become that at first glance it would appear that there were over a dozen gods bearing the name Horus, some of which are mentioned below.

Haroeris. Worshipped at Letopolis and at Pharbocthos, Haroeris' name in Egyptian was Har-Wer – Horus the Great or Horus the Elder. To the priests of Letopolis he was also known as Horkenti Irti – Horus Who Rules the Two Eyes – whilst at Pharbocthos, he was Hor Marti – Horus of the Two Eyes. His birth was celebrated when the sun and moon were in conjunction (at new moon).

In the Pyramid Texts, illustrations show Ra, the great sun god, with his sons Horus and Set either side of him. Horus represented light and Set darkness. In the eternal battle between the two gods, Set rips out his brother's eye and is in return castrated by Horus. In later texts the battle is between Set and his nephew Horus the son of Osiris, and not Horus the Elder.

Harakhte. Harakhte meant 'the god on the horizon'. Horus was the first state god of Egypt, but in early times he appeared to have become so confused with Ra that the two gods exchanged places, with Ra eventually becoming known as Ra-Harakhte.

Behdety or Bedhey. Behdety or Bedhey was worshipped at Behdety in Edfu. The myth linking Horus and Edfu tells of an occasion when Ra-Harakhte, who was with his army in Nubia, heard of a plot against him led by Set. Ra-Harakhte sailed down the Nile from Nubia to Edfu, where Set had assembled his demonic army. Ra commanded his son Horus to fight on his behalf against his enemy. This Horus did, rising up into the sky in the form of a fiery disc and flying over the land, slaying the demonic followers of Set wherever he found them. To commemorate Horus' valuable service his father Ra gave him the title Horus Behdety, Horus of Edfu.

Behdety was usually represented in the form of a winged sun disc and may be seen carved above temple gates and other places. He is also present in battle scenes where he flies protectively above the pharaoh in the form of a great falcon holding the ring of eternity. (That was what Bear was trying to tell me during my fast at the Indian sacred ground in the United States, mentioned in chapter 1: he had been there when the pyramids were built. The aliens were gods to the Egyptians.)

I asked White Arrow what was the object or person referred to as 'the Keeper of the Shapka'. 'It is the key to the Forbidden Kingdom,' was all he would say. I wondered to myself what *that* meant. 'You carry the key, Little One. You are the Keeper of the Shapka. In time, Little One, you will understand.' I did not *want* to know what he meant, but I had an idea. It had to do with the drawings of the Coptic writings I had done.

Zipper waited for me to finish my notes. 'Again, I would like to see you tomorrow,' he said, stretching his hand out to me in a loving gesture. I held my hand in his. There was a tremendous feeling of warmth and love. I thanked him once again, and Bear and Eagle, then they left.

Next day, 5 March 1993, I was writing my journal while at the hairdressers – that was how hectic things were getting! I was extremely tired. There was little time; I was having trouble keeping up. On top of everything I had my clients to see. My body ached and I was getting headaches, but I knew that was just the strain of the work. I needed a break, but I knew it would not be possible for a while yet. White Arrow, please show me what to do with the words, I wrote. Help me with all this, White Arrow.

I was booking the trip to Egypt for the middle of May 1993. It was only eight weeks away, and so much was unfinished! I knew White Arrow and the aliens would not be pushing me so hard unless it was very urgent. I could not fold now, but I also could not take much more.

On 6 March, Zipper came, and Alien Girl appeared with a book. 'Zipper,' I started, 'could I have all the words at one go today?' He smiled. 'I feel it would be better for both us,' I added. He took the book from Alien Girl and opened it. Bear and Michael were now also there.

I was beginning to realize what White Arrow's father meant when he said they were amongst the highest in the galaxy, now that I was aware of the fact that Bear and Eagle had been regarded as gods by the people of Egypt. But what did that make White

Arrow? He was far more important than I ever could have realized, I now knew that, too. Zipper started to show me the next sequence of words.

SHQURST	FERH	SYTRETTE	CUQTHE	At Saqqara speaks a jacket in Coptic
MUAQDE	FUQSTEQUER	TI HI	QST	It is part of a dowry and will be good in the future
FEISH	QUETTI	MUTUQET	PHUREH	Ti – of him the Lion there is a portion/share
SEIRQTER	FINESHQTE	QUESTET		At Matariyah there is a young goddess where there is a portion
MUADEE	PHYFISQE	SESQTER		Cairo Saint get ready for reward from young goddess
DUESTRE	FINQSTE	WYENFIZH		A portion in village of Giza

'These go with the last words I have given you,' said Zipper (the last set was SYRETQETE FUH MORQHSET SHURMETTE PUSHQTE DESHUQE). The pharaonic words belonged to the kings of Egypt thousands of years ago. The Arabic words were written phonetically, needing translation into modern Arabic. 'Thanks, Zipper,' I said.

'You're welcome,' he replied. 'You will find what you are looking for in these letters.'

Then he opened the book again and showed me a drawing (*see* figure 6.1). This was new to me. I did not understand it at all. 'Nor do you need to, Little One. You will find there will be many drawings that mean nothing to you, but in time you will be taken to people who will understand and will give you the true meanings for you to tell the world. All of these writings are sacred and come from many years ago. You are to go to St Mary's Church in Cairo when you first arrive there. We will speak more before you go, but for now I have given you enough information. Put them together. When you have finished, come to me and I will help.'

Then he stood up and continued, 'No, you don't have to come tomorrow. Today I have given all that is necessary.'

'Thanks again, Zipper,' I replied.

'We will give you strength and help,' he added. I knew what he meant. We all then said our goodbyes and parted. Zipper said he would see me soon.

HIERATIC WRITING

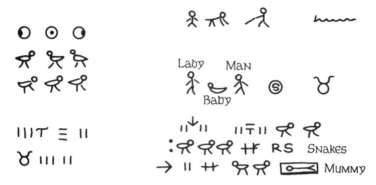

The SiGN LaNGuaGe – HIERATIC oR THE TRuTH backed iN black to be safe, Not to be taken advaNtaGe of, aNd Not to cause harm aNd that is cleaR iN the drawiNG of the FATHER, the SON, aNd the HOLY GHOST – aNd it is old peRiods symbols aloNG the planets histoRy

TRaNslated iNto ENGlish, 25 July 1994, by Abdel Hakim AwayaN

Figure 6.1 Hieratic writing (1)

François arrived later, to go through some of the words. I discovered that the first word of the Arabic, Saqqara, was the name of the place where they built the first pyramids, before those built at Giza. It was also the first place I was to go to on my trip to Egypt. Also, there was a temple of Coptic writings which was in ruins, and most of the surviving work there had been moved to Cairo. I now knew where to go. Also, at Saqqara they had keepers, and I felt sure I was to see them. Would they know what the messages meant?

It was understandable that White Arrow, Bear and Eagle would take me to the first pyramids ever to be built. Only the last Arabic words were still to be found, and hopefully that would complete the information we needed for the journey. Also, very importantly, François and I found out that at Matariyah there is a tree called the Virgin Tree, where Mary and Jesus had apparently rested on their journey. There was talk of a keeper there who read Coptic. I would have to go there.

On 9 March, White Arrow said that Zipper wanted to see me in the back room. Bear appeared, then Zipper, then Alien Girl. I said hello to Zipper, who acknowledged me. He was reading something. I talked to Bear in the meantime. 'I know now what you meant when you said during my fast in America, "I helped build the pyramids".' He nodded his head in agreement.

Michael and Eagle materialized. 'We will help,' they all said together. They had heard my silent prayers for help and I knew I would be sure of their protection. Zipper now looked up. Not more words, I thought to myself. He showed me the tree I was to visit. 'You are to walk three and a half times around it. When you have done this, stop and look at the tree and wait.' Wait for what? I thought. Faith, Ann. Strength and faith. I will do it for them when I get there.

White Arrow spoke. 'I will bring news of importance to you soon. I will protect you.'

'I know, White Arrow.'

'Do not worry, Little One. Everything has been taken care of.' There was tremendous love in the room.

'QRESTUAE PQULLE', Zipper said. 'We are taking you on an important trip. It is for mankind, and you will be safe. We will all be with you.'

'Thank you, Zipper.' I looked around the room and thanked them all.

Zipper continued: 'We will want to see you this week, as often as possible. This has to do with the trip – and other things.'

'Okay,' I replied.

Zipper then stood up and put the paperwork under his arm. 'I will return.' He stretched out his arm and touched me. 'Call on the medallion for strength.' I was going to ask him about the medallion, since I had recently clearly seen him in it. But before I could ask, he was already answering. 'Yes, you are in direct contact with me,' he replied. He waved goodbye and they all left together.

· 7 ·

The Second Teacher

It was 10 March 1993. Zipper spoke first. 'These now are for you to take to Egypt. No one is to see them until you have been there. We will show you who to go to.' He handed me a drawing with more letters (*see* figure 7.1). (Figure 7.2 shows the translation.) The drawing was of a pyramid again.

'The Coptic writing received is on parchment paper buried somewhere in Egypt. The writing I give you with numbers is from Imhotep, which he wrote when he was alive,' said Zipper.

I was finding the latest words very difficult. They were in very old Coptic and needed to be translated. I now knew there were three sets of pyramids I would have to visit before the jigsaw was complete. I just hoped I could keep my strength up. I had never worked so hard in my life. Thank God I had such a wonderful husband – Tony knew it was hard for me, and when I got irritable with him, he knew I did not mean it.

Suddenly, Zipper and Michael appeared in the room, then Alien Girl with Eagle. Then the Lion was there, White Arrow's father. Zipper had the book with him. Not more words, Zipper, please! These last few have been difficult enough! Zipper changed his colour, but only for a few seconds.

I asked Michael how he was. 'Fine', he replied. We did not often get a chance to socialize because the workload was so time-consuming. Eagle spoke: 'Do not worry. We will be out there tonight.' I knew what she meant – when we met out in the back garden I felt closer to them. I thanked her.

'Soon you will see the light,' Zipper said, shutting the book.

'Zipper, how far does that book go back?' I asked.

'In this book many things of long ago are recorded. It holds the

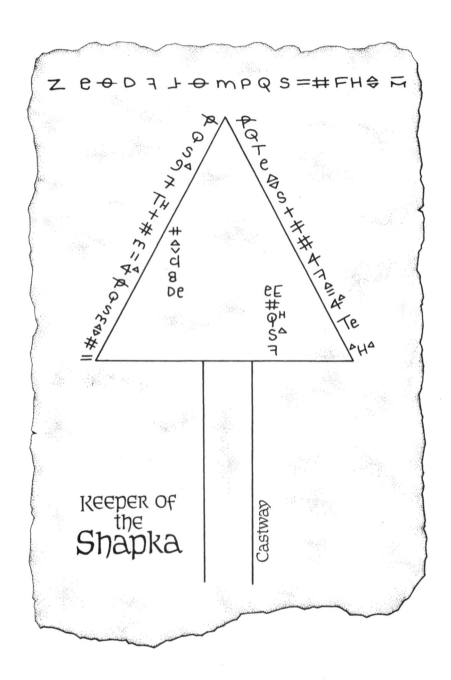

Figure 7.1

Site Universal Key

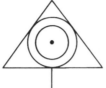

The Binds within the double circle
within the divided Triangle —
The Fire that holds the Essence of
the DIVINE —
The Gold that purified in the Flame of
Initiation —
The Eye of God in the capstone of
the PYRAMID —
The Measure of the Mastery
IMMORTALITY

The chambers to be found within the GIZA
HALL of RECORDS shall be many and varied,
something PYRAMID shaped, or having a
PYRAMID within a PYRAMID. Others shall be a
tetrahed or three sided. Still others shall be
Cone-shaped, even spherical or CRYSTAL shaped.
Many will have no defined walls at all, being
ATTACHED to, but NO PART OF, this Physical
Plane.

This is a translation by Abd. El. Hakim Awayan of
Nazlet el Samman village, next to the GIZA PYRAMID
whom WHITE ARROW led me to.

Figure 7.2

key to many things of the future too. We are taking you to find the book. We will show you where it is. It will help the world know of us and of many other things – but most of all of White Arrow. Yes, it is the book that you are going to Egypt for. Much is written that people have not found before, and in it are recorded many events.'

I knew the book in Egypt must be ancient. Would it be written on parchment, on a wall, or what? 'Will I recognize the book?' I asked him.

'Some know of the whereabouts of it, but only those who are sworn to secrecy – and they are the ones who will lead you to it.'

'If they know, Zipper, why don't *they* get it?' I asked.

'They know of its whereabouts. I didn't say they know *exactly*.'

'Sorry, Zipper.' Of course, White Arrow would have taken care to make sure that possibility did not exist.

'These people we shall take you to know of your coming. They are waiting. They also have great faith in their God and will only give it to the right person who shows them the keys. You hold the keys. The journey is long. The keys are in parts. One person knows one thing, the other knows another, but we will lead you.

'When you find the book you will take it to the world. Bear and Eagle will show you the way. It is *their* work, on behalf of White Arrow and his father. I will speak more tomorrow. It is better this way, so that you digest it bit by bit. I will see you later.' With that, Zipper and the aliens left.

Then I heard White Arrow. He spoke to me softly. 'Do not worry, Little One, everything is planned for your visit to Egypt.'

'I know, I trust you, White Arrow, but *who* are you?' I asked.

'One day, Little One,' was his reply. I presumed he would tell me when he was ready – or when I was. All I knew was that he was here to help the world.

'I love you, White Arrow,' I said. He smiled and left.

At last! François had found all the words. It was 13 March. Now all I needed to do was try to understand it all, and then I would be ready for Egypt. At long last I knew where to go.

SYRETQETE	secrets/herbs
FUH	mouth
MORQHSET	of the palace
SHURMETTE	inlet
PUSHQTE	blessings or offerings
DESHUQE	small house of Daher

In other words: 'Secrets will be spoken of the palace inlet, blessings at a small house.' The rough meaning of the remaining block of words, reading downwards, was: 'At Saqqara speaks a jacket in Coptic. It is part of a dowry and will be good in the future. Ti – of him the Lion there is a portion/share. At Matariyah there is a light/young goddess where there is a portion. Cairo Saint get ready for reward from young goddess. A portion in village of Giza.'

Saqqara was my first place to visit. I did not understand it all, but I knew where to go. The rest would be revealed later on. So my instructions were laid out in front of me. I was to go to Saqqara, Matariyah, Cairo and the village of Giza.

On 15 March I made the booking for Egypt. I had a feeling this trip would not be the one where I would find the tomb the aliens wanted me to show the world, but I would follow the directions they gave me and see what unfolded. I would probably have to return later. Tony was not very happy about all this; he was worrying about my safety, but I assured him that White Arrow would look after me. It was to Tony's credit that he chose to trust that this would be so; he never stood in my way.

Zipper wanted to see me. He appeared around noon with Alien Girl. I was starting to get a bit worried that they were not going to come, since they arrived later than expected. Still, it taught me not to take anything or anyone for granted on this journey. Zipper smiled. 'We won't leave,' he assured me.

'I know, Zipper, but . . .'

'No buts', said White Arrow. 'Look and listen.'

Zipper was getting some papers ready. I interrupted to ask his help with a word. I told him the word and he spelled it out. Then he showed me what looked like a globe of the world. He then gave it to Alien Girl. Bear and Michael arrived. Then Zipper brought in the book and I waited for his instructions. He gave me more words:

PHURHUS	TUMAB	GHUAD'D	FHERUPH	SULTEMB	FEMURHS
QESBERAS	NEIMUS	KUENHQS	SUPHEUR	FEURHS	PUEMUES
TUMBABS	SUESUEMS	KUM BEUS	TI	THOUERHES	

I had thought the previous words had been all I needed for Egypt, but apparently not! I got the feeling that these words continued from the previous ones – perhaps it was more information to instruct and help me when I got there.

Old Arabic	Modern Arabic	English
PHURHUS	BARAHA	place
TUMAB	TAMAM	perfect
GHUAD'D	GAADA	main path
FHERUPH	FARABI	second teacher
SULTEMB	SULTAN	king/ruler
FERMURHS	THEMARA	fruit
QUESBERAS	QUESBARAH	using the plough
NEIMUS	NAMOUS	gospel
KUENHQS	KANAS	besides me
SUPHEUR	SAPOUR	patient
FEURHS	FARAS	horse
PUEMEUS	BAHIMA	domestic animal
TUMBABS	SHA SHAMS	door of the tomb
SUE SUEMS	H HAM BEA	King of the Sun
QUM BEUS	KAUM B'HAS	courageous people thanks to God
TI		Ti the deity
THOUERHES	BAJOUR HUA	incense

Properly interpreted, this meant: 'Follow main path to perfect place – rewards from king (pharaoh) Imhotep, besides me, White Arrow and the aliens – with patience, these people of great courage, thanks to God, with the king, will show me the door of the tomb of Ti. Incense is his.'

Zipper stood up. 'I will see you later.' With that they all left.

On 15 March François confirmed that the Egyptian lady would be my guide for four days while I was out there. Meanwhile, the date had changed to 13 May. But there was still much to do!

By 19 March I found out what QRESTUAE PQULLE meant – at last! It meant 'In the knowledge of God'. This was an acknowledgement of the spiritual orientation of White Arrow and the aliens. Also, the drawing of the pyramid with words (figure 7.1) had been proved to be Coptic, so I would have to wait until my visit to Egypt to get an explanation of it.

I hoped that meant everything was sorted out now – but who knew with this journey? Now all I had to do was put all the words together – the aliens had strung together a cleverly mysterious thread of clues! At 3.30pm they asked me to see them. The medallion had changed colour.

'Hi, Zipper.' He was already sitting down in the back room with Alien Girl at his side. Then Bear, Michael and Eagle appeared. I was first with a question: 'Zipper, I need to know some answers to the words you gave me. Firstly, who was, or who is the "second teacher"?'

'Imhotep,' came the reply. I had had a feeling it was him, but I was glad to have it confirmed.

'And "fruit"?' I asked.

'It means the fruits of your journey.' I also asked about the word 'king' which related to Imhotep. 'Imhotep was a king in his own right,' said Zipper.

'Who is Imhotep, White Arrow, and what has he to do with our journey?' I asked.

'All will be revealed in time. He is very important to our journey. He has helped us in the past and is to help us in the future.' I knew very little about Egypt and its kings, so I needed to find out about Imhotep. Once again, I was taken aback that such important people were to help me on the journey to Egypt.

Imhotep and Ancient Egypt

The early pre-dynastic Egyptians lived in villages scattered along the banks of the Nile. They existed in isolated communities, cultivating crops and keeping domesticated animals such as dogs, goats, sheep, cattle and pigs. There was no unified leadership, although they probably combined together under one or more leaders to meet a challenge from nature or from rival groups. Eventually, these scattered communities coalesced into the two kingdoms of Upper and Lower Egypt, about 3168 BC. Upper Egypt was the dominant kingdom, setting the pattern of pharaonic Egypt.

During the Third Dynasty, Zoser (Djoser, Tchesar) came to the throne. Prior to his reign all buildings were constructed mainly of mud brick, with some stone incorporated in the form of flooring, lintels and jambs. However, Zoser's chancellor Imhotep (c2680 BC) was pre-eminent in his time and renowned in later ages as an astronomer, architect, writer, physician and sage. It was he who invented building in dressed stone, as shown by the Step Pyramid he built at Saqqara, where his name is carved in equal pride of place with that of the king. This pyramid complex, made entirely of cut and dressed stone, was the wonder of its age and set the standard for all subsequent Egyptian buildings.

It is said that the temples at Philar and the series of magnificent stone buildings that arose at Kom Ombo, Edfu and Esna in Ptolemaic and Roman times were built to an architectural plan which was supposed to have been revealed in a codex that fell from heaven at Saqqara in the days of Imhotep.

Imhotep was also an early high priest of the sun god at Heliopolis, where his title was Chief of the Observers, which suggests that his role was connected with astronomy and observation of the stars. He was later deified as Imuthes, a god of wisdom and healing, and was celebrated throughout later Egypt as the virtual founder of its culture. His achievements became legendary among later generations of Egyptians, who regarded him not only as an architect but also as a magician, an astronomer and the father of medicine. In Saite times he was elevated to the status of a god, being considered the son of Ptah.

I now understood. I asked Zipper if there were any more words, and to my great relief he said I had enough for the time being! 'These words will help you on your journey for us. I will tell you when I need to help you next.'

'Thank you, Zipper,' I said – and I meant it!

Bear suddenly growled a greeting. I said hello and he put out his hand in friendship. Zipper then stretched his hand out, gently patted me on the knee and said, 'I will see you tomorrow', reminding me that I was to return to the ship. Then: 'Do not worry about the medallion.'

I had earlier been worrying about getting the messages from the medallion right. One colour meant I was to see them, another colour that I was to travel, and I was becoming confused. He continued, 'Later, when it is used more often, you will then remember.'

'Thanks, Zipper,' I replied. That was a relief. Then they vanished, except for White Arrow.

'I am proud of you,' he said. I did not know what I had done to cause that, but nevertheless it made me feel it was all worthwhile and I thanked him for saying so.

At last, I had a weekend break by the coast with my family, without whose love and support I could not have done so much. I was soon back, however. I was due to go up on the ship shortly, but White Arrow appeared and I took the opportunity to speak to him alone – a rare thing in those days! 'White Arrow, I know what the journey is about – at least I *think* I know. You're here to save the trees and prove who you are, but I really do not know *who* you are, except that you are returning as an alien. Is that right?'

There was a pause, then White Arrow answered. 'Yes, Little One, I am a living being who has travelled many light-years to come here for my father. I am the Son of God. It is not enough now to send a man to Earth to seek to demonstrate proof to mankind of the miracles that will take place. Mankind will fight such a man as myself. Time will be wasted. Time cannot be wasted because of Mother Earth and all who live on her. So we have chosen *you* to introduce me to your people. Through you we will show the powers of God, my father.

'When the time comes for mankind to believe, then I will present myself through you. But for now I have to put much on your shoulders. I am sorry, for I know how hard you have worked for me. You have shown faith that no other person could have given. Yes, Little One, this is why you have been chosen. But remember the plan.'

My mind went back to what they had once told me of my previous life with White Arrow. 'But surely,' I said, 'the faith I have comes from the past, so if I have always had the faith then it does not make me special, White Arrow'.

White Arrow smiled, understanding my dilemma. 'I know what you are trying to say, Little One, but even when you were born you were still given free will, and we had to wait to see when the time came whether you would give and trust as much. You have not failed me. Do not fear the future, Little One. Yes, it will be hard and many will try to stop you, but remember I am here and your friends the aliens will protect you for ever. In Egypt much will happen to you but it will only give you more strength for the future. Believe what you see, for many things will be shown to you and miracles will be demonstrated for you to take to the world.'

'White Arrow, you're putting an awful lot of trust in me . . . ,' I said. It was rather a silly thing to say. I really had no need to worry if White Arrow assured me that he would protect my family and myself. What am I doing questioning that? I thought. I know he will look after us. I was being self-centred. Here was I complaining, and what was White Arrow doing? Saving the world. 'White Arrow, I really mean that, and I promise I won't grumble any more about our not having the time together that we used to have.'

There are times when I realize how foolish I am, and this was one of them. White Arrow seemed to be aware of my inner conflict. 'Do not worry, Little One. In the future we will have times to talk. Remember, I am always with you.'

· 8 ·

Paperwork!

As I arrived on the ship my attention focused on the window. From where I was standing I could see out to the Earth and some way beyond. The room was in darkness. The only light was coming from the stars and the reflected light of the Earth's atmosphere. The Earth moved into view and I just stood and stared. To me, this view itself was a miracle – being on an alien craft and seeing the world from space.

I could see the aura of the Earth's atmosphere. For a moment I wondered where my house was, and I just laughed to myself at the thought – the galaxy spread out before me and here I was, trying to spot my house! I turned my gaze towards the stars. Everything looked so peaceful and beautiful from here. I could have gazed for ever, but I heard movement and turned round to see White Arrow behind me.

'Come,' he said and pointed me to my lit-up chair. He walked towards the window and stood there, looking out at the Earth below. I watched him. I felt a sudden gush of love and pride, proud to have been chosen to help him in this work. His apparent importance in the heavenly scheme of things had never once changed my experience of him. He was, and is, always kind and gentle, a man of compassion. He is our saviour.

I felt rather humble and small. There were the five aliens who had been chosen to help White Arrow. There were White Arrow and his father, and here was I, a very ordinary person, sitting with the Highest in the galaxies.

White Arrow turned to me and smiled, his blue eyes twinkling. He looked happy today. I was glad too, thinking how upsetting it had been, the day I saw his tears. I began to think how hard this whole task must be for him. But I am only a mortal, and what seemed hard for me was nothing to what God can do.

Suddenly, the room lit up and Bear, Eagle, Alien Girl, Zipper and Michael entered through the door to my left, greeting me as they all came in and sat down. Alien Girl rose from her chair and passed some notes around – none for me this time. I sat watching White Arrow's father's chair, expecting it to light up at any minute. White Arrow was standing at the side of it. I looked past him to the window, longing to look out at the marvellous view again, but I knew I should stay seated.

Then Zipper spoke to me. 'You understand the instructions we have given you for Egypt?'

'Yes, Zipper. I understand most of it, but there are still a few things I am not sure of. One is, why Ti?'

'This we will show you when you go,' he explained.

'Nothing is to happen this time though, is it?' I asked. I hoped he would say no (and put me out of my misery), but he ignored the question and busied himself with his notes again.

Bear was next to speak. 'I will instruct you when you get there.' I already knew Eagle would be with him. I had a feeling I knew the reason for returning to the ship this time, but I could not be sure. White Arrow had said the ship was my home – that was a comforting thought.

Everybody was busy reading their notes, so I took the chance to examine the room more closely. I still had the feeling that it had been designed to make me feel comfortable and at ease for my visits to the ship – a touch of home from home.

Just then the chair started to light up. White Arrow's father arrived. Everyone stopped what they were doing. Alien Girl collected all the notes from the table and sat down. The chair started to move and, within seconds, there was White Arrow's father.

The crown on his head was shimmering in so many colours that it took a moment for my eyes to get used to it. There was an incredible holiness in the room. I could feel it and breathe it. It was inexplicable; I felt instantly compelled to bow down on my knees to his holy Presence. It filled the room. Words cannot begin to describe the overwhelming power and divinity of his aura. I wanted to give my thanks to him, but he knew how I felt. I sat in awe, and waited for him to speak.

'Ann Walker, you have been brought here today about Egypt. On this journey many miracles will be performed. These miracles will be for mankind. They will happen to you. You must accept them. Do not be scared of the responsibility connected with them. Others will watch these miracles that happen to you. Bear and Eagle, with my son, will protect you out there. When you need me, use the staff. Do not be scared of the journey, for I will be watching and my protection will be with you. I want you to prepare yourself for this trip, for much will happen. I will leave now. Thank you, Ann Walker.'

The chair moved round, then the colours went. I sat there amazed. *He* had said thank you to *me*! Dazed, I looked over to White Arrow. We arrived back home – my visit to the ship was over.

My quandary over the trip to Egypt was not resolved, however. On 9 April, I asked Zipper: 'May I ask if I'm going to experience anything or find anything when I go to Egypt?'

'Much will happen on your journey while you are there,' is all he would say. I had known that he would not give much away, but it was worth a try! I had the feeling it would be my return trip to Egypt which would be the most important. Zipper reminded me about the Amazon – there was later to be more to all this, in South America.

'Please, Zipper,' I said. 'Let me do Egypt first!'

He laughed gently and sat in the chair. He turned and spoke to Alien Girl, then walked over to White Arrow. It looked as if they were hugging each other. I know what a hug means on Earth, and I presume its meaning is universal. Zipper walked back to the chair, sat down and smiled at me. He is such a loving person! I knew I would miss him when the journey was over, but I would have to put it to the back of my mind for now.

Zipper spoke again. 'In the following four weeks we have much to talk about and do for Egypt. Bear and Eagle will be with you. Much instruction will be given to you before you leave. You will follow this in order for the journey to be a success. So I will go now. White Arrow or the medallion will tell you when I want to see you.'

Then a cross appeared – a very old cross. I do not know why they showed it to me. Zipper then left, with everyone following him. I turned to White Arrow and said to him, 'Thanks for the help over the past few days. I'll need your strength on this journey to Egypt.' White Arrow had assured me he would help. He smiled and said, 'Do not worry, Little One. Everything is all right.'

After Easter, on 13 April 1993, Bear wanted to see me about Egypt. Zipper was sitting in the chair opposite me, but Bear was not there yet. 'Where's Bear, Zipper?' I asked.

'He's coming', Zipper told me.

Then I heard Bear's familiar deep growl. Now I could see him. I said 'Hi' to him. He still could not get out of his habit of speaking in his own language, but I knew he was saying hello back. Unusually for Bear, he had brought notes with him this time. I glanced at Zipper in surprise. Then Bear said to me, 'Go to Saqqara and visit the tomb of Ti. As you go in, look on the left-hand side of you. When you enter the third room or passage look at the drawings. On paper, write what you see and keep them for the future.'

'Do you mean one of the drawings will mean something in the future?' I asked.

'Yes, all is for future work. Before you go I will tell you what to do on each day,' he replied.

'Are you saying that's all for now?' I asked.

'Yes. Remember each message, for it is important for our journey,' Bear said.

'Bear, before you go, what about the words I have to take?'

'I will lead you to the right keeper,' he explained. Thank goodness, I thought. How am I going to get all of this done in just four days in Egypt? But I sensed that what I was to learn in those four days would be important for a future visit. When I looked up again they had all left.

Some days later, on 18 April, I felt bad all day. I had a sore throat and was still very tired from all the work. I went to the White Arrow Spiritualist Church, which we had opened in his name in 1984, and while I was there I received healing. While I was receiving it I saw a bright light and I knew it meant the light was showing me the way.

Suddenly, White Arrow appeared. He went over to a picture on the wall which showed footsteps in the sand. It alluded to a well-known parable, the one about Jesus walking with someone on the sand. There are two sets of footprints while he walks with him. The person with him despairs that he can only see one set of footprints some of the time. Has Jesus forsaken him? Gently, Jesus points out that there was only one set of footprints – *his* – because he was carrying the person through difficult times. White Arrow showed himself with me on his shoulders, implying that he was carrying me. I felt like crying, my heart filled with joy.

A few days later, on the morning of 21 April 1993, I was sitting having a few moments on my own before Tony my husband got up, when Sitting Bull came in. This sounds preposterous, I know, but very little surprises you when you are working with the Spirit, I assure you!

'Soon you are to meet the leaders,' he said.

A question entered my mind. 'Do you mean leaders on Earth or from other worlds?'

'You will bring the two together,' Sitting Bull replied. Then he left.

That afternoon I had to see Bear about Egypt. I sat down in the chair, exhausted. Zipper was there first, then Bear came in. I said 'Hi' to both of them, and apologized for not concentrating, as my mind was on other things. They understood. I was worrying about Egypt. Not long to go now, and I had to make sure everything was in place.

Zipper got down to the business at hand. 'Listen to Bear,' he said. So I turned my attention to Bear.

He spoke. 'On the second day I want you to visit the Virgin Tree. You have been given some instructions, but I want you to see the keeper. Offer him money – it is a way of thanking him for his services. Show him all the paperwork, including the one Zipper said not to show anyone in England. He will be able to lead you on to the next part. Then go back to your hotel room. What you have been told will help you again in the future. We will meet again.'

'Thanks, Bear,' I said as I watched him go. I knew they were both in a hurry. They both said goodbye and were gone.

'I hope I get this right for you, White Arrow,' I said, but he just smiled, his teeth gleaming. He seemed very happy. I wished he would tell me why.

'I'll see you later,' he said, and suddenly he too was gone.

On 23 April I was in the hairdressers. I had such a busy day ahead that I had asked Bear if I could see him while I was having my hair done. He had wanted to see me the previous day, but due to pressure of work I could not, so he agreed to see me there. If the people there knew what was happening, they probably would not believe it!

I greeted him, and I sensed Zipper's presence but I could not see him. Bear spoke. 'After Matariyah (the Virgin Tree), on the third day I want you to sit near the window of your hotel and look towards the north. The following day I want you to visit the village of Giza where you will visit the Holy One, and show him all you have and tell him of the things you have seen. I want you, before you go, to bring me all the words you have, and we will show you what they mean.

'When you return from your trip we will once again sit and prepare you for your next visit. The information you bring back will help you on your next journey to Giza. Be prepared for the changes it will bring. I promise that the journey you follow you will come to understand, but we must give it to you slowly, for too much at one go will only hurt you. It is too much for you to carry alone.'

I thanked Bear. I knew he could stay only a short time. I turned to White Arrow and asked, 'Can you help with the words?' I was so worried I had already forgotten what Bear had said, that they would help me in a week's time. I realized belatedly what I had done. 'Sorry, White Arrow,' I said.

I was beginning to be impatient and frustrated by it all. I so wanted to know what the words meant and what lay ahead of me, but I also knew that patience was part of the journey. One cannot rush White Arrow or the aliens.

Later, the aliens wanted to see me out in my back garden. White Arrow had not said what it was about. It was 8.40pm and I had just got back from our church, where I had been working. Zipper appeared. 'I hope you like your picture?' I asked him. 'Yes,' he replied? I had been working with Jimmy, an artist, describing White Arrow and the aliens, so that we could have an artist's portrait of everyone for *Little One*, which was nearly ready to be published. The drawing of Zipper was very accurate.

I knew how Jimmy had achieved this. He had told me that he was making good progress generally, but that when he tried to draw Zipper the first time he was unhappy with the likeness. He did not know why, but he had the feeling it was 'like a passport photo' – nothing like the real thing. His next attempt, however, was actually Zipper's image – Zipper had traced it on paper without Jimmy knowing, and the other aliens also traced their pictures – and this worked better. I was pleased, for I wanted so much to let the world know who I was talking to.

'Why have you asked me out tonight, Zipper?' I asked him. Before he could answer, Bear, Eagle, Alien Girl and Michael appeared, then White Arrow's father. I saw the staff first.

'I will be with you on your journey to Egypt. Remember to use the staff,' said White Arrow's father, and he pushed it forward to me. I took it from him. It was lit in colours of yellow and white. 'It is yours.'

'Something will happen in Egypt,' said the father. 'You must keep it to yourself until I tell you to tell the world. My children will take you to a place where many secrets have been kept for centuries. They are for the world, in time. Be prepared for me to show you something which, on your return to Egypt, will open the tomb. You will not understand me today, but you will understand on your return home. I will go now, until my return.' White Arrow's father then left.

White Arrow spoke next. 'We have much to do. Before you go you must sit with me every day and I will show you things to do.' Zipper got up and said, 'I will see you tomorrow.' Then he, Bear and the rest of the aliens left.

On 4 May 1993, I came to talk to White Arrow. He brought up the subject of the Virgin Tree again. I waited for him to speak. 'I want you to go to the Coptic church and see the priest. Show him your drawings and tell him of your mission. Tell him of me. Tell the truth as to why you have come. At the tree, stop and follow the instructions we have given you. Do not fear the events that are to take place. Tomorrow I will tell you more,' he said.

White Arrow had arrived alone, and I wondered why none of the other aliens were here. 'Do not worry, Little One. They have not left you, but they come only when necessary,' he replied. I understood. 'I will say one thing, Little One: if any harm is to befall you, I will tell you so you can avoid it, so do not worry over paperwork.' I wondered why he had said that.

I had been getting into a real panic with all the work I had in order to prepare for this trip. I was so busy with the organizing that I sometimes forgot just how much help I was going to have from White Arrow, his father and the aliens. They had all reassured me recently – and really, what more assurance could a person wish for? Yet I was still panicking. But I am only human, sometimes *very* human. I thanked White Arrow again, then he stood up and said, 'We have finished now, Little One. Take these notes with you, so you will remember.' He left.

That evening I saw François, and we put all the messages together, some with what we hoped were their meanings. The way it came together, it looked as if something *would* happen on this trip – and it made me nervous. I had thought I was only going to get the feel of things in Egypt, in preparation for the second visit. But no, there was to be action.

I had to see White Arrow the next day. When I entered the back room he was already there waiting. He could see that as the date for the trip approached I was getting more nervous. He just smiled at me. 'You know, White Arrow, I'm not an explorer,' I said, somewhat flustered. He just laughed, his white teeth gleaming, and then said, 'We will go to Cairo. Now, on this journey I would like you to visit the church where Jesus Christ rested. Here you will just sit and pray. A vision will come, of great importance to you. You will understand at the time.'

Suddenly, Zipper appeared beside White Arrow, then Bear, Michael and Eagle. White Arrow continued by saying, 'Follow the words when you are there. They will be of great help afterwards. For two nights you will sit by the window and look towards the north. You may that day visit the places we have mentioned.

'This is just the start of your journey. The last day of your visit is very important. You must tell the head man everything about me, and he will be able to help us on our journey. He holds the cup to you.' I *thought* I understood!

'Although this journey is different to the visit to the Indians, it will be more successful. I'm sorry it's hard work, but you will be rewarded well.'

'I do not want rewards, White Arrow, as long as I can help. I will be safe though, won't I?'

'You will be safe, I promise,' said White Arrow, again reassuring me. I thanked him, and with that he and the others left.

· 9 ·

Why Me?

By 7 May, everything was ready for Egypt. I was in the back room, waiting for White Arrow, and he appeared. 'Little One, I will be preparing you for your journey to Egypt. Once again I say, no harm will come of you.' I felt White Arrow's father's presence in the room too. Suddenly he appeared and spoke to me.

'My child, you are in safe hands. This journey will help me to help my people. You have done well for my son. Do not be afraid of what is to be shown to you when you are there, for I will be with you.'

He held out the staff. I did not want to let it go because he was holding it with me. It was the first time I had ever been that close to his holy Presence and it made me feel so humble. I was actually holding the Staff of God with him holding it with me! No words can explain how it felt. It was beyond words.

White Arrow's father spoke again. 'Soon, Ann Walker, we will be showing the world of our existence. My children will show the people of the Earth the love that has been sent by me. Thanks to your faith all is possible. Do not be afraid. Remember, you must not tell the world until I say, and it will be difficult. But I trust you. When the time comes, then the world will believe the words you have written are true.'

He turned and left. I did not know what to say. I looked at White Arrow. He was smiling, again, his white teeth gleaming. 'I do love you, White Arrow,' I told him. He put his finger to his mouth as if to say there were no words to be said. He knew how I felt.

'Where are the aliens, White Arrow?' I asked. I had been seeing White Arrow on his own most of the week. I had thought that perhaps the aliens were leaving – one day they might.

'Do not fear, Little One. They will not leave you,' he replied. 'While you are on Earth, Little One, the aliens and I will be part of you, until the time you leave.'

'Thanks, White Arrow,' I replied. At least *that* was one problem I did not have to worry about! But what did this say about when I was to leave?

Then he added, 'When you come back you will be as one with us all.' I wondered what he meant, but at the same time I did not want to know. I had enough to think about.

By 9 May we had found out as much as we could about the words. They seemed in order, but the demotic text and other drawings I would have to sort out later. The messages daunted me a bit, but I tried to put that to the back of my mind. Everything was as ready as it could be.

Tomorrow was to be the start of a seven-day stretch of going out to the back garden to meet the aliens. I had done this since meeting them in January 1992. I would have to continue the meetings in Egypt. Suddenly, White Arrow appeared and said, 'It's all right, Little One. I will give you my strength. The world owes you much for the tasks you have done.'

His father was around. I could feel his presence. I heard him say, 'My staff will be with you.'

'Thank you for reassuring me of your presence with me in Egypt,' I said.

There was something about this trip, a feeling, but I could not put my finger on it. Was I going to see White Arrow another way? There was *something* – I could feel it – but I let it go, for I knew I would not get the answer to that from him.

Next day I thought to myself, two more days to go, and I'm off to Egypt! I've done all that I can at this end. It's up to White Arrow, his father and the aliens now. This trip is already much harder than the visit to the USA was. I had come out to the garden while it was still light because I was so tired.

Zipper arrived and said, 'You have done well, Little One.'

'But I've done nothing yet, Zipper,' I replied.

'You've done more than you think, believe me.'

Bear and Michael arrived, then Alien Girl. She had brought some notes for Zipper. I hoped he had no more notes for me! Zipper sensed my dismay. He rested his hand on top of my head, in a loving gesture. 'Not till you return,' he said kindly. Thank goodness, I thought. It's amazing, I'm hardly with them five minutes and I start to feel better! It's almost like a tonic being out here with them. Their love gives me new strength.

White Arrow nodded in agreement. 'You have done well,' he said.

I looked at him and asked, 'Why all the pats on the back?' He laughed gently at my surprise. White Arrow is not one for giving credit lightly, so I *was* surprised. But I greatly appreciated their thanks.

Bear put his hand on mine and growled in his own language. I did not understand it, but I felt it meant good wishes. I watched as he talked to Zipper. Zipper was giving him instructions for Egypt. How I knew this I am not sure, but he was. That implied that Zipper was in command of them all. I did not know why I was so surprised. Zipper had always acted that way anyway. I laughed at the thought and looked at Zipper. 'I'm only joking,' I told him. I felt his love flow through me.

Eagle was here now. Zipper then spoke. 'In Egypt, we will all be with you. Look towards the sky on the night of the 17th.' I promised him I would.

'The journey will be successful,' said White Arrow.

'Good,' I replied. I was somewhat relieved.

Although it was still quite light outside I could see the tunnel clearly – the tunnel was their means of coming to visit me when we needed to meet. You could call it a kind of inter-dimensional passageway from their ship to my back yard!

Zipper suddenly pointed his finger at me. It was emitting energy, showing me white. I knew he was giving me some sort of healing for my fatigue. I seemed to be managing, even though so much was going on.

'I hope you're all pleased with your pictures,' I said. Bear grunted, reminding me that his portrait was not finished yet. 'I'm sorry, Bear. I'll ask you at another time. But what about you three?' I asked, turning to Michael, Alien Girl and Zipper. They all agreed that the portraits were good. I was pleased, because I really wanted the world to see who I see, for they are in many ways like us. They love and laugh and care. The only two differences are their bodies and their inability to hate or destroy. They come only with love.

Zipper laid his hand on my arm – it was his way of saying thank you. 'Soon, I will have to share you all with the world, but I feel very privileged and happy that I met you first,' I told them.

Zipper started to make a move. 'Is it time already?' I said. I looked at my watch. Twenty-five minutes had gone already.

'I will see you tomorrow, Little One', said Zipper, and he started towards the tunnel. The others followed.

I watched as they entered the tunnel. 'Goodnight,' I said softly.

'Come, Little One,' said White Arrow. We went indoors.

On Tuesday, 11 May, I opened the back door to go out, and Eagle and Bear were already standing waiting. Zipper was in his usual place looking over some notes he had with him. He turned and greeted me by laying his hand on me. As he did that Bear did the same thing. Then Michael appeared, then Alien Girl. I could see the tunnel, even though it was still quite light outdoors. I had had a really good night's sleep and, although things were hectic, I felt a great deal better. I was just going to ask White Arrow a question when he said, 'Look and listen!' I left the question – one does not argue with White Arrow!

White Arrow smiled at me and said, 'You still do not know what power you have behind you.'

'Yes, I do realize, White Arrow,' I said, 'but sometimes it's frightening to have all this knowledge.'

'Have I not promised to protect you?' said White Arrow.

'Yes,' I said.

Suddenly, White Arrow's father came. The staff appeared. He spoke. 'Use it at the tomb. It will show you the way to go. The journey is important to mankind. Those who are linked to you, Ann Walker, while you are on Earth, will be protected with you. Your family is protected by the Highest. I have spoken.' I thanked him from the depths of my soul.

I always worry about the safety of my family, and he must have known. 'Till tomorrow, Ann Walker,' he said. Then he left. I watched as his robe disappeared. I was so honoured by his presence that it left me wondering, why me?

Zipper put his hand up. Then he put it down. I never knew why he did that. Bear was talking to him. Eagle stood nearby, listening. Alien Girl was taking notes with her finger. Michael was just standing there. If only people could see this amazing group, I thought.

'Hi, Michael,' I said to him. 'How are you?'

'Fine, Ann,' he replied. 'Send my regards to Tony.'

'I will,' I said. 'Are you happy where you come from?'

'Very much,' said Michael. 'Love there is different to your

world. I have much more to offer your world now than when I lived on Earth before,' he continued.

'Tell me, Michael, have you been an alien before?'

'Yes, Ann. But now I have come to Earth for a single purpose. *You.*'

I looked at him. All this was too much to take in, so I just let it wash over me. As far as I am concerned I am just an ordinary human housewife who has an ability to talk to the spirit world and the aliens. If I could help White Arrow, his father and the aliens, that was fine. That was all I needed to know at the time.

White Arrow put his hand on me and smiled. I must have seemed pretty bewildered by it all sometimes. They had all done so much to reassure me. I looked over to Zipper, then Bear, then back to White Arrow. Then Zipper said, 'Do not worry. In Egypt we will show you what to do when you're there.' With that he got up and walked to the tunnel, waving back to me at the same time. 'See you tomorrow,' he called to me. I watched as the others followed him.

'Come,' said White Arrow.

· 10 ·

Egypt

It was Thursday, 13 May, when we went to Egypt. I got up at 6.30am – I needed time with White Arrow to finalize things before Tony got up. I put the kettle on, grabbed the paperwork with the instructions and drawings, sat down and waited for White Arrow. I needed to know if I had everything he needed me to take. This trip was important, like all his trips, but somehow I felt it was *more* important this time.

Val, my friend and helper, was coming with me. People had been worried about our going on our own – two women alone in Egypt. I tried to explain that we would be all right because I had White Arrow, and Tony *almost* accepted that. But, as always, he would worry wherever I was, so I arranged with him that I would phone every day. Being a clairvoyant's husband must be a bit like being an astronaut's wife!

White Arrow suddenly appeared. 'Hi,' I said as he sat down in his usual manner. 'I think I have everything.' He nodded his head in agreement. Bear was also there. I read the list of places to visit. Saqqara was on the first day, then Matariyah, then Cairo and lastly the village of Giza. Would I find them all on this trip? I hoped so.

I could hear Tony getting up. White Arrow vanished. I had a busy time ahead before I left for the airport, so I made sure everything was ready for 2pm, our departure time. We arrived at the airport with plenty of time to sit and have coffee. Soon it was time for us to depart. The flight was good. I had promised White Arrow I would sit with Zipper and the rest at 7.10pm, and this is what I wrote:

It's 7.10 and I'm flying over Italy on my way to Cairo. As promised,

Zipper is beside me. If only the people on this flight realized that there was the presence of an alien here, let alone White Arrow!

'This trip is important to us all. We will show you things that are important to the world,' said Zipper.

'But this isn't the trip for the tomb door, is it, Zipper?' I asked him. He said nothing, but I knew in my heart it wasn't.

Michael is here, and Alien Girl. I wonder how far their ship is from here. 'Not far,' replied Zipper. I hoped not that near! That's all I needed, for them to turn up! But I was joking. I knew this was not a game, but at the same time nothing would surprise me.

'Have a good night's sleep tonight,' said White Arrow, 'for tomorrow will be the start of an important journey.'

Zipper laid his hands on mine and said, 'Remember, we are with you. Call if you need me, for I will be there. We are your friends, special friends, and we thank you for your faith in us. It is important that you write every night from now on till the 17th, that you stay in communication with us.'

White Arrow's father is here. I wish I could let the people on this plane know he is here! He shows me the staff and I thank him. 'Ann Walker, I thank you', he said to me.

Why? was the first thing on my mind. I should be on my knees to him and thanking him! I would do anything and go anywhere for him, for my body is his body, my soul is his soul – yet he thanks me! Although I do not see him, I know he is putting his hand on my head. Now he's gone.

I turn to White Arrow and he smiles, then puts his finger to his mouth as if to say 'Quiet'. Zipper is holding my hand and looking around. I don't know if he has been with other people before but he acts as if he hasn't. Now he has gone off down the aisle of the plane. I don't know where he's going. No, he's on the way back now – I think he was just having a look around. I see Michael and Alien Girl behind him. 'Remember, use the medallion if you need my help,' he says. I thank him and he just vanishes, the other two with him.

White Arrow says, 'Enjoy the journey. I will speak tomorrow. Sleep well tonight, Little One.'

'God bless you, White Arrow,' I said. He smiled and then vanished.

We arrived at the hotel just after midnight and I phoned Tony to tell him all was well. He was happy I had arrived safely. I got undressed for bed and went out onto the balcony. Our hotel faced the Nile and the view was beautiful. As I breathed in the air I looked up to the sky and prayed silently, Help me, God, on this journey.

It was 2am when Val and I finally crept into our beds, exhausted. It took a long time before I dropped off, and my sleep was restless. I woke up before dawn, wide awake. Much as I tried to go back to sleep, I could not. I looked at my watch: 6.15. It's no use, I said to myself as I crept out of bed, trying not to wake Val. I slipped into the bathroom and washed and changed. After I had finished dressing I sat outside on the balcony. By this time it was light. I watched the city wake up.

In front of me stood the boat that takes people down the Nile on evening trips. Towards the left of the large boat were much smaller ones, on which families lived. There were cars already on the road – another day was starting. I felt drained from having had a bad night, but I could not allow myself to dwell on that. My thoughts were on Saqqara and Ti, for that was my mission for today. I had my notes in front of me and thought about the guide I had hired for this trip.

All I knew about her was her name, Hala, and that she had been highly recommended to me through François. I had spoken to her on my arrival and we had arranged a time to meet. François had made all the arrangements for me. Would Hala be able to help me with the drawings and words, besides taking me to the required places? I prayed she could, for it was so important to me that the words and drawings could be proved right; then it would help White Arrow.

I had about 24 pages of writings. Some of them we had mastered and understood, but others were a mystery. Would I succeed in finding out what their meanings were? White Arrow appeared suddenly and said, 'Everything is ready. You will understand most things by the end of this journey.'

'I hope so, White Arrow.' He vanished.

At 7am, Val awoke, and as soon as she was ready we went down for breakfast. We sat for a while enjoying the food and returned to our room to get ready. I had everything ready and we waited for Hala. Soon after 11 she arrived.

Hala started to say what she was going to show us for our short stay. She knew nothing of me except that François had asked for her help on the demotic drawings. So I had to interrupt her proposed schedule. 'Hala,' I began, 'I am sorry, but these are the places I need to go to.' I showed her the piece of paper with White Arrow's instructions. I did not know how she would take it, so I felt the best thing to do was to tell her the truth about the situation, from the start.

I spoke for a while, explaining some of my reasons for being here and showed her some of the paperwork I had brought. She was quite eager to help, but a bit unsure as to why exactly I was here. We sat on the bed together discussing it. She promised that she would help with the demotic drawings, and the rest if she could. I thanked White Arrow for bringing me help. Her eyes gazed at some drawings from 1,500 years ago, hieratic writing (*see* figure 10.1), and she worked them out. She sat on the bed engrossed in the writings and words. She had the meanings of most of them, but she could not understand 'RS' and 'H' and told me so. Suddenly, White Arrow appeared and said through me, ' "R" stands for "Ra" and "S" stands for "Sun God".' Hala sat back astonished. I could see it took her breath away.

'Of course!' she said. 'That is something new I have learned today.'

I smiled at her. 'Don't worry. He's always full of surprises.' Hala regained her composure and moved on to the sign/letter 'H'. She had no idea what it meant.

White Arrow moved forward, and told me to pick up the pen. 'I have told Little One to write it this way, as "H", until I meet the right person.'

The written symbol was changed to look more like 'π', the Greek letter 'pi'. Hala looked on in disbelief. She immediately understood the sign. What shocked her was that she knew the papers I

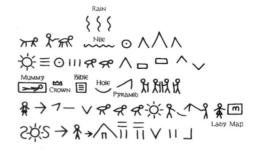

This is an Earth Crystal Grid Energies = directing Mental Will Energy to bring through visions from Other Realms and Dimensions in to PHYSICAL MANIFESTATION

Translated into English by Abdel Hakim Awayan

Figure 10.1 Hieratic writing (2)

had brought from White Arrow were authentic, and his final touches made the messages clear. Also, as White Arrow promised, he had kept the messages secret until he was sure he could trust the people involved. Hala was overwhelmed. I must admit that I too was taken aback.

In one stroke White Arrow had kept his promise concerning my safety. Hala said that the writings were secret, known only to a few Egyptians, and that if I had shown them to the wrong person they would have been very suspicious of my motives, as only Egyptologists would know of this language. How did I come upon these writings? What was I doing with them?

This was evidence for Hala that I was indeed in contact with another force, for without years of study of Coptic, which very few people know, where else could I have received such drawings? To me, it was the first miracle. This was my first day in Egypt, and here, in front of me, stood a young lady telling me that all this was not imagination but demonstrable *fact*.

Suddenly I remembered White Arrow's words before we left. 'Don't worry about the paperwork,' he had said. Now I knew what he had meant! Only the right people would get to see the real meaning. He would reveal it to them when the time came. I too had learned something: White Arrow would deliberately insert incorrect symbols until he was sure the person he was dealing with could be trusted to help him – protecting his work, and protecting me at the same time.

Hala was very moved by it all and I was just as touched. She told me that the doctor at her college had said the demotic drawings I had sent were to do with the construction of a pyramid, and also that the first part was missing. I knew this was true, for only I had it – another safeguard. So Hala worked on the beginning. We agreed that if I left the drawings with her when I went home she would get someone to help me complete the message. There was only so much she knew, but without doubt she verified that they were demotic pictures. To me, however, a miracle had taken place, for how could I, Ann Walker, know of such languages and write them unless I was truly in contact with White Arrow and the aliens? What other explanation was there?

Hala informed me that the driver was waiting, so we got our things and I put the book of words and pictures away safely. As we left the room I asked Hala if we could go to the Virgin Tree in Matariyah. Hala said we could not, as it was in Upper Egypt, ten hours away by bus. I hid my disappointment, but as we went down in the lift to the foyer my mind was in a panic. How had I got it wrong? I had not done enough research on the Arabic writing! I had got it wrong for White Arrow.

'I am so sorry, White Arrow. I will have to come back again and go to Upper Egypt next time,' I said to him. I felt terribly disappointed, but I still had to carry on and try to do the rest for him. Yet I felt I had let him down somehow with one word, 'Matariyah.'

I could hear Val speaking to me, asking if I was all right. I told her I was fine and put on a brave smile. Although I felt I had failed, I was determined to do my best to finish the rest of the instructions.

As we left the hotel Hala pointed out to us various landmarks and sights. I could feel the hot sun and felt better. Not all is lost, White Arrow, wherever you are, I thought. At least we are off to Saqqara. Hala introduced us to the driver, Mohammed, then we set off. The excitement of being in Cairo lifted my spirits and I felt happier.

We listened to Hala as she pointed out places we were passing. She also said to us, 'Tomorrow I will take you to the Hanging Church in Cairo. Also, we will visit the Coptic Museum and see if we can get someone to help you with your Coptic words.'

'Great,' I replied, once again getting excited for White Arrow. If only I could authoritatively prove the validity of the writing I had! If I could, it would mean everything I had written was true. I told White Arrow again that I was sorry about Matariyah.

'Do not worry, Little One,' he said. 'You will understand all at the end of your journey.' He did not seem upset, and that pleased me. I had moreover promised I would return if he needed me to, so I sat back and relaxed.

This is what Adrian Gilbert has contributed concerning Saqqara.

Saqqara

Saqqara was the ancient burial ground for Memphis, the capital of the united kingdom of Upper and Lower Egypt. As such there are graves there going back to well before the Pyramid Age. It was, however, still occasionally used throughout most of Egyptian history. The Step Pyramid of Zoser (Third Dynasty) is the most notable feature, but there are other pyramids there from the Fifth and Sixth Dynasties. The pyramid of Unas (last king of the Fifth Dynasty) is the earliest known to have texts inscribed on the walls.

Imhotep, known to the Greeks as Imuthes and identified by them with their own god of healing Aesclepius, probably lived in the time of Zoser. He was revered as the father of architecture and inventor of the pyramids. It is more likely that he was a great priest who was initiated into the concepts of architectural science by the gods, who may have been extraterrestrial entities. Little more than that is known about him except that he was a healer. Given that he worked closely with Zoser, it seems likely that his tomb would be near that of the king at the Step Pyramid of Saqqara.

Today Hala was taking us to see the Step Pyramid, which had been erected around 2700 BC. She told us many other statistics and bits of general information as we continued our journey to Saqqara. We were travelling down Pyramids Avenue, a very long road, when suddenly Hala started to tell me about the tombs in Central America. I did not say anything about my going there one day, and I was surprised she should mention them. But this journey was to be full of surprises, and this was just the first day!

I heard her say that there is a connection between the tombs in Egypt and those in Central America. The same writings had been found in tombs in both these areas. The ancient pioneers in Mexico were thus linked with those in Egypt. The jigsaw was fitting together: I now knew the link between them both and why I would have to go to Mexico one day.

We arrived at Memphis, the ancient capital, and stopped to have a look round. We looked at the statue of Ramses II. As I walked towards it, absorbing the sight of it, my mind went to the aliens. They were the same height. I knew in my heart that the great pharaohs knew of the aliens, and somewhere there was a tomb that would verify this. I told Hala.

I had told her I was in contact with aliens and that I also knew Eagle was Isis and Bear was Horus, the Egyptian gods of thousands of years ago. As I stood in front of this massive figure I knew I was on the right journey. Here would be proof one day of the existence of White Arrow and the aliens. I took some photographs and walked back with Hala to the car.

'Do not show anyone the papers you have brought with you,' she whispered to me. 'They are dangerous.' She had said nothing like this in the hotel room, so I looked at her surprised. She then said, 'Please, at the moment, do not tell anyone my last name. The Egyptian government will think I have given you secret papers.' I must have looked surprised, for she said, 'What you have brought here the outside world does not know of. Only the Egyptians know of it.'

Again, White Arrow's words came back to me. 'You will be safe with the paperwork.' My first thought then was, had I hidden them well at the hotel? Then I shrugged my shoulders. I hoped that Hala was reading too much into it, or maybe I was too afraid to think I had anything so important on me. She mentioned it three times that day, but I still could not see why.

Finally we arrived at Saqqara. We walked towards the temple and Hala told us about its history. I listened to her and was fascinated by it all. As we walked forward I suddenly had a vision of someone being carried in a chair by four men. The vision was there only for a second, then it went.

As I carried on walking I spotted Bear. He was pointing to the left of him and I wondered if that was the way Hala was taking us, but instead we went in the opposite direction. I asked Hala what was in the direction Bear had pointed to, but she did not seem to know, so I left it. He had vanished, so I could not ask him what he wanted me to do – but at least I knew he was here with me.

We entered a great arena, and in front of me stood the Step Pyramid. I knew this was important to Bear and Eagle. I videoed it and stood and looked. Hala was giving us information on how it was built, but my mind was more on taking everything in. I knew I had to try and remember everything for when I returned to England – that was when the hard work would begin.

I turned to Hala after a few minutes and listened to her. Once again she told us the pyramid was erected in 2700 BC, it stood 65m high and there were six steps to it. Below it, underground, were shafts between 61 and 68m down and 21m across. I made notes for when I returned home.

Suddenly, a sandstorm blew up. As we walked along, Hala said it was impossible to go to the tomb of Ti, but we could return on our last day, on Monday. She would arrange for a man called Mohammed to bring us in a hired car, as she would be working that morning. I told her the arrangement would be fine by me. As long as I saw Ti's tomb it did not really matter when I went.

Then all of a sudden Hala stood still. 'Ann,' she said, 'could you help me with a dream I had two nights ago?' Now, I had told Hala only that I knew White Arrow and the aliens. I had not told her that I actually knew five of them. I had only mentioned Bear and Eagle. She went on to recall her dream. 'My grandfather came to me,' she began. 'He had died some time ago and in the dream he beckoned me to the window. As I looked out I saw six angels standing there, all in white. The one to the left was holding six white arrows. He told me to tell my mother not to fear. They were small angels in white robes.'

I stopped in my tracks. I knew it was White Arrow and the five aliens, and I told her so. 'That dream was them telling you about their existence, and about me coming here,' I said.

Hala reflected. 'Yes, now I have met you . . . and judging by what you were telling me before I told you about my dream . . . well, it all makes sense. It is right.'

We walked back to the car, deep in thought. It was only my first day here and so much was happening. If I wanted White Arrow to give proof of his existence, then today I was getting it. We got in the car and drove off to find somewhere to have a meal. The driver joined us, and I found him to be a very nice man. We chatted for a while, and after we had eaten we drove back towards the centre of Cairo to our hotel.

On the way back we saw the Great Pyramid at Giza in the distance. Hala pointed out the pyramids to us, and as I looked I could see a ray of blue light coming from them, and then pink. Within a few seconds they were out of sight. I did not know if we would see them tomorrow or the next day – I wondered what to expect when we did.

Hala dropped us back at our hotel and asked if I would meet a friend of hers later that night. She said she would pick us up at 9pm.

'Val, if nothing else is to happen on this trip, at least I have found proof of some of the writings,' I said. That was what I *thought* I had come for – that, and to feel my way around before the day came when I would open the tomb. But if I had known what was ahead of me in the next three days I think I would have run away!

After we had both had a relaxing bath, we still felt exhausted from the day's events and decided to have an early night. Hala rang. I asked her if she minded if we did not see her friend after all, since we had lost so much sleep the night before. She said it was all right with her, and she promised to pick us up in the morning.

Before I could go to bed I had to go out on the balcony. I had promised White Arrow I would do this until 17 May. This is what I wrote:

Friday evening, 14 May 1993. I'm sitting on the balcony in front of the Nile. We have been to Saqqara, but I have to go back on Monday to see Ti. I had such a bad night last night – only three hours' sleep – that White Arrow said I would miss out on the things I had to see because of lack of concentration.

I will write about the trip later. I'm waiting for Zipper and the rest. White Arrow is here and Zipper has just arrived.

'There is much for us to do. You are being prepared.'

'For what, Zipper? I feel something is going to happen, but what? I don't know what.'

Zipper nods his head. 'Later.' He wasn't going to say.

Bear and Eagle have just arrived, with Michael and Alien Girl. Zipper is sitting in front of the balcony on the rail facing me. I am so tired! I will be glad to get to bed and I hope I'll sleep. I don't want to hold them up on their journey.

I look at Zipper. Even here, thousands of miles away from home, he's still writing! I watch as he passes Alien Girl some notes.

Eagle is very close. What people don't realize is that the great statues in Egypt are the same size as the aliens. When I saw them today I realized the connection. People just thought the kings were made that big to show power. They weren't, and Zipper agrees with me. What else is to come on this journey?

Zipper has more drawings, but I can't do them tonight – I'm too tired. I ask if I can do them later. Zipper agrees. I have some hard work to do here – today was the start of it. I just hope I have the strength to do it for them!

I would love Cairo if it weren't for the work side. It is a beautiful place, but my priority must be White Arrow's journey, not a holiday for me. Even so, I am glad of the experience of it.

I think I panic a bit in case I miss something they're trying to tell me, but Bear comes in and says, 'Do not worry, Little One, everything is in hand.'

'Soon we go,' says Zipper. I know he is thinking of me, knowing how tired I am. 'It's okay, Zipper,' I tell him. He places his hand on me and love rushes through my whole body. Then he shines a light from his finger and points it at me. I feel he's giving me strength for my journey. Zipper suddenly moves, and as he does so Eagle comes in and says, 'Do not fear, Little One, you have the highest,' and she steps back.

Zipper says, 'We will be with you tomorrow and we will see you tomorrow night.'

'Okay, Zipper,' I say.

'Sleep well, Little One,' said White Arrow. 'Tomorrow is a new day.'

After I came in from the balcony I got into bed and chatted with Val. I now had proof that all the words I had been given in other languages were right. Everything so far was going according to the instructions – so why was I going wrong with Matariyah? All I had to do now was find proof of the Coptic writing and what it meant. I prayed I could. But neither of us had the answer, and I was too tired to work it out that night. As my head touched the pillow I fell sound asleep.

· 11 ·

The Holy Vision

I woke up early. It was 6.45 but I felt refreshed from a good night's sleep. I got up quietly and went out on the balcony. White Arrow was already there waiting. 'Hi, good morning,' I said, looking out across the river. 'It's lovely, White Arrow.' He nodded his head and looked across, following my eyes. We stood in silence for a few moments, the magic of Cairo taking hold of us.

White Arrow turned his gaze to me. I sat down. I said to him, 'I hope you were pleased with yesterday, White Arrow. I know I am. Although I always knew you were right, I know it for sure now.' I was referring to the writings.

White Arrow smiled, then said, 'There is much more to witness on this journey. Remember, I will be with you.'

I smiled back and was about to ask him what to expect today, but I knew he would not tell me so I left the question unasked. 'Sorry about Matariyah, White Arrow,' I said. He just smiled. There are times when I just do not understand him. Had I not got a word wrong? He just smiled and said, 'I will see you later.' With this he vanished.

I sat and watched the city. It was quite peaceful. I knew we had a lot to do, so I got up and woke Val. We both washed and dressed and went to breakfast. We talked about the previous day and wondered what was to happen today.

The people here were lovely and made us very welcome. We decided to have a half-hour walk before Hala came. We did not want to venture far as we were in a strange country and I was nervous of getting lost. We returned by 10am and Hala arrived downstairs 15 minutes later. We grabbed the notes I had brought with me, the video and cameras, and with our sun hats on, we left.

In the lift going down, my mind was on the Coptic words. Please God, help me find the truth. We were going first to the Hanging Church, then on to the Coptic Museum. I was eagerly looking forward to that, to see if we could prove the veracity of White Arrow's writings, so by the time we met Hala in the foyer I was quite excited.

She hugged us both. She had hired the car for two days and confirmed that Mohammed would take us to Ti on our last day. It was not long before we pulled up in a narrow street in Old Cairo. 'We are here now,' she said. 'They also call this St Mary's Church.'

More proof: 'You will go to St Mary's Church,' the aliens had told me. I took a deep breath and got out of the car. The heat hit us straight away. We followed Hala through the gate to the church. As I stepped into the opening of the courtyard I could see at the end of it the steps leading up to the door of the church. In the courtyard stood two large palm trees linked together. In between them was a piece of wood as if to hold them together. Around them was a small square wall. I stood and looked at it all for a moment, and then felt a familiar jolt in my stomach.

We walked to the tree. Hala was telling us that this was one of the places where the Virgin Mary had rested with the infant Jesus. Then we all leaned forward and took turns putting our hands on the tree. I thanked God for allowing me to be there. We stood awhile, while Hala carried on telling us about it.

Then Val asked me if there was something I should be doing at a tree, and I remembered I had to walk three and a half times around one (as per the written instructions). I had forgotten about it because I was not at the place where I thought I should do it. It should have been in Matariyah, or so I thought.

However, White Arrow had asked me to do it, and even if it was the wrong place I would do it anyway. There were half a dozen people in the square, but we were the only foreigners. Not that it mattered to me – I would have done what White Arrow had asked me to do even if thousands had been there. So I just walked around the tree according to the instructions. Val videoed me doing it. As I finished doing the three and a half circuits I stopped and waited – for what, I did not know. I shut my eyes and waited.

Suddenly, I heard the words, 'You have the holy vision.' Nothing else was said.

I looked at the tree. I did not know what I was supposed to be looking for, and there was nothing there, just the tree. I moved on towards the steps leading into the church, puzzled by those words. It did not make sense, so I shrugged my shoulders. Knowing White Arrow, it would be made clearer at a later date. Hala sat on the top step, explaining the history of the Hanging Church, and I sat on the step in front of her.

Then all of a sudden, to the right of me, appeared Moses. How I knew that, I do not know! I just knew it was him, and he was holding the staff. I told the other two he was here and nothing was said for a few moments. Naturally, it was a unique and privileged experience.

I looked at Moses, puzzled as to why he was here. I asked Hala if he was important in Egypt. So much was happening to me it was hard to keep up with it all and to remember what I had learned in the Bible.

'Yes,' Hala replied. 'Moses lived in Cairo when the pyramids were built. He had a new religion and took it to St Catherine [in Sinai]. He climbed the big mountain at Sinai, where he received the Ten Commandments from God.'

I listened to her whilst looking at Moses. Then he suddenly vanished. I thought no more of his visit. As I entered the church I said to White Arrow, 'Help me not to let you down, White Arrow.' I could not see him but prayed he had heard me. We looked round the church. It was beautiful, with such a lovely feeling about it. The doors inside were made of cedarwood and ivory, and there was a beautiful painting of the Virgin Mary and the baby Jesus, among other pictures. Hala told us the church was built in the 3rd century and renovated in the 10th.

I told the others I wanted to sit alone and pray for a while, so I left them and went to the seats near the altar and knelt down. 'God, please show me a sign that I am doing the right things for White Arrow.' I knelt for five minutes, but nothing happened. I could feel nothing – unlike in the USA, where God gave me a sign that I had passed my test. This time I could feel nothing at all. Just then, White Arrow said, 'Look behind you.'

I looked and saw a picture of Jesus on the Cross above the door. Was this the vision White Arrow had spoken of before I came to Egypt? I now knew White Arrow is the Son of God, but I still could not allow myself to believe I was helping Jesus – I had blanked it out of my mind. After all, I was only Ann Walker! Only *special* people would be chosen to work for such a man. White Arrow is more than that to me, but to say to the world, 'Hi, I work with Jesus

Christ,' that is different! And frightening. But White Arrow knew of my fear and understood me more than any man. Everything White Arrow has done for me and shown me has been done gently and slowly.

I looked at the picture for a few seconds. Then I got up off my knees and looked around the church. It was lovely. Hala saw I had finished praying and called me over. She was standing near a door. I walked over to her.

'Ann, look,' she said, pointing towards one of the pillars supporting the church. There must have been about 24 pillars altogether. I looked at the one she was pointing at and there was a picture of a woman. Hala said, 'I have come here with tourists at least a hundred times. Some time ago I was told there was a picture of the Virgin Mary on one of the pillars. I have been looking for it for some time now, but I've never found it – until today. That is the picture of the Virgin Mary.' She just could not believe it.

I went to have a look at it, puzzled as to why she had not seen it before. It was quite a large picture – almost half the size of the pillar – so it was not as if one could easily miss it. I put it to the back of my mind, but at the same time I felt especially humble and privileged that White Arrow had brought me here. My mind started drifting again, thinking about the Coptic Museum. I felt I could not be at the right church, for nothing of particular significance had happened which could help White Arrow.

Hala said it was time to leave, so we followed her outside. There was a little shop selling gifts and I stopped to buy a few things for my granddaughter. Then I walked back into the courtyard. I was talking to Val and Hala about how lovely the church was, asking Hala if we were now going to the Coptic Museum. As I looked towards the tree I suddenly saw a lady by the side of it, a spirit lady. Something made me say out loud what I could see, as if I had to. I quickly asked Val to write everything down and turned back to the lady.

She was digging at the ground near the tree. She was hitting it and pointing towards it. I knew she was angry. I could not understand what she was doing. She looked very tired, and she was in dark clothes which made her look older than her years. Then she started to water the tree, and for a few moments I watched her, bemused by her actions. Maybe she was the keeper of the tree. Before I could think any more she beckoned me to her. 'Let me water your feet for your journey,' she said to me.

I walked towards her and climbed up beside the tree, and she watered my feet. 'You can go now,' she said, so I stepped down and turned round to face her. 'You are here. You are at the right place,' she said.

What did she mean? She was telling me, you are here, at the right place, Cairo. Then she pointed to the tree. I looked. What was she trying to say? Was something buried there? Papyrus paper, perhaps? I did not know, and somehow that did not make sense.

Then she showed me herself with child, pregnant. I knew she was not old, just tired. 'I have travelled in time to give you this message. The tomb will be opened. I have brought you this message from my son. I will leave now,' she said. Then she vanished.

Once again I repeated out loud what I had seen and been told. Then I asked Val if she had managed to write all of it down. She confirmed that she had. I was puzzled by it all, and so were Hala and Val. She must be the keeper of the tree. She could not be the Virgin Mary. I was at the wrong church. And White Arrow had not told me this was going to happen – or had he? In my instructions he had written 'a young goddess'.

What I had not realized was that in Egypt they sometimes refer to the Virgin Mary as a goddess, but this did not convince me – had not most people who had seen the Virgin Mary seen her in a blue dress and looking like an angel? Here, I had seen a lady who had dug at the ground as if in anger, and had looked tired. What I could not understand was the water. It was as if I was missing something. As if she was trying to tell me something of great importance, but I could not see what it was.

I put it all behind me and we left for the Coptic Museum. On the way there I prayed that someone would know the last missing link – the Coptic writings I had brought with me. If I could get proof of their authenticity, I knew I would have completed my current journey for White Arrow.

When we arrived at the museum, Hala went and spoke to someone in authority. She came back five minutes later with a man. He showed us up a flight of stairs and went straight to a book that was in a glass cabinet. He spoke to Hala for a few minutes, and she acted as interpreter. I had my book in my hand ready to show him. Hala started to tell us about the book in the glass cabinet. The man had explained to her that it had been written by one of the apostles and had been found in the arms of a baby girl. My mind went to the book that I had brought with me. I remembered the demotic drawings. I opened it, and the last couple of drawings were of a girl holding a Bible, and next to that one of a baby in a pyramid (*see* figure 11.1).

I turned to Hala and said, 'Yes, I have drawings of that,' and showed them to her. She was taken aback but said nothing. She carried on asking the man if he could read Coptic writing. The book of the apostle, was it in Coptic? He said no. Hala said that was all right, we would find someone. So we followed her. We did not even take time to look at the museum. It was as if Hala knew that it was very important to find someone to verify those words.

Out in the grounds of the museum, Hala took us down a narrow passageway hidden behind the back streets, and we went down some steps to the Church of Abu-Serga, St Sergius, where the Holy Family had taken refuge for three months. We were told by the keeper there that they were knee-deep in spring-water, in a place underneath the church, for all of that three-month period.

We stayed there about ten minutes. Then we walked back to the gate where we had entered the museum. Hala stood talking in her native tongue to the guard, asking him if there was anyone available who could read Coptic. I was still clutching the book tightly in my arms, praying that someone would know what it meant, or at least verify the Coptic words.

Then the guard called over to an Egyptian man who was walking by. He was carrying a briefcase and walked with a distinct limp. He had two women with him. He turned out to be a scholar who worked there. Hala introduced herself to him, then straight away explained that we needed someone to help us. They discussed the issue in their own language.

Meanwhile, the women accompanying him were getting anxious, saying in their native tongue that he should hurry, otherwise he would miss his train. Hala later told us that he told them to leave if they so wished, and that 'these people' (meaning us) needed to know something which was more important. How on Earth did he know?

The two women left to catch their train, and he introduced himself, still using Hala as interpreter. After Hala had spoken to him for several minutes he looked at the paperwork and told her that he actually did not know what the words and pictures meant, for it was not the form of Coptic he knew. My heart sank. But then he took out his pen and asked for some paper to write on, telling me, through Hala, that I could write to some other people who

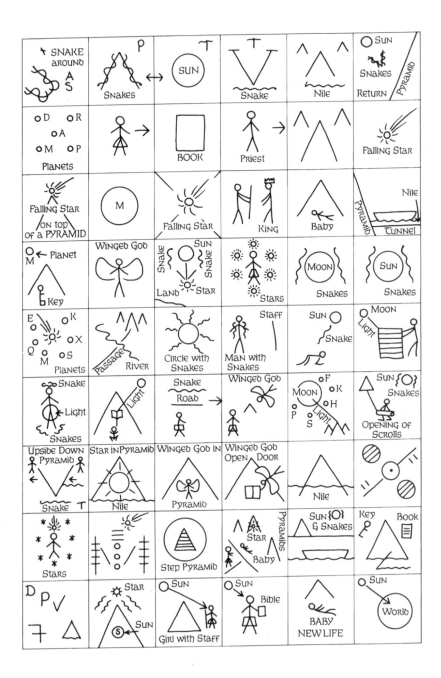

Figure 11.1 Hieratic symbols

might be able to help. He gave us the names and addresses of two people to contact.

I thanked him warmly for being so helpful. The guard, who had been listening, spoke to Hala. She later said that he had told her to go to the large church on the other side of the museum. He pointed the way to her. He told her to try to see the priest. Hala was amazed by all of this, and I wondered why. She later told us that people habitually interfere or are unhelpful. According to her, it is usually very hard to find people to read such words, yet the right person seemed to be available at the right time in our case – the scholar being there when we needed him, and the right guard being on duty. It seemed everyone wanted to help us find the Coptic words – as if they knew it was somehow important.

We walked down to the large church on the other side of the museum. We tried to see the priest, but he was not there. We were told to come back in the morning. One of the hardest things to do is to see a priest in Egypt; people are very protective towards them. I prayed that White Arrow would help me speak to him.

We walked back to the car. I told Hala that there was another pyramid built below one of the Giza pyramids – White Arrow had shown it to me in the demotic drawing. 'When are we going to Giza?' I asked.

'Tomorrow,' she replied. 'We have to be back here at the church at 9.30 to see the priest before the service.'

Then she paused for a moment and said, 'Ann, these papers you carry . . . I will explain. Many can come here and draw pictures that they see, but what you have, people do not see. Only the Egyptian government would know about them. They are secret, I know that.'

It was beginning to worry me. I was about to turn to White Arrow to speak to him, but I changed my mind. Nothing could convince me until I had proof. Although I knew she was worried about this secrecy, I still needed proof, so once again I pushed it to the back of my mind. So much was happening that I was finding it hard to take everything in, but if I could get proof of the validity of the Coptic writings I knew I could prove to the world that everything White Arrow had said and drawn was true. That was all that was on my mind. To White Arrow everything had to be fact. Although the journey was so far proving to be successful, I felt that there was more.

We stopped to have dinner. I told Hala I had to take pictures and videos of the pyramids, stones and steps. White Arrow had told me to do this. Then Hala said she was having a few personal problems of her own, so we had a session with White Arrow, which helped her. There was something she had to do that night and I told her to call on White Arrow. 'But I don't know him,' she said to me. Then White Arrow said through me, 'Everyone knows me.'

I was used to White Arrow, so what he said did not affect me, but Val and Hala noticed what he had said. I explained to Hala that this trip was in order for me to feel my way forward before I could open the tomb, and that I would have to study the pictures I was taking when I returned to England. But something inside was making me think there was more to this.

Suddenly, Bear spoke: 'I haven't finished yet.' White Arrow smiled but said nothing. Then we left the restaurant and Hala dropped us off, promising to see us at 9.30 the following morning. We sat downstairs for a while, then went to our room.

As I sat on the bed, the memory of that morning came back. The lady at the tree: I felt the water had played an important part, but what had she been trying to tell me about it? I could not be convinced it was the Virgin Mary, although she had shown me herself with child. When she came to Egypt, Jesus was two years old. Surely if the Virgin Mary was there, Jesus would have been there too? The water bothered me – I knew she was trying to give me a message. I could not think any more, and turned to Val.

Val reminded me of what Hala had said about the stone. I had been telling Hala earlier in the car that White Arrow had said that a stone from another planet had been put in the Great Pyramid. Hala had just looked at me in astonishment and confirmed that she had heard stories of such a stone. I think I must have looked more surprised than her.

I went outside to write.

Saturday evening, 15 May 1993. 'Do not fear the events that are going on,' said White Arrow. 'They are all part of the plan to show the world the truth of your pathway, that they will believe who I am, through you. You have done well. Two more days of events, then you can rest.' After this trip I will know that nothing is ever impossible! I thought about his words.

'White Arrow,' I said, 'I know now how important this trip is to you.' He is just standing there in front of me. I have learned more about White Arrow and his miracles in the past two days than in the last 14 years. Things that have surprised even me!

Zipper and Bear have appeared. White Arrow comes behind me and says, 'Watch and listen.' Zipper stretches out his hand and lays it on me. Suddenly, Alien Girl appears at his side and he gives her something. I can hear Bear growl, then I see him. He is also in front of me, next to Zipper. Suddenly, Michael appears with Eagle. Once again, White Arrow says, 'Watch and listen.'

Zipper is talking to them, but I do not know or understand what he is talking about. Then all of a sudden I hear 'Giza'. I am going there tomorrow. Why are they bringing it up tonight? White Arrow suddenly says he will bring help. The Coptic writing was still on my mind.

Both Val and I are exhausted with the events that are taking place, but it is necessary to solve this question. 'We will show you something of importance tomorrow at Giza. Part of it you know.' I presumed Zipper was referring to Bear's drawings.

'I told you not to worry. Have I not proved that in the past few days?'

'Yes, Zipper.' All of them have demonstrated that I was not to worry. But I also know that it was having White Arrow with me that meant I hadn't missed anything.

Zipper puts his hand on me and says, 'Soon we will go, but remember, we will be with you at Giza. Tomorrow night, wherever you are, look towards the north.' I still didn't understand what he meant by this – but at the beginning of the trip to Cairo I didn't understand the first set of messages and I do now, so I'm sure I will know in time.

'Come, Little One,' said White Arrow.

Twenty-five minutes later Val and I got ready for bed, both exhausted. So much was happening that it was tiring me mentally, but we had only two days to go. I was wondering what to expect tomorrow. As I climbed into bed I suddenly heard White Arrow say, 'Hala is speaking to someone about you, to do with the work.' I told Val what White Arrow had said. Very soon I was asleep.

Hala Opens Doors

It was Sunday, 16 May 1993, the third day of our Egyptian trip. I was up early as usual and sat on the balcony.

'Are you happy, White Arrow?' I asked him.

'Yes,' he replied.

'You're very secretive, though, White Arrow,' I told him. I was used to him telling me things which were about to happen, but on this trip it was as if I had to find out for myself. 'I'm pleased for you, White Arrow. We have found so much to prove you're right.' I looked at him. You're doing very well so far, I thought. He just stood looking across the Nile. I sat and watched him, this man whom God had sent to help the world.

The more evidence he obtained, the more I would have to share him with the world. But much as I love him, I could not keep him a secret anymore. Soon the world would know about him, this man God calls his son. To me he is just White Arrow, the most caring of all. No human could love and care as he does and I knew the world would love him as much as I do.

'I hope, White Arrow,' I said to him as he turned towards me, 'that you won't leave me.' I knew I was being selfish in saying this.

Then White Arrow said, 'Little One, you have been chosen to help me. You will always be special to me.'

'Am I being so selfish in asking you, White Arrow?' I asked.

'No, Little One, you are human, and humans always fear. But do not fear. We must continue our journey.' I laughed to myself. White Arrow never wasted many words. 'I will see you later,' he said and left. There were other questions I was going to ask, but he obviously knew this and had no intention of telling me the answers, so I got up and woke Val.

Soon it would be time for Hala to arrive. The events of the previous day were in the back of my mind, yet my thoughts were on the present. White Arrow had told me to tell the priest about him, but yesterday Hala had told me that we would have great difficulty in seeing the priest, so I prayed we would succeed today. However, I would not be able to see him privately. So today I just prayed that at least we could show him the words. This was my last and only chance, for this man could read Coptic, and if I could not see him it meant I would have to research somewhere else – and where, we did not know. Time was running out.

I picked up the book and we went down to the foyer to wait for Hala. She was late and apologized; she had been held up. 'We will still go to the church, but because we are late we'll have to wait till after the service to see the priest,' she said. My stomach was churning with excitement and hope. At the same time my mind was telling me, don't be disappointed, you have tried, no more could be asked of you. We climbed into the car and drove off.

Hala was quiet for a moment. 'Are you okay?' I asked her.

She looked at me, then said, 'I was going to ring you last night. I was going to ring you because I was scared. I was puzzled.'

'You should have done so, Hala,' I told her. 'Why, what was the problem?'

'After speaking to you last night I went to see another friend of mine. She also is a tour guide . . .'

I must explain here that the guides in Cairo have to study and learn for years about the history of their country. Hala herself had studied for six years. It is hard study, for they have to know everything that is necessary to help people understand their history. Hala had told her friend what she had witnessed at the tree the day before, and her friend had told her that in their old Bible the Virgin Mary, with the baby Jesus, had fled to Egypt and stopped at the tree. Mary was tired from the long journey and thirsty.

'At the tree she became angry at God. She was thirsty, but more than that, her baby needed water and there was none. She kept hitting the ground in anger and digging with her hands. God heard her, and as she dug, water came forth. The Virgin Mary gave Jesus water first, and then she watered the tree, for the tree had given her water and had saved her baby Jesus, so the tree was more important than her.'

Hala carried on, 'I told you the day before yesterday that

Matariyah was ten hours away by bus. What I didn't know was that the place I took you to was the *original* Matariyah. Many, many years ago they decided to name a new town Matariyah – that is the one ten hours away. White Arrow was right!' Her words hit me like a lightning bolt from the blue, flashing light over everything.

I heard a sob – it was coming from me. I turned towards the window, tears filling my eyes. I must not cry. I must not cry. I was so shocked. I had witnessed a miracle. It *had* been the Virgin Mary! She had appeared and had even watered my feet. I managed to compose myself, then turned to Hala and Val. What could I say? The only words I could find were, 'I'm glad White Arrow was right.' All three of us sat in silence for a while, stunned, and then Hala said she understood what I was going through, for she had already had the shock earlier.

'We will be at the church in five minutes. Get your notes ready,' she said. I was glad. I did not want to think about what had just happened – not yet. It was too much to take in. So by the time we got there, I was back to my old self again. Within five minutes we were in the church. I thanked White Arrow for lending Hala to me, but I was also worried for her. She was young, and I hoped White Arrow would give her strength to cope with all these events.

We climbed the stone steps and entered the church, then joined the other people praying. Once again, I asked God to help White Arrow in his search. Then I stood up and looked around. There was beauty everywhere and delightful singing from two women and two priests. Like the other church, it was very old, with pictures of Jesus and the disciples everywhere. We all lit a candle. Hala is a Muslim, and she asked me what she should do, for she wanted to light a candle also. I showed her what to do and she lit one. By the time we had arrived the service was halfway through, so we did not have long to wait. Val and I joined the queue and took the cup of wine and bread from the priest. Hala stayed behind to talk to the head priest. She called us back to join her.

The priests were very well protected, but Hala was persistent and the priest stopped to talk to her. I was very nervous. Hala sensed this, took the book from me and gave it to him. She showed him the two pages of Coptic writings. He looked at the Coptic words – the first on a drawing of a pyramid with letters and numbers around it (*see* figure 7.1, page 66), and on the other side eight words written in Coptic (*see* figure 5.1, page 50). He looked at me over the top of his glasses – a kind and wise man.

His eyes showed me that he liked me, although his words frightened me.

'These are Coptic Latin words. It is a combination of Coptic Greek and Coptic Latin. It is magic.' We later worked out that he meant it comes from another world – also that it is very dangerous. 'It is also mathematical, a prescription. There are 24 letters from the Greek alphabet and 7 Coptic letters, plus mathematical numbers.'

He flicked through the rest of the pages, looking at them all, knowing each and every page was important. He stopped at one page then pointed to two words: QRESTUAE PQULLE. I had written them under the instructions White Arrow had given me before I came. I had not translated them. I told him I knew what it meant and he waited for me to say it. 'It means "in the knowledge of God" '. He nodded in agreement, then shut the book. He handed it back to me and I thanked him. I held on to the book tightly, my heart racing. I had found proof that established that all White Arrow had said and written was true. I thanked God.

We left the church in silence. I had encountered two miracles in one day! As we got back in the car and drove to the pyramids, my mind was upset, confused and frightened. I had not fully taken in the potential consequences of finding such proof – and here was a Coptic priest telling me the Coptic was correct. It finalized in my mind that the report in *Little One* was right, that our world *is* in trouble. So instead of being happy, I could feel righteous anger swelling inside me, a feeling of frustration over the state of the world.

As we drove past several tourist buses near the pyramids Hala caught sight of someone she knew. She said she wanted to show the book to a Greek guide who was a friend of hers, to see if she could interpret what the word and numbers meant. Although the priest had verified that they were Coptic, he had not told us what it all meant.

Val and I went towards the Great Pyramid, and I did everything White Arrow had told me to. It was important that I did not miss a thing, so I videoed it and took photographs in great detail. After this we walked towards a small wall where we could sit. The anger I felt inside came out – I was full of fear at the enormity of it all. I thought of Hala and Val, who had witnessed all of this, but my anger was with White Arrow. Sitting in front of one of the seven wonders of the world made little difference. How dare he put so much responsibility on me! How dare he! I could not carry all of this. I never realized, even though he told me that what I was carrying around was so important, and what danger I could be in. I felt like crying and told Val how I felt. How dare he put this on me! So much had happened since I had arrived that I felt I could go on no more.

'Where are you, White Arrow?' I said out loud. As I said the words he appeared. I could hear Val saying to me in the distance, 'Use the staff, Ann.' In my anger I had forgotten to use the staff. Then White Arrow said, 'Little One, there are still other things to happen before you go home.'

'White Arrow, no more. So much is happening, and you really cannot expect me to carry all this on my own.' I was of course forgetting that I was not on my own, for I had White Arrow and the aliens with me. Straight away, White Arrow's father appeared and around him stood Zipper, Michael, Alien Girl, Bear and Eagle. He spoke, and as he spoke he held the staff towards me. I took it. As I held it in my hand it was bright white, then pink.

'Do not fear, Ann Walker. I am of the staff. My son is with you. Do not fear, for it has been taken care of. Trust me, Ann Walker, for I am here to save the world. I know you are angry, but your faith has overcome your anger previously, so I know you will follow.' I looked at him. No matter the enormity of it, no matter how I feared, I loved him and his son. My anger evaporated. He left and the staff left me, too. White Arrow's father had appeared in his cloak and crown, but as usual I could not see him.

White Arrow sat next to me. 'I'm sorry, White Arrow,' I said to him. I knew he understood. After all, I am only human, and I had never felt more so than now. Then he said, 'Hala will find you more answers to your questions. She will find someone who will tell you what it means.' I looked at him amazed. I found it difficult to believe anyone could have had so many miracles happen in just a few days, and here he was telling me more was coming.

'Little One,' he said, 'I understand that you could not tell the priest, but next time you must tell them who I am. Refer to me as the Son of God, because I have many names all over the world.' I was puzzled, for that was what I had always called him. But I did not dare dwell on it, in case I faltered in my work for him. Was there something I was missing? 'The priest you saw would not have feared, had you told him so. He could not say much,' explained white Arrow, 'for he did not know who you were.'

'I'm sorry, White Arrow,' I said.

'No, Little One, it was not your fault, and I knew you would not tell him. But you will meet others, so I tell you this for them. The vision you saw yesterday, Little One, was to prove to the world that I am the Son of God, that those whom I bring [pointing to the aliens] also work for God.'

I just could not entertain seeing Virgin Mary at this time – that was the most heavy of all burdens to carry. I had witnessed and seen Mary on this journey, and I just could not believe she had come to see me. There had been something she was trying to tell me, to tell the world, yet I still could not work out what it was. The water kept coming back into my mind. I knew I had to go home and digest it all. White Arrow knew this and said no more except 'I will see you later' before he left.

Just then, a man with a camel came up to us and asked me if I wanted to have a ride. I do not know how it happened, but I felt the load lift off me, and the worry disappeared. Val and I went for a short ride. I found myself laughing – something I had not done since arriving here. I knew in my heart that while White Arrow was with me I had nothing to fear.

We looked at the pyramids once more and then went to look for Hala, who was sitting in the car waiting for us. It was very hot and I was thirsty – my first thought was for the bottled water in the car. I drank half of the water, then put it back. 'I have something to tell you,' said Hala.

The fear I had felt earlier had left me and I felt prepared. After the last few days, nothing could surprise me any more. 'Ann,' she began, 'my friend has told me the writings are factual. The drawing you showed me at the hotel room is π. The key to getting into the tomb you have already written down – only you have the key to opening it. The Pythagorean mathematical theorem means '3.14'. It is all in the map you have of the pyramid – but it's top secret information.'

I sat silently, my mind on White Arrow. When you do something, it's never by half, is it? I thought. I looked back at Hala, who went on to say, 'Also, Ann, my friend commented on the two sets of figures in the pyramid diagram. They mean that the 33cm between the two sets of figures represents the 33 years that Jesus Christ lived on Earth. The secrets of life are here. They are Coptic Latin numbers.'

This validated what White Arrow had said: in the tomb is

evidence of the past and future, the secrets are in there and the writings in my possession could open it. Hala started the car and drove us a few hundred yards before parking it again. I had to try and put everything I had learned aside for the moment, although one thought crossed my mind: Jesus Christ had kept cropping up – he had something to do with this journey. Once again, I put it to the back of my mind – it was just too much right now.

I asked Hala if there was a village of Giza. It was just one more thing I had to do before I left Egypt – that is, besides Ti. But she said, 'No, I have not heard of it.' So I left it. Once again I said sorry to White Arrow – everything he had instructed me about had happened, except the village of Giza . . .

As we got out of the car we could see the three pyramids and the magnificent Sphinx. I knew the Sphinx was important. I had to take close-ups of it. Apart from Saqqara and Giza, the Sphinx was very important for White Arrow to show me the way to open the tomb. I looked at the Sphinx in wonder. The feeling there was remarkable. I still had a job to do, to video it, so I took the camcorder out and started shooting. We were permitted to photograph only one side of it and were not allowed close, so I videoed it with the zoom – twice, so I would not miss anything. Then we left.

'I will help you always,' said Hala. 'But I must tell you: I have to go and see my teacher and ask him if it is all right. If he says no, I promise with all my heart that I will find you someone who can. I want you to promise we will stay friends always.'

'Of course, Hala, I understand,' I said to her. Hala, a Muslim, had just witnessed things to do with Christianity and miracles. My heart went out to her. Val had been close to me on my trips – she knew some of the things White Arrow could do, and this trip had affected her deeply. But poor Hala! She must have been more than shocked to get so much proof. 'Hala, you have done so much for White Arrow and myself. I will never forget you. Go to your teacher, and ask him.' She leaned over and cuddled me.

We stopped for dinner. We sat and talked for a while, not once bringing up what had happened. We just enjoyed ourselves and then left for Hala's mother's house. Val and I were made very welcome. Then Hala took us back to the hotel. She promised that Mohammed would be there at 10am. Val and I just dropped everything when we got to our room and flopped onto our beds, exhausted. We chatted about other things.

I was tired, but I still had to go out to see the aliens. Looking northwards from the balcony seemed important to them, but as I stood and looked I still could not work out why. Maybe on my next trip it would make sense. I sat and wrote.

Sunday 16 May 1993. This trip has proved beyond doubt that White Arrow exists. I can only say it has been a stream of miracles, some dangerous, but I have to trust White Arrow for my safety in the future. Zipper has just appeared. He says, 'You are more relaxed now. Now we can get on with the real work. Look to the north and wait. I will be back.' Michael is here. I don't know why I have to look to the north, but I'm just waiting.

White Arrow is here and says, 'Do not worry, Little One. Everything is all right.'

'I was scared, White Arrow,' I said.

'I know, Little One, but I will look after you, I promise.' I know he will.

White Arrow's father is here. 'You have done well, my child. You have done much for mankind. Soon comes your reward.' That puzzles me, for I feel I have had more rewards and miracles than anyone would go on their knees for. 'When you go home, Ann Walker, our work will begin. You are ready. Remember the staff is with you. I will return.'

Zipper is back. 'Why the north, Zipper?' I ask him.

'You will understand in the future.'

Michael then speaks. 'You know you are different now?' I didn't particularly feel different. 'You have been touched by the hand of God.' I don't understand. I am still stunned, denying the enormity of it all, for my sanity's sake. I turn to White Arrow. Suddenly, Bear appears, and Eagle.

'White Arrow, what does Michael mean?'

'I will tell you another time. It is not the right time for you to know what Michael means.'

Zipper appears and puts his hand on me. I feel the love go through me. I love these people so much and I hope their message will get through to the world. Without Val's support I think I might have failed them, for too much has happened to take in – so I'm glad she came.

Zipper suddenly says he has to go. 'See you tomorrow', he said, and vanished. Michael is still here, with Bear and Eagle. 'I will be with you at Ti', said Bear. I knew Eagle would be with him.

White Arrow says, 'Come', and they go.

We crawled into bed and sat chatting; we would both miss Cairo – a city which never sleeps, with a heart of its own.

Before I fell asleep I thought about Val. She had come into my life in the 1980s, helping me on all my books. As time went on she became a close friend and witness on all my journeys – not once did she fail me. Whatever I forgot, Val remembered; she witnessed every move I made, and her help became invaluable. She had a young family, and all of them had put their trust in White Arrow, never stopping her from spending hours and days helping me. White Arrow had chosen well! He gave me a friend to share the load when it was too heavy.

She grew to understand me as we followed the journey – when I needed humour she gave it, and when I was sad she empathized. But most of all, she loves and trusts White Arrow, her faith greater than I could have hoped for. I was blessed to have her walking alongside me on this journey, and I lay there, feeling great appreciation. Then I dropped into slumber.

· 13 ·

The Juggler

It was light when I awoke. I turned over and saw Val stirring. I got up and went to the bathroom, shouting to Val to wake up. We had another busy day ahead of us. But we had to do a bit of shopping first – it was the last opportunity to pick up presents for our families. I phoned Tony and my daughter and told them I was all right. He was pleased, but more pleased that I would be home next day! Val and I had breakfast, then we waited for Mohammed. I had my book with me in case anything happened to it.

Mohammed arrived dead on time. He was a nice man. His English was pretty good, so we could all understand each other. We had been talking for about ten minutes on our journey to Ti at Saqqara when I decided to ask him if there is a place called the village of Giza.

'Yes,' he said.

'You're joking?' I was taken aback. 'Are you sure?'

'Yes. After we have gone to Ti, I will take you there on the way back.'

I was over the moon. I had not failed White Arrow! I put my head back on the headrest, completely relaxed and pleased. I had felt so much better after White Arrow's father had given me the staff.

Suddenly, I remembered White Arrow's instructions for Ti. 'Take pictures of the wall to your left as you enter the offering room at Ti. I will show you what to look for when you return home. When you leave Ti, look to the north. You will come back within 12 months. This and all other trips will be important to mankind. On the third trip we will succeed in finding the tomb.'

Just then White Arrow appeared and said, 'You are safe, but be careful to whom you show these things and to whom you speak, for they might steal from you and it will only hold up the future.'

'I understand, White Arrow. But you will have to tell me who to go to.'

'In time,' was White Arrow's reply. 'When you leave Ti, take the sand in your hands and look towards the sky and thank God.'

White Arrow would have his own reasons for requesting that, so I told him I would not forget. I looked at some of the places we were passing. Then Mohammed spoke. He was pointing something out to me, but all I could hear was 'Michael Douglas' – I was remembering a film I had seen.

Back in February, Zipper had told me of a man on stilts, a juggler, the number five and a corner, also about someone who either believed in the Spirit or worked with spirit beings. I had completely forgotten this. Now White Arrow was bringing it back to my memory. The film I was remembering was called *The Jewel of the Nile*. I had watched only the last ten minutes of it. Michael Douglas and a woman had been walking down a hill following a man ahead of them, and the woman turned to Michael Douglas and said something like, 'Do you want to know who or what the Jewel of the Nile is?' He said yes, and she said, 'He is . . .', and pointed to a man ahead of them.

I sat back wondering why White Arrow had brought this up in my memory and what the film had to do with this journey. Then I looked at Mohammed and, without thinking, I asked him how tall he was. 'Six foot four,' was his reply. The man on stilts – I just knew *he* was it. It was the aliens' way of describing a tall man. In the film, Michael Douglas had worked it out that way; that was why White Arrow had brought that part of the film into my mind. Then I thought of the juggler. I looked again at Mohammed. Could he help me solve the riddle of the five and the corners? If he could, then he would be the juggler, juggling the things they had given me in his mind.

'Mohammed, could you help me with something?' I asked him. 'I'm trying to unlock some clues concerning the number five and some corners, and they're linked with the village of Giza.' I had not known of the connection with Giza, so it must have been White Arrow working through me.

'Five could mean a street,' said Mohammed, 'but five in Egyptian. When I take you to the village I will ask. The corners I do not know of, but we will wait till we get there.' I thanked him.

If he could find me the answers, then I would know he was the juggler.

We enjoyed the rest of the journey there, and before we knew it we were at Ti. Mohammed introduced us to his brother, who kept camels. I had not realized we could only get there by horse or camel. The things I end up doing for you, White Arrow, I thought. He was not around, so I do not know if he heard me or not.

The brother's name was Sheban. He helped us onto a camel. With both of us in tow, he rode off to Ti, about ten or fifteen minutes away.

Adrian Gilbert wrote the following on Ti, the man.

Ti

Ti was an important court official who served under three pharaohs. He married a woman of royal blood, and his children were considered to be royal. He was overseer of the building of the pyramids of Abusir. These small pyramids lie between Saqqara and Giza. You can just about see them from a little bit in front of the Unas pyramid. His titles were Lord of Secrets, Superintendent of Works, Overseer of the Pyramids of Abusir, Counsellor of the Pharaoh and even Royal Hairdresser.

What seems to me significant is that he must have been involved in the transfer of power that occurred at the end of the Fourth Dynasty and the beginning of the Fifth. This is the time when something happened between the building of the pyramids of Giza and those of Abusir, and power was transferred to a new line of pharaohs from Heliopolis. These pharaohs are believed to have been triplets, the sons of a priestess. It could be that Ti was around at the time when the gods (extraterrestrials), who may have had a hand in building the Great Pyramids of Giza, departed and left Egypt in the hands of new rulers.

Sheban told us that Ti had been a medicine man. I was not really surprised. It seemed to fit, but I really had no idea why Ti was so important to White Arrow. He had told me nothing, except to go there – and I was there now. White Arrow's father had told me to use the staff when I entered Ti, which I duly did.

I had my video and camera with me, although as a rule the Egyptians do not allow filming. As I entered the offering chamber I asked the guide whether it was all right to video. He said yes, but told me not to let anyone see me. Luckily, we were the only ones there. I was videoing a lot, but only because I wanted to make sure I had got everything for White Arrow. I was surprised the man was allowing me to take so much – he was a bit nervous – but I thought it was because he wanted a large tip. After I had shot everything I thanked him and gave him extra for allowing me to do it. I wondered if the staff had played a part in this stroke of luck.

We were then to go to the Tomb of the Sacred Bull. Although I did not need to go, it was somewhere that Sheban took everyone. This time we had two camels – Sheban had found another man, Allah, with another one. I sat behind the new man, and Val sat with Sheban on his camel, and off we went to the Sacred Bull tomb. I did not know why – it was not in the instructions – but, just in case, I took more pictures. As we left I remembered that I also had to video the north of Ti, so I did that, then went to the sand. I bent down and picked some up in my hands and looked up. 'Thank you, God,' I said quietly. 'Thank you for everything.' Then I turned to join the others.

I do not know why, but I asked Allah a question. 'In your religion, do you pick up the sand and thank God?'

'Yes,' he replied, without hesitation. I knew then why White Arrow had told me to do it. We returned to Mohammed, tired, dusty, hot and very thirsty. He was sitting inside a large open tent which had tables and chairs. We ordered cold drinks. Mohammed had a bad throat, so Val offered to give him healing. He accepted her help willingly; I knew then that he knew about Spirit.

I had had some notes about a tent and a flute, and I asked if the flute was important. They said, 'Yes, we go to the desert and play the flute to God.' I deduced from this that one day I would have to go into the desert. I had not really worked out the full message, so maybe the flute meant something else. But knowing my luck with White Arrow it would not surprise me if I ended up in the middle of the Sahara. It could only happen to me, I thought, and I laughed to myself.

Mohammed's throat and head felt better and we went back to the car. I said to him, 'Are you going to take me to the village of Giza now?'

'Yes,' he replied. 'It is not far from your hotel.'

I prayed I would find out what the five and the corners meant, and also why White Arrow wanted me to go there. I rested my head back and enjoyed the ride. We stopped at a railway crossing and watched the trains pass. As we sat there some schoolchildren came around the car and we spoke to them until the second train had passed. Then we were off again. Mohammed reminded me of my brother – their features are so alike.

It was not long before Mohammed said, 'We are here.' I looked out and there stood a building. Across the front were the words 'Village of Giza'. It was a museum – a floating one, run by Professor Hassan Ragan, which was concerned with the making of papyrus. There was also an island there called Jacob Island. We could not stop for long, but Mohammed promised that he would tell Hala how to get here and I made up my mind to return that night – White Arrow had said 'Go to the village of Giza at night.'

As I was looking, Mohammed said to me, 'Ann, you wanted to know what "five" and "corners" meant. Look . . .' I looked where he was pointing. Across the road stood five single blocks of flats, and each of them had their own corner in the road. There were five corners – we counted them. I worked out the message, thanks to Mohammed. I was sure I was at the right place, but I had to wait for White Arrow to tell me, to make no mistake. But I knew for sure that Mohammed was the juggler. I thanked him warmly, and when we arrived at the hotel he gave me his address and I promised to write to him.

That evening we were to visit Hala's grandmother, and Hala was waiting in the hotel foyer for us. She wanted me to bring the book so that it could be copied for her. She promised to carry on helping me. I was going to miss her, and I would never forget her.

We arrived in time for dinner and her grandmother greeted us warmly. Afterwards I spoke to Hala about what White Arrow had told me. He had said that part of building the pyramids was done according to the patterns of the stars. Hala agreed. She confirmed that the pharaohs used astronomers to calculate stellar formations for the siting of the pyramids, and she reckoned the stars would help unlock the pyramid. Everything White Arrow had told me was being confirmed. She then said that the map belonged to the Great Pyramid. The Coptic words and numbers had given its exact size.

It was known that there were secrets within the Great Pyramid, secrets White Arrow had mentioned before I came. But the Egyptians were frightened of what these secrets held, so they did not really want the tomb opened. I just had to pray that White Arrow could find a way of showing the Egyptian government that it was for the good of humankind, for I would need their help.

We left at about 8pm to go to the Village of Giza. When we arrived it was dark and the place was shut. It had closed at 4. White Arrow had insisted that I go at night, but why? He must have known it would be shut. Hala spoke to the guard. I wanted to take some pictures and the guard said it was all right, but I was surprised when he beckoned me to follow him inside the complex. He allowed me to take as many pictures as I wanted. I knew that White Arrow would not bring me here without a reason, although I would not know that reason until I returned home. I would have to study the pictures – Hala promised she would help me. We went back to the hotel.

Hala was in tears and I hugged her, promising we would return, and I would ring her when I got home. Val and I packed our cases and bags, and then I returned to the balcony to write.

Monday 17 May 1993. Zipper is here already. I am so tired. We have had so much to do, but it has been wonderful. I'm pleased for White Arrow that the trip has been successful. Zipper says he has some important pictures for me when I get back.

White Arrow is here and I know he is pleased. I didn't let him down. Bear is here, with Michael and Eagle. Eagle tells me I have come far. The messages will get easier because I have learned. I presume she means I understand some of them now.

'Thank you, thank you, thank you, White Arrow and you all for allowing me to help you. I love you all and you know that I am proud and humble that you have chosen me,' I say.

Zipper, Bear and Michael put their hands on me. Their love goes through me. For this moment words are not needed, just love and trust.

'White Arrow, I love you and I thank your father for sending you to me.' He looks at me and I can see the love in his eyes. Again no words are necessary. 'I will do my best to follow you and help you help the world – I promise. I will always be here for you all,' I say.

It goes very quiet, then Zipper says, 'Look to the north'. I see nothing. I don't know yet why the north is so important, but when I return to England I will go over everything and then maybe I will understand. I look at them all. Zipper puts his hand on me and says, 'We have much work to do.'

'I know,' I reply.

I have to forget the miracles and get on with the work we have come to do. I will miss Cairo and the magic of this journey. But I will be back to help White Arrow prove he is the Son of God.

Zipper suddenly says he has to go – but I do not understand, for he's only been here 15 minutes tonight. Bear comes forward, saying, 'We will see you tomorrow.'

As we got into our beds Val phoned to book an alarm call. We were to leave at 6.15 in the morning for the airport.

I was in a deep sleep the next morning when I heard the phone go. It was Hala. She just wanted to say goodbye again. She had hardly slept all night, thinking of what had happened in the past four days. 'I am more than grateful to you, Hala,' I told her in all sincerity. I am not the best person to talk to at 4.45 in the morning, but I wanted to tell her that most of all. 'I will phone you on Sunday, Hala,' I told her.

'You promise?' she said.

'Yes, I promise,' I assured her, and said goodbye.

I dragged myself out of bed, half asleep. Val had already gone to the bathroom, so I went out on to the balcony for the last time. 'Goodbye, Cairo,' I said silently. 'I will return.'

We had breakfast and waited to be picked up for the airport. I felt sad leaving and promised myself I would return for a holiday one day. I had a window seat on the plane. As we waited for the plane to take off I looked out of the window. White Arrow suddenly appeared but said nothing. 'I'm pleased everything went well for White Arrow, Val,' I said. Val agreed. 'You know, this book is going to be massive by the time I come here again, what with all the work in between, the writing and drawings.'

White Arrow spoke: 'You know I asked you to walk three and a half times around the tree and you wondered why?'

'Yes,' I said, intrigued.

'You were walking my footsteps when I was on Earth.' My stomach sank. 'You were walking the 30-odd years I was on Earth.'

'Then you *were* Jesus Christ?'

'Yes, Little One, I was. When you came back to the tree and spoke to my mother, the reason you could not see Jesus was because I was already with you. This book is for the message my mother brought to the world through you. The message was to do with the water and the tree and the tomb.' I knew I had missed something. The tomb I knew, but the water kept coming back to me.

'This is my mother's message. She was showing you that the tree had once provided her with water, water to save me, the Son of God. Without the tree I would not have survived. My mother knew this, so she watered the tree in thanks for saving that life. She brings back the same message: without the trees mankind will not survive. My mother, Mary, asks you to tell the world to save the trees, for the trees will save you, the world.'

I sat and looked at him. I knew in my heart he once was Jesus, but I could not accept that such a man would choose *me*. I had accepted he was the Son of God – but once upon a time he had been Jesus, and this I had to accept too. I knew it to be true.

Suddenly, he said, 'Remember my father told you about the walls of Jericho?'

'Yes, I remember, White Arrow,' I said.

'When you were at Giza, the walls of Jericho came down.' I wondered for a moment what this could mean. 'It means,' said White Arrow, 'the truth can now be told, that nothing can stop it.' I understood, and silently I thanked the Virgin Mary for her message for the world.

Once again we had come back to the trees, the force of life. I was to pass the message to the world, for it was for the world that this book was being written. White Arrow had brought the truth to the world in Cairo – and the miracles with it.

Once again I turned to White Arrow and said, 'Whatever happens to me, I will pass your message on, for I know you speak only truth.'

I returned home. For a while I tried to put it all behind me. I had to get used to what I had witnessed. I finished writing up the material and turned to White Arrow, wondering if he was going to say anything. One thing I knew was that I had not gone to Cairo for the tomb. This was to come later. White Arrow had taken me for the message the Virgin Mary sought to give to the world.

Then I could hear White Arrow saying the words once again: 'In many languages, QRESTUAE PQULLE – in the knowledge of God.'

'Our father, who art in heaven . . .'

· Part Two ·

· 14 ·

On with the Work

Zipper shut the book. 'It didn't take you long to find me more work,' I said – I had not been back more than a week. I now fully understood the urgency of this journey, so I really did not mind – it was just a matter of fitting in so many other matters as well.

'We will give you all the strength we can to help you. Please do not fear us.' Zipper was referring to Harry, a ufologist who had remarked the day before that he was still not sure if the aliens were here for good reasons. I had been angry about that.

White Arrow then spoke. 'Little One, everybody has a right to their own thoughts, and Harry does believe in me and my friends. Many questions will be asked, but in the end I will prove through you that the aliens *are* the world's friends, that they are here to help the people of the world. Never fear such questions, for I will have the answers.'

'I don't fear, White Arrow. I just get angry! I know you are all good.'

'Yes, Little One, but you have had time to work that out. Now it's other people's time to find it out for themselves.' I understood. I would have to stop expecting people to believe as fervently as I did.

'But I am scared, White Arrow, of people on Earth,' I admitted. 'There are some who will not want me to have such knowledge. But I promise one thing: I will not run away from this journey. I have given my promise, and I will keep that promise, whatever lies ahead. But how do we open the tomb? That is the next question.'

'Patience, Little One. We will show you.'

'I know, White Arrow, but how are we going to get permission from the Egyptian government? Mind you, I guess I'll worry about that later . . .' I realized I had months ahead to work out where the tomb was, let alone open it. There was a lot of work yet to do with White Arrow and the aliens.

'I will want to see you daily, Little One,' said White Arrow. I wondered how long that would be for. White Arrow simply said, 'We will see.' Then he showed me the sign of the cross. Yes, after Egypt I would have to accept that he had indeed been Jesus Christ.

'I will see you tomorrow, Little One,' said White Arrow.

'Yes,' I replied, thinking of the months of hard work ahead. I just hoped I could cope with it!

On 24 May I spoke to Hala, who told me a professor was looking at the drawings for me. She had also found out that there was talk of a secret tomb under the Great Pyramid – it was said that it holds the secrets of the world, which is what White Arrow had told me the previous year. If evidence is ever needed, he is providing it. I asked Hala to check on the book at the Coptic Museum to find out if it was found at Saqqara. I also asked her find out more about the Village of Giza – I needed to know more. I was sure it was not the village of Giza that White Arrow was referring to, but I would have to wait for White Arrow to guide me there.

A few days later I saw Mrs Prince, who was going to get me some maps. Hala had recommended that I get a permit to dig near the pyramids, but to get a permit one must tell the Egyptian government where one is going to dig, and I really did not know at the time. Later, White Arrow told me I must tell no one where I was to dig until he said so. So I would have to be careful.

On 30 May, White Arrow appeared in front of the television while I was watching a film, something he never does unless it is very important. I went to the back room and waited for him. Zipper was there already – I had not expected him. White Arrow stood beside him. I wondered what this was all about.

'Soon an event will take place,' said White Arrow.

'Is it to do with the spaceship?' I asked.

'No,' replied White Arrow, 'but whatever it is, you must come to me before you explain.' Explain what? I was puzzled. 'A man is coming. He is of great importance. He will be able to help us on our journey. You must be ready for his arrival.'

'Is he on Earth?' I asked.

'Yes,' replied White Arrow. 'In the coming months much work must be done on Egypt. This man can help.'

'Am I to trust him?'

'Yes,' replied White Arrow.

I could only guess that this man was coming very soon. I could not think who he could be. But then 'soon' could be a couple of years to White Arrow, so all I could do was wait. 'I hope I say the right things for you, White Arrow.'

'I will be there. Do not fear, Little One, for I will *be you* when we talk.' Good, I thought.

On 1 June White Arrow called me again. Bear was with him. There were a lot of events to take place this year. 'You will put by one day every week for us, for we have much to show you,' said White Arrow. I promised him I would make Saturday or Sunday free. He smiled.

All of a sudden, an Egyptian king appeared. 'We have brought him to help, like the Cherokee Indian.'

'Who is the king, White Arrow?' He did not answer, so I left it. In time, I was sure I would know.

White Arrow said, 'We will talk again tomorrow.' Zipper waved, Bear growled. I suddenly saw Michael, but they all left.

'I didn't expect this, White Arrow,' I said, referring to the appearance of the king. He smiled and put his hand on my shoulder. It was obviously important to him. 'I promise I'll help, whatever you ask me, White Arrow,' I told him.

'I know you will.'

Later, I was upstairs saying my prayers, asking for help to carry the load, when suddenly I heard White Arrow's father speak: 'Call on my staff.' I did so. For the first time the staff appeared in white, yellow and pink. I felt humble. The load lifted for the day and it made me stronger.

By 8 June I had finished writing about my first visit to Egypt, so I could now concentrate on the next journey. Zipper was already present. Bear and Michael, Alien Girl and Eagle all came in together. It was good to see them. White Arrow said, 'Watch and listen.' Alien Girl gave Zipper what looked like a book, but not one I had seen before. It was white. The king appeared next to him. Zipper was looking through the book. Bear seemed to be talking to him but I did not know what he was saying.

Eagle sat down. Michael was silent at first but then said hello. Zipper opened the book towards me but I could not see clearly what he was trying to show me. He got up and came over, using his finger to draw something, then went back and sat down. I did

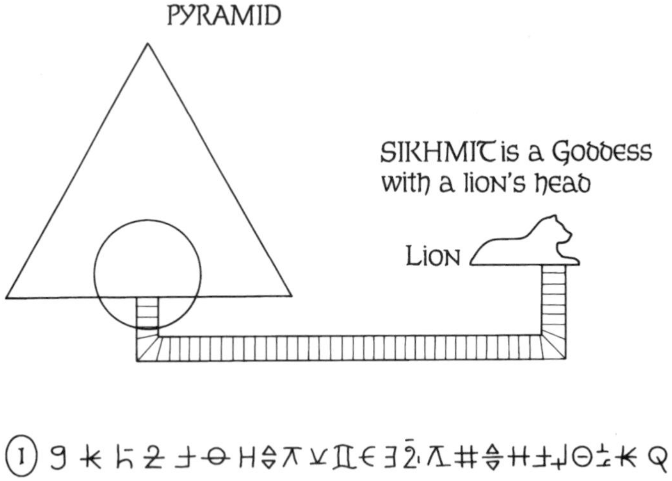
PYRAMID
SIKHMIT is a Goddess
with a lion's head
Lion
1

Figure 14.1 Zipper's first drawing

his drawings as if they were directly transmitted through my hand (*see* figures 14.1 and 14.2). I did not understand, but the writing looked the same as the Coptic Latin. White Arrow suddenly said,

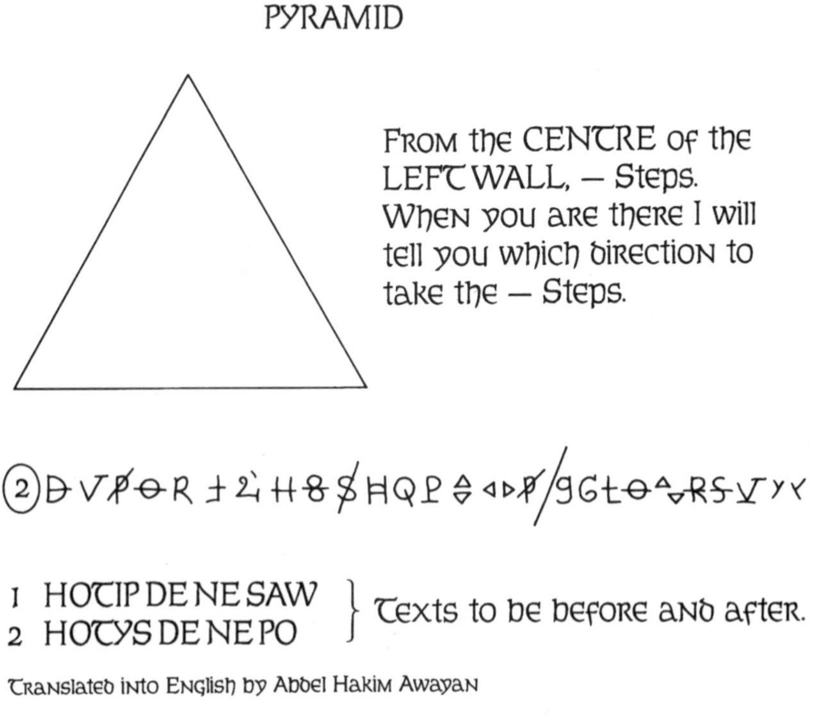
PYRAMID
From the CENTRE of the
LEFT WALL, – Steps.
When you are there I will
tell you which direction to
take the – Steps.
2
1 HOTIP DE NE SAW
2 HOTYS DE NE PO
Texts to be before and after.
Translated into English by Abdel Hakim Awayan

Figure 14.2 Zipper's second drawing

'I will bring the right person to you.' Just then I felt the presence of White Arrow's father. Then I saw him holding the staff.

'You have done well, Ann Walker. I thank you for your faith.' Once again I felt humble in his presence. 'Soon I will show you a miracle. This miracle will come through you. After this, the world will not doubt my presence. Through you, my son will appear. Do not fear, for all will be made clear on your journey. You have helped my son greatly – you will not be forgotten for this by mankind. I know you seek no reward, but it is my command that you receive it.' He held out the staff. 'Take it, Ann Walker, for it will serve you well.' I took it, watching it change in colour. He left.

I turned to White Arrow. 'If there is something else to happen, please warn me, White Arrow.'

'It is all right, Little One, you will be prepared,' he replied.

Then I said, 'Also, White Arrow, if in future there's any change for the worse, do tell me. You promise?'

'I will,' said White Arrow. He looked at Zipper and said, 'Is that all?' This surprised me – he had never said that before.

Zipper replied, 'That will do for today.'

He got up and moved towards me, with Alien Girl in tow. He started to do something with the medallion. He took it off me, then put it back on. 'More power,' was all I heard. Then I watched him and the others leave.

'We will come back tomorrow, Little One,' said White Arrow.

Two days later, I found I needed to talk to White Arrow. I could see all of this getting too big. I wondered if I could cope. I could do the writing and talk to the aliens, but now I would have to let the public know about all this too – and that is where I wondered if I would be able to manage. I would have preferred just to publish the books and be out of the public eye, but I could not see that happening; White Arrow seemed to need to talk through me in public.

He had just arrived. 'White Arrow, what is next? Am I strong enough to cope?' I asked him.

'Little One, the journey is hard and what I expect of you seems impossible, but I will never let you down.'

'It's not a question of you letting *me* down, it's me letting *you* down,' I said quietly.

'For 14 years I have been with you and watched and protected you. Not once have you let me down,' replied White Arrow. 'I have chosen well.' Judging by the way he said that I knew he wanted the subject dropped.

'There will be many things coming through to you about the tomb,' said White Arrow, 'but, for now, just write them down and I will bring the facts later. There will be many more meetings than usual, for we have a limited time for our journeys. Do not worry about the people around you – I will take care of them. What you must do is concentrate on the writing. I have much to bring to the world and it is urgent that we waste no time. Time is what is important in saving the Earth. We have a planet and the human race to save – so if it seems I am working you hard, do remember that it is for mankind.'

'I do know that your mission is urgent,' I said.

White Arrow put his hand up and said, 'It is the hand of God we work for. Between us we can do his work.' After a pause he said, 'I want you to see the aliens at four o'clock in the back room.'

At 4pm, Zipper was already waiting. Michael appeared just after I sat down. White Arrow just said, 'Wait and listen.' Alien Girl appeared next to Zipper. She had the same book as before. Zipper took the book. Suddenly, an ambient redness appeared around us – I did not know why. Then it went. Zipper was looking at the book, saying nothing. I could feel Bear and Eagle around. Bear suddenly said that I would have to return to Egypt – there was important work to do there.

'I can't go yet, Bear,' I told him, although I knew he was aware of that. White Arrow knew that I would have to learn everything first. I could hear Bear grunt. Then he laid his hand on me. Eagle just smiled in a greeting fashion. Looking at them all, I felt so lucky: here were the kindest and most loving people in the universe, all here on a special mission – and they had chosen me to do it with them.

Once again, White Arrow said, 'Look and listen.' Zipper opened the book in front of me. As before, I could not see it clearly. Zipper got up and came over to me, pointing his finger at the page (*see* figures 14.3 and 14.4).

'That is good,' said White Arrow as I drew the pictures. I thanked him. 'No, Little One, this is the first step.'

Zipper was trying to get my attention and held the book up again. There seemed to be words on it: CENQTREUSY EIGUPETY EUNA. He put the book under his arm and said, 'I will see you later.' I

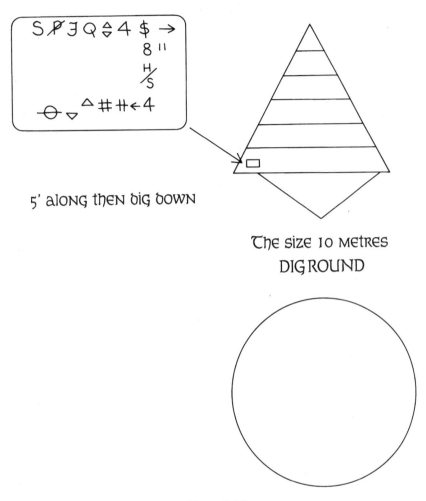

5' alONG theN big bOWN

The size 10 metres
DIG ROUND

Figure 14.3

caught a quick glimpse of the king. I thought perhaps he was going to say something, but he vanished with the rest.

By 13 June I was getting tired again, but I had to carry on. The problem was that other things were cropping up and I wished they would not. Bear had come in yesterday asking me to do some pictures for him, so for the first time I called on the medallion for him – I must have remembered Zipper telling me to. Bear did not arrive, but I was sure he would.

'White Arrow, where am I going to get these people to help me work out the secrets of opening the tomb?' I asked him.

'Have patience, Little One. There are many other words we

SAQQARA the STEP PYRAMID

CENQTREUSY EIGUPETY EUNA
Year of Study – Go on Pilgrimage
(Translated into English)

Figure 14.4

must have before we bring help to you. It is better to have the whole jigsaw than just part of it. So, for now, please write it all down. When we've finished I will bring the help.'

Bear arrived. I asked him, 'Did you hear me call on the medallion, or were you coming anyway?'

'I heard you,' replied Bear.

'So it *did* work?,' I said.

'Yes, Little One, it worked.' Good, I thought.

'This is what I want you to draw,' said Bear. He did the same as Zipper, but instead of pointing a finger, he put his hand on the paper (*see* figure 14.5).

I had found the answer to one of the messages – or part of it, anyway. I was to go to the pyramid at Giza. 'Thank you, Bear. Thank you.' I was beginning to understand.

'We still have much more to do, but this helps you to understand,' he said.

'Come, Little One,' White Arrow suddenly said. 'There are other things we must discuss.'

Bear waved. 'I will see you later,' he called. Then he vanished.

'I want you to ask François to tell you the meaning of the word DEYCOURES,' said White Arrow. Then he asked me to phone Hala – it was urgent. I thought it was to do with the journey, but when I rang her she had a problem. White Arrow knew, and he wanted to help. That was so nice of him.

The following day, we found the meaning of the words CENQTREUSY EIGUPETY EUNA – 'year of study, go on pilgrimage'. Presumably it would take one year before I came to know the full story of where the tomb and hidden secrets were.

On 15 June, I was to make contact through the medallion. I had

It is five words in a PYRAMID, taking the middle
of two other PYRAMIDS and that PYRAMID has
the symbol of the SPHINX, and the centre of the
PYRAMID which is located a square like a diamond
cut surrounded with four words pointing that the
key beneath the statue of the SPHINX, and that is
what WHITE ARROW has mentioned —
WHITE ARROW has found resistance not to
expose the key.

Translated into English by Abdel Hakim Awayan

Figure 14.5 The main pyramid at Giza, as drawn by Bear

not been told to do it this way before. Zipper appeared in front of me. I was suddenly *in* the medallion. I could see sky. I knew it was hot and I felt sand around, like a sandstorm. I was on the path going towards the tomb of Ti.

I thought I was going to the Step Pyramid, but I was not. I could see the steps down to the tomb. I was now in the tomb, where I had taken the pictures. It was as if I were watching myself. I seemed to be looking for something. I looked up towards the light coming from a window above the pictures on the wall and watched to see where it fell. It fell near the pillars. I remembered that I had taken some pictures of the pillars – White Arrow had told me to do so. Someone was coming. I stood in the corner. There were three people, with a guide. Others were outside. I looked around. Had I missed anything?

I did not know why White Arrow had asked me to go back to Saqqara. I had not regarded the pillars as important, and yet they did appear to have some significance. I was suddenly near to where there had once been a statue of Ti. What was I looking for? I felt there was something behind the pillars – perhaps a room. As I stood there I could not see what White Arrow was trying to show me.

I was suddenly outside the tomb. The day was lovely and the sandstorm was gone. I was walking away now. I felt the sand getting into my shoes. I was wondering where I was going, when suddenly I was in the temple leading to the Step Pyramid. Then I was standing right in front of the Step Pyramid. I could see it clearly and felt I should go nearer. I started to walk slowly, not sure what I was supposed to be doing or looking for.

I came back to the room. I was not in Saqqara any more. 'White Arrow, what is this all about?' I asked. I tried to calm down. How could I be in two places at the same time? I put it to the back of my mind – the important thing was what they showed me. I would have to look at every picture I had taken in that tomb.

Zipper had gone. Everything was quiet. I knew there was not any more and that I would not be using the medallion again that day. I asked White Arrow to help me with the word DEYCOURES. We knew it meant 'light' and 'bell'. Light meant vision, and bell meant church. Vision and church. I felt I had only half of the message. 'Did the message mean I would have a vision at the church?'

'Yes,' replied White Arrow.

Then he gave me SAUQQRAE CUEVESA/PLUSUESU. By the next day

I had discovered that it meant 'Saqqara', 'achievement', 'spirit'. The message was therefore roughly 'The Spirit will achieve at Saqqara'. I now knew one of my first journeys was to be to the Step Pyramid and Ti. I thanked White Arrow.

· 15 ·

Meetings Beyond Time

It was 19 June 1993. White Arrow wanted me to go to the ship. When I got there, the room was in darkness. Only the light from the stars outside lit it up. I was becoming increasingly relaxed with each visit I made to the ship. I saw White Arrow by the window and walked towards him. He told me to look out. I saw the Earth and as usual it took my breath away. Suddenly I was outside the window with White Arrow. It was just like floating, but at the same time it was not – it is difficult to express what it feels like doing these things!

I looked around me, a bit afraid. White Arrow just carried on looking, so I followed his gaze. I could see a cluster of stars in the distance – it was beautiful. Yet I felt I was missing something. What was he trying to show me? I had been out here before, but not this long.

Just then, White Arrow held my hand and we walked forward. This was all strange, and I was nervous. 'Where are we going, White Arrow?' He turned to me and smiled, but I felt it was a sad smile. It worried me to see White Arrow like this. I did not know what was going on. Wherever I was going to, I did not get there, for suddenly I found myself in the chair, back in the meeting room.

He was standing at the bottom of the table. The room was lit up now. Suddenly the door opened and they all entered – Eagle, Bear, Michael, Alien Girl, then last of all Zipper. He was carrying something in his hand – again it looked like paperwork. They took their usual chairs. Papers were passed around, but this time not by hand. One minute they were with Zipper, the next they all appeared laid out in front of everybody, including me. Once again, as I looked at the paper it reminded me of an X-ray. I looked to

White Arrow for an explanation but he was talking to the rest of them, so I sat back and waited.

Then White Arrow spoke. 'You will go to Saqqara. There you will find a book and the key to Giza. Here lies Imhotep, for he took our secrets with him to be revealed at this time. I want you to look at the picture in front of you today. You will not understand what it means yet – when the time comes to use this information your mind will already know it, and you will know what to do. Only then will you remember what you have seen today.'

I bent forward and looked, absorbing the words and pictures. I knew it would be locked away in my memory until it was time to use it. Since I usually wrote things down, I could only think that no one else was to know. After a few moments I leaned back and looked at White Arrow. I asked him, 'Why did you seem so sad out there, White Arrow?'

'I am sad for my people,' he replied. I knew he was talking about the Earth. 'What hurts them hurts me, and what hurts Mother Earth hurts me,' he said.

'I know, White Arrow,' I said. There did not seem to be much more for me to say. I looked at the others and said, 'With your help it will be all right.' What else could I say or do? I was just Ann Walker, but my heart went out to White Arrow and the aliens.

White Arrow spoke: 'At Matariyah, you will eat the dirt at the tree and you will bring back with you the seeds of the earth. You will dig near the tree.' I looked at him. Yes, I would do all those things, but I wondered why.

Suddenly, the lights went out, then came back on. I could see aliens behind the wall, but only for a split second. Then the wall was normal again. I looked back at the table. They had all gone, except Zipper, Michael and White Arrow. They had gone when the lights went out – I did not bother asking how. White Arrow and Zipper spoke for a few moments. Michael was just listening to them. Then they both got up and left – this time by the door.

Now there was just White Arrow and me. I felt strange and excited for a moment, without knowing why. 'Come,' said White Arrow, and we left. Instead of returning home we arrived in another part of the spacecraft. There were aliens at computers. White Arrow went to a picture on the far side of the large room. There was a lot of activity going on and the aliens I saw were like those in the medical room, only taller. I followed White Arrow everywhere he went. The floor felt soft, like walking on cushions.

White Arrow was pointing to a very large map. There were lights going on and off. In front of the wall was an alien sitting at another computer, which seemed to control the map on the wall. The room suddenly went dark and everything went quiet. Only the large map was lit up. I knew it was the Earth. One minute it was a detailed close-up, the next minute one could see it as if from orbit. This map could just zoom in to the Earth, showing pictures from every angle as the ship orbited the Earth.

I suddenly spotted a rainforest on the map – I do not know which one. Then it was gone. Another picture, then another appeared on the screen. I turned to White Arrow. He was watching the screen. He looked at me and smiled, that he turned and his hand pushed something on the computer behind him. The alien who was sitting there just looked at the screen as well. Although I was fascinated by it all I wondered what we were doing there. Suddenly, White Arrow said 'Come,' and before I knew it I was home.

'What was the big screen about, White Arrow?' I asked.

'It helps us to know what is wrong with the world and where the main problems are. You saw it can pick up even the inside of the Earth.'

'Can you get close-ups of *anything*, White Arrow?' I asked.

'Yes, even your house, Little One. The main reason is to know where the major problems are, like fault-lines and other things. At a later date I will show you more, but for now it is better to show you things slowly.' That I understood, for that was White Arrow's way.

On 23 June, Bear was with me. He had been around for a couple of days, which was unusual; as a rule, I see the aliens only at certain times. But it was nice to have him around.

'We must get back to Egypt,' White Arrow suddenly said, then Zipper appeared with Alien Girl.

'I want you to write this down,' said Zipper. 'ZEZUENPH TUEBUEL TI EUES VUEA GOEPUTELY ZEGULY TI. SUESUPTLY II.'

Old Arabic	Arabic	English
ZEZUENPH	ZAMZAMA TA	gathering, funeral, cloth – come
TUEBUEL	TUM BAHAL	tomb, barren (empty)
TI		Ti
EUES	AYES	I want
VUEA	HA'A	her

GOEPUTELY	COPTALI	of the Coptic people
ZEGULY	ZAGALI	popular Arabic poem
TI		Ti
SUESUPTLY	SHA SABTALI	King of Saturday
II		two/the second

Then White Arrow spoke. 'Go back to the medallion. Go back to Ti. It is important.' I looked at the medallion. It was green, then black. I had seen it black before but I could not remember if I had seen it green.

Suddenly, I was back in the desert, walking towards Ti. I walked down the steps and bent down to walk through the same small tunnel, then I was back in the room again. Why was Ti so important? Why did they keep bringing me back there? No one was there – no tourists – I was on my own. I went to the wall of the paintings that I had videoed before.

White Arrow appeared next to me. 'Tell me what to look for, White Arrow,' I said to him. I leaned my hand on the wall, as if feeling for something, but what? I then put both hands on the wall and moved them along it. I suddenly felt cold – I did not know why – but I carried on. The sun was coming through the window. 'What am I looking for, White Arrow?' There had to be something there to help White Arrow, but why would he not tell me? Why did I have to find it myself? There was *something* there, I knew that. I followed the wall round, but then I stopped. I came back to the left wall, then changed my mind and followed around, with my hands still on the wall, feeling for something. I was now where a statue stood.

I thought of Ti. I stood on the place where this statue had stood and looked around me. It was not a large room. There was something important about the place where I was standing, I could feel that, but what was it? I would have thought it would be more important to be at the Step Pyramid than here, but there had to be a reason for being just here. I looked at where my feet were, and across to my right. There had been another statue there. I thought it might have been of Ti's wife. I would ask Mrs Prince and Hala when I returned.

I sat down. Why was the place where I was standing important? What did the pictures opposite mean? Did the two connect in some way? There was an answer somewhere, involving the pictures on the wall and the place where I was standing, but even if there was an answer, what had Ti to do with the Step Pyramid and Imhotep?

Everything was quiet. I was feeling the side of the room, but nothing seemed to be important. Suddenly, the king appeared. I was taken aback! He was just standing there; he *looked* like a king, but I was not sure. He was the same one the aliens had brought to me some time before. He had a long hat on. He had a longish nose and looked very regal. I just sat and looked at him, and he at me. I did not know what to do or say – I think I was too startled. But at the same time I was excited. He started to look around the room. I watched his eyes. He suddenly turned to me, catching me looking at him. He smiled and looked back at the wall. Then he was looking through a peephole in the wall at the statue of Ti. Then he turned to me and spoke in a language I did not know. He stopped and spoke in English.

'I'm sorry,' he said. That was nice of him, I thought. Then he said, 'Return tomorrow. I will be here, waiting.' I was back home.

Two days later, the medallion went green and I returned to Ti. The same thing happened. I walked towards Ti and entered the tomb until I reached the room again. It was empty. I was lucky to be on my own to concentrate on what I was there for. I sat where I had been the last time, waiting for the king to arrive. White Arrow suddenly appeared – I always felt safer with him around. He was looking up at the window as if looking for something or someone. He turned and said to me, 'I will return later, Little One,' and vanished. The king then appeared. He stood below the window. I watched again as he looked around the room. Suddenly, he disappeared through the wall leading to where the statue of Ti stands – we humans have to look through the peephole to see it.

Still sitting, I waited for his return. I felt excited, wondering what he was going to do and say. A few minutes later he returned. A chair appeared out of nowhere and he sat on it. The back of the chair was high. He wore what looked like a white skirt coming down to his knees, with gold and silver sandals. His hair was black and gleaming – it was then that I realized he did not have his hat on. He was wearing a white jacket braided in gold and silver, which made the colour of his skin show up. His hair was tied back and very smooth. There was something around his neck, but I could not see clearly what it was. He beckoned me closer; I moved and sat a few feet away from him. I guessed he was in his forties. He smiled as if to say, it's all right.

Suddenly, he said: 'White Arrow has sent me to you to help

show you what you must do and to help you understand. I will
help show you the secrets we left behind us – many secrets people
of your time do not know exist. I can show you the way: the rest
is for you to follow. During your journey to the tomb I will appear
at certain times to show you things that will help in your search.'

'Can I ask you a question? Why is Ti so important?'

'I will show you,' he replied. 'Patience, Little One.' I was taken
aback for a moment, wondering how he knew White Arrow's own
name for me. Then I realized it would be the name White Arrow
would have introduced me by.

He looked around at the walls again, then suddenly he picked
up some paper from the floor, which I had not noticed before.
What he was holding looked like the papyrus I had seen at the
museum. He sat writing on it for a while with something I could
not recognize – it was not a pen. He was drawing as well as writing
and I waited for him to finish. I sat and looked at him. He seemed
friendly, a man of authority but also a man who would listen. I
suddenly felt a bit cold and shivered. He looked up and smiled,
then went back to his paperwork. Somehow I knew I had to return
home and come back the following day. I took one more look at
him and left.

On Saturday, 26 June, I returned to the tomb of Ti. There were
people leaving. I watched them pass me and then I entered. I went
and sat down where the statue had once stood and waited for the
king to return. I wondered if the words I had last received were to
do with today; I would wait and see. Again I felt cold, although I
knew it was hot outside, for the sun was shining through.

Why did I suddenly feel the earth shake? An earthquake came
into my mind, but all went still again. Suddenly he was there; he
just appeared from nowhere. He stood near the wall and said
nothing. Then three people entered; one was the keeper. I sat and
watched the king. I knew that nothing would happen until they
left. It was not long before we were on our own again and the chair
appeared. He walked over and sat down.

'I am Imhotep,' he announced. My stomach churned. I was
talking to one of the most famous people in Egyptian history! He
had built the Step Pyramid and helped the kings of Egypt build
Giza. He looked towards the window, then turned to me. 'We have
much to talk about,' he said. 'I will teach you and show you many
things.'

Suddenly White Arrow was at my side. Imhotep bowed his

head to him. 'Listen to his every word, Little One,' said White Arrow, 'for his words are of wisdom and he is here to help you on your journey. Remember, I am here, even if you do not see me.' I understood. I got up and walked over to Imhotep, then sat on the floor and waited. He picked up the paper he had had the day before and started to write. As he did so he turned and looked at the drawings on the wall, saying nothing.

'There are two things I want you to do today,' he said softly. 'I know that you have no experience of Egyptian ways or of pyramids, so I will show you slowly what to do, for it is important your journey is understood by you. First, you have pictures you took when you first came to Ti. I would like you to look at them. It is better I show you on your pictures rather than here because it will save you time.' I would study them later.

'Each picture tells a story,' he said, pointing at the drawings on the wall. 'Some mankind knows of, but there are also many secrets painted there that man does not understand. These were done on purpose so they could not find our secrets. This tomb is special to me.'

'Why?' I asked. I had thought it was Ti's tomb.

'You will know in time. The second thing I wish to show you is this . . .' and he held up the paper he had. I suddenly felt White Arrow's presence and turned round. He was sitting behind me.

'Write what you see, Little One,' said White Arrow.

I turned round. Imhotep was placing the paper on the floor in front of me. He knelt down, holding it at each end to stop it rolling up. I looked at it, trying to understand it. It was not in my language. I stared at it and wrote it down (*see* figures 15.1 and 15.2).

'You will be taken to someone who will be able to decipher it for you. It will give the world proof that you are indeed in contact with me. There are more words, and when we have found the right person I will give you the rest.'

We stopped. He looked towards the entrance and I heard people coming. He put up his hand and said, 'Stay.'

I looked for White Arrow and he was standing there. 'Come, Little One,' he said, and he beckoned me to stand at his side. We waited for the people to go. I could see Imhotep just standing waiting. Soon the people left and we all sat as before. I wondered why they did not do all of this when no one was about, but White Arrow and Imhotep must know, so I did not question it.

I looked at the paper once again, but this time it was a different

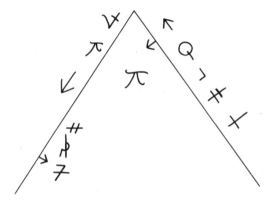

This is a local cluster configuration = The Key to the Energy configuration of both the present existing and future potential Sacred Sites at Giza, Saqqara, is found in SESHETA – a Goddess.

Translated into English, February 1996, by Abdel Hakim Awayan

Figure 15.1 A local cluster configuration

sheet. I must have come to the end of the first sheet. Suddenly a young Egyptian girl came in carrying a drink, and gave it to Imhotep. I watched him drink it and hand it back to her. Where's mine? I thought in jest. That was probably my apprehension disguising itself behind humour. No one laughed. I looked back at the picture. Imhotep's feet caught my eye – I liked his sandals and thought, wouldn't it be nice if I could get a pair like that

Secret IMHOTEP

This is an EARTH CRYSTAL GRID LOCATION

Translated into English by Abdel Hakim Awayan

Figure 15.2 Imhotep's secret

myself? But I did not look long. I knew how precious time was to them.

I was getting a headache and rubbed my eyes. It was hard to understand all this, and I knew I could not. Again, I wrote what I saw, and I was asked not to reveal it. The words were to stay secret for now.

I heard White Arrow say to Imhotep, 'You have done well.' 'Tomorrow I will return with Little One.'

'Thank you,' said Imhotep and he bowed his head. He looked at me and said, 'You have much faith. It is good they have chosen you. Thank you.' And he went.

'Come, Little One, we must return,' said White Arrow. I came back. I did not realize I had been writing for one and a quarter hours – time went quickly when I was working for White Arrow! 'I want to speak to you later,' said White Arrow. 'Rest for now.'

Later, when White Arrow returned, I said to him, 'White Arrow, how am I going to get help in all of this?' I was referring to the Coptic Latin, although I was really asking whom I could trust.

'Leave it to me, Little One. I will take you to the right people,' he replied.

'You know, White Arrow, soon people are going to know about you, and I'm glad but also scared about how they're going to take it all and whether they'll believe me. After all, I'm only Ann Walker!'

'They'll all believe, Little One, trust me,' said White Arrow.

'I do trust you, White Arrow, but it's *people*. I only hope they forget *me* and remember the reason why you've come – to save the world.'

'I am the Son of God and mankind will believe that, Little One, for I will show them the miracles they seek.'

'I'm sure you will, White Arrow, but I hope they don't argue like they did when you originally came as Jesus Christ. Why do people not accept God's help when it's so freely given? Why do they argue? I will be judged when this story is told and I'm not scared of telling it, White Arrow, but they will judge me and tell me it is impossible. Why can they not look further than me and see that something else is there?'

'Little One, I have taught you never to judge mankind!' said White Arrow.

'I know, White Arrow, but I worry so much that they will delay in saving the world,' I said.

'Have more faith in my children, Little One. As they read the words you have written they will see much more than you think.'

'I hope so, White Arrow,' I said.

Tony and I had taken our family to the coast that day, and I had been sitting on the beach watching a ship laying pipes for sewage. My thoughts had been on the pollution out at sea. What could Ann Walker do on her own? I turned to White Arrow and said, 'We must have help from the living.'

White Arrow smiled and said, 'I have seen into the future, and many will listen and help. You are not on your own, Little One, for soon I will bring many.'

'I thank your father for bringing you, White Arrow,' I said. He said nothing. White Arrow had once given me my life back, and a chance to be happy with my family after a long time of despondency – for this I will give my life for him, and whatever is to be done will be done.

Later that same day (26 June), the medallion went green, then red. I knew Zipper was around, with Bear, Eagle, Michael and Alien Girl, but I had to return to Ti for Imhotep. He was waiting – the medallion was telling me that. Before I knew it I was back in the tomb. It was light but I knew that no one would come – why, I am not sure. I simply felt it was shut.

I had learned that day that I would have to return to the Virgin Tree on my next visit to Egypt. The message 'vision' and 'church' came back into my mind. Was I to see the Virgin Mary again? No, I thought. I had already had her message for the world. I looked at White Arrow, but he said nothing. Then my thoughts went back to the tomb where Imhotep was waiting.

White Arrow stood behind me, with all the aliens – I did not know why they had come today. Imhotep was sitting in his chair. I sat in front of him and waited. He smiled. 'Welcome,' he said. Then he looked at White Arrow. Words were said but I could not understand them, for they were in his language – and White Arrow was clearly a linguistic expert. I heard Bear growl and Zipper put his hand on my head, then they all left. Just Imhotep and I were left in the room, with White Arrow.

'You will listen carefully,' said Imhotep.

'Yes,' I replied.

He produced more paper. 'You will get a detailed map of Saqqara and bring it to me.' I promised I would do that. He walked over to the wall where the statues had once stood and pointed behind. 'Here is a tunnel which will lead to where I was buried. Here is where there are secrets to Giza and many other secrets. Here will lead you to the Step Pyramid.' Then he said a strange thing: 'Mother Earth will help.' I did not understand, but I was sure that in time I would.

Imhotep carried on talking. 'After my time there was a book written and hidden amongst the treasures. It is a most sacred book. It will help you with your journey. I will show you where it is, but first I must show you the way to it. It will be difficult, but this was meant to be, for we had to wait for you. The book had to be kept in a safe place from humans.' I looked at him. How was I supposed to do all of this? The Egyptian government would not allow me just to come and do what I liked. I turned to White Arrow, but then I thought, what is the purpose of asking? White Arrow would know how and whom to bring.

I turned to Imhotep again. He said, 'For today, that is all.' I got up and bowed my head to him out of respect.

'Come, Little One,' said White Arrow. It was time to leave Ti.

I had learned that day that I would have to go into the desert on my next visit, very early in the morning. I would arrange it. In addition to this, something had struck me: when Zipper and the rest had come to Ti, Imhotep had not looked at all surprised. It was clear that the ancient Egyptians knew about aliens – Imhotep had always been completely matter-of-fact at their presence.

· 16 ·

Unas

It was 27 June 1993. I would now have to go back to the aliens, for there was so much to do, and to learn about opening the tomb. 'Do I return to Ti, White Arrow?' I asked.

'Yes, Little One. It is important that you follow Imhotep.'

The medallion was going green and blue and I knew it was time. As I returned to Ti, I was surprised to see Imhotep standing outside. He beckoned me to follow. I could feel the heat. Four camels and about half a dozen people were standing at the entrance. We were walking around Ti when Bear appeared at my side. I suddenly wondered whether I should count my footsteps and then thought, no. After all, I did not know how far we were going.

Imhotep was tall and slim, and took large strides, so it was difficult keeping up with him. We passed Ti and moved some distance away, but we could still see it. Imhotep suddenly stopped and pointed downwards. There was nothing but sand all around me. I stood at his side and looked back at Ti. How far were we from it? That was important, for I knew something was buried where we were standing – what, I did not know – and I had to know exactly.

'Bear,' I asked, 'can you ask him to give the exact measurements in English rather than in his language?' Bear spoke to him for a moment, then White Arrow appeared and joined in their conversation. I could see them clearly, Bear towering above them. He looked larger today. I sat on the sand and waited. White Arrow sat beside me, then Imhotep, then Bear. We sat in a circle and Imhotep drew in the sand (*see* figure 16.1).

Suddenly, Imhotep said, 'Take the same distance as you took to

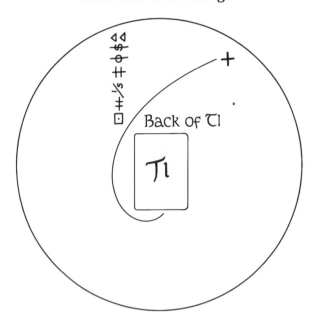

This is a Major Hall of Records Site, Primary
Time Capsule for the Present Soul Influx's
History And Initiations, Keeper of the Beacon has
the Emerald Jade Gemstone Temple
Translated into English, February 1996, by Abdel Hakim Awayan

Figure 16.1 Imhotep's drawing

get to Ti.' He meant the camel ride I had taken to the tomb. He
brushed the sand over, taking all the writing away, and stood up.
He pointed towards the Step Pyramid and said, 'This will lead you
there.'

'Is there a tomb here?' I asked.

'Yes,' he replied. We all headed back to Ti. My legs felt as if they
were aching, but I thought, that's daft, it's only my spirit here! We
arrived back outside Ti. Imhotep walked into the tomb.

'Come, Little One, we will return,' said White Arrow. I was back
home again.

So much was happening. I was going to need a lot of help in
opening the tombs, but who would I get to help me? I was just
going to have to put my trust in White Arrow.

On 1 July, I was back at the ship. There was no one there but
White Arrow. I saw him by the window and walked towards him.
I stood by him watching him look out towards the stars. He turned

and smiled at me, then put his arm around me and pointed out to the sky. I watched a falling star go by. The sight of all this was breathtaking and I watched for a while. There was some mist around the Earth.

Just then, the lights came on and I walked towards my chair. White Arrow sat in his father's chair. I waited for the aliens to come. 'Not today, Little One,' said White Arrow. 'I need to talk to you about your journey.' Why on the ship? I thought. Who knows how White Arrow thinks!

'This journey is hard and dangerous. What I have already expected of you has not been easy, but what is to come will be harder. I want you to know that, whatever lies ahead, I will be at your side. No human has ever been asked to do as much as you are doing. I need to show my people miracles so they may come to believe that the Earth and her people are in trouble – and I need you to help me. You have done more than well – but it is the future which matters. Will you trust me enough to take care of you? I have to tell you that the journey into the future will be difficult.'

'Are you trying to tell me that I now have a choice of coming off the road or of carrying on with it, White Arrow?' I asked. He just looked at me. I knew the answer to my question, for it is in his nature to care and to warn me of problems to come. I already knew in my heart that the road was going to be hard and dangerous, but had he not given me 14 years with my family? 'No, White Arrow, I will follow you. I will not turn away, for I trust you and love you.' He smiled.

I knew he feared for my safety with regard to other people, but I was willing to take my chance, to deliver the messages that White Arrow and his father chose to give me. White Arrow was not telling me I had a choice, for he knew my decision – but he did need to warn me. He just looked at me, then beckoned me to join him at the window. His eyes on the Earth, he said, 'My people have called. I must answer, but this time through you, for it will take too much time to do otherwise.'

I never questioned White Arrow. He knew what he had to do and I would do whatever he asked me, despite my periodic worrying and self-doubt. I looked at the Earth, thinking how lucky people were to have White Arrow watching over them. He put his hand on my arm and said, 'We will return, Little One.' He had asked his question of me and had got his answer. Now it was back to work.

A few days later, on Sunday, 4 July, Tony and I were out in the garden. Earlier, White Arrow had told me of my next test, in January 1994. I was to go out to the Great Pyramid in the early hours. While out there something would be shown to me. I presumed this would constitute the next instructions for my journey. I was wary about what might happen out there. Nothing would surprise me, but this time there would be only the guide and Val with me.

I had a lot to do before January. I could see there was going to be much going on in 1994, but I would have to wait and see. Suddenly the medallion was going yellow. I did not know what yellow meant or whether I had seen it before. I turned to White Arrow, who said to me, 'Wait. It will be explained.' So I left it.

'Are *you* all right, White Arrow?' I asked.

'Yes, Little One. There is so much to do.' He seemed concerned. Then he added, 'No, I'm all right, Little One. Sometimes I look at your path and see the responsibilities you have, so it is natural that I worry over you. Your heart is big and words hurt you – that is what I am concerned about. Humans sometimes cannot handle change, and they could fight you about it. They might even damn you for it. There will be times when you will wonder whether it is all worth it – words can bring much pain. I know you will not turn away from your path, but it will hurt, and what hurts you hurts us. We can protect you in many ways, but not from people's words.'

'White Arrow, I will remember what you have said today, and I promise I will judge no one, for it is only fear that makes people say damaging things – and if they do hurt me then I will turn to you for guidance rather than to my tears. If I cry I will still carry on, because of what is at stake. As long as I know you're at my side, does it really matter what is ahead? The only thing I ask of you is that my family be safe.'

'This I can promise, Little One. That has already been taken care of.'

'Then I want nothing for myself but to help you, White Arrow,' I said. He put his hand on mine, then he showed me himself on the cross, in his former life on Earth. I knew what he was trying to say.

'It's different this time, White Arrow. You are coming back in a different way and they will know it is you. If they treat me the way they did in the old days then we will be too late to save the world

– and I don't believe that, otherwise you wouldn't be doing what you are doing, White Arrow.'

'Little One, you have much faith in mankind. That is good.'

'Only because I can see mankind needs you. All men and women inherently believe in your father and need him. I have to learn to trust humans, White Arrow. I *have* to. If I don't, then I have failed you and them.'

'That you will never do, Little One,' said White Arrow. He smiled and said, 'Now we have much work to do, and the journey must be done quickly if we are to succeed.'

Zipper suddenly appeared and the medallion went yellow. 'Why is it yellow, Zipper?' I asked.

'I will explain. The yellow is for you. The medallion can heal as well.' There was a pause. 'You must take a journey.'

'Where to, Zipper?'

'I want you to find a book. It is called *The Face Behind The Mask*.'

'I will try to find it, Zipper,' I said.

'Is it an Egyptian book?'

'Yes. When you have got it, come to me and I will tell you what to read.'

'Okay, Zipper.'

'I want to speak again tomorrow,' Zipper said.

Then Bear spoke: 'We have to finish the last drawings – and I have new ones for you.' I had promised Bear I would do them this week. Also, I was to get maps of Egypt, detailed plans of Saqqara and Giza. In the coming months I would have to study and learn about everything I was to do. I also had to bring in experts – I had to trust White Arrow to help me with that.

Suddenly, I was back at Ti. The medallion had turned blue. I entered the tomb, found my way to the room and sat down where I usually sat. White Arrow was with me. I watched him looking at the drawings on the walls while we waited – presumably for Imhotep. It did not feel warm and it was not sunny outside. I could see there was a sandstorm, so no tourists would be here today. White Arrow went and stood by one of the pillars. I suddenly smelt a sort of perfume, but then realized it was incense. Where it came from I did not know.

Just then, Eagle was there. She was just sitting, her long dress covering her body, her long golden hair hanging down, her eyes wide open. I never liked looking straight into her eyes – I did not know why, for I knew she meant no harm to me. Then Imhotep appeared next to

WHITE ARROW was careful of MANKIND'S safety from destroying expected from other Stars and he sees to resist that disaster is to create living creatures in certain spot on our Planet – to ease the Destruction by growing trees and by clearing dams and STOP fear – with no threat among the people.

Translated into English, 25 July 1994, by Abdel Hakim Awayan

Figure 16.2

her, sitting on his chair. They spoke for a few moments, then she suddenly left. I wondered why she had come today.

White Arrow touched my shoulder and said, 'Follow me.' We walked past Imhotep to the small corridor that led into the chamber. What was he doing? He stood and pointed to a wall on the side of the wall I had videoed. I could not see clearly so I decided to draw a picture of where we were. I wondered if the chamber was hidden from humans. I drew the picture, but it was hard to understand what White Arrow was showing me. With this particular drawing I had a feeling that this was not to be shown to the public until the time was right for the tomb to be opened.

Imhotep joined us. I left the drawing, then went back to it. White Arrow returned and stood at the pillar. Imhotep sat in the chair and beckoned me to sit in front of him. He looked at me for a moment, then picked up the paper. It was rolled up and he laid it out in front of me. I drew what I saw (*see* figure 16.2), but I was sure there was more to it. Why was I feeling there was a complex or village hidden there? I had to go now – there were things I had to attend to. White Arrow understood, and I promised I would return.

Moses had been on my mind. I had been wondering about him and what his connection was with this journey. I knew that there was definitely a connection between White Arrow and Moses. Did Jesus stay in Egypt when he was older? Did he go where Moses had been? I would have to wait until White Arrow told me more, but I did remember that Moses had worked on the pyramids. The whole thing puzzled me at times – but as White Arrow told me, I needed patience! I knew I also had to find the Temple of Isis at Saqqara. I would have to go there when I returned to Egypt.

I was soon returning to Ti – or so I thought. I looked at the medallion, waiting for it to take me there, but I turned up somewhere else! It was under the ground. There was a dark hallway and an archway above me. I saw sand falling down, a trickle of it, and it was cold. It seemed no one had been here for years. The stone wall looked very dark. I was walking down the hall. White Arrow was with me, and I turned to look at him.

As he stood by the wall he suddenly changed into Jesus, then back to White Arrow. 'Don't do that, White Arrow, please!' I said. It was bad enough being here, somewhere strange, let alone seeing White Arrow transformed. I knew he had once been Jesus, but over the years I had become used to him being just White Arrow. He returned to being White Arrow, and my attention turned back to the tunnel. It reminded me of the Tomb of the Sacred Bull, but I knew we were not in that tomb. 'Where am I, White Arrow?'

As I spoke I saw a woman down at the far end beckoning me to come forward. So I walked towards her. It felt strange, and I wondered why I was here and not at Ti. I did not want to be here. I was scared. It seemed a long corridor, but I saw light at the end of it. Thank goodness, I thought. What was strange was that I felt I was somewhere holy – as if it were some sort of church. As I got to the end I turned and there was a small hole leading out into the open, through which I had to crawl. As I came out, there was something in front of me – a hill or maybe a pyramid – but I had to squeeze past. I could feel the heat.

I crawled back inside. I felt I had to see where I had been. The walls looked as if they were made of marble. As I looked closer there were markings of some sort, but I could not see them clearly. I had a feeling someone had once hidden here – why I felt that I did not know, yet somehow I knew I was right.

'White Arrow, why have you shown me this place?' I asked.

'Follow me,' he said. We went back to where I had arrived and he carried on walking. Suddenly I saw Moses. I was so confused by it all! White Arrow and Moses met and spoke for a few moments. Moses had the staff with him. He was just the same as when I had seen him on the steps of the Hanging Church in Cairo.

All of a sudden, Moses bent down and went into something. I was a few feet away, so I could not see clearly. White Arrow beckoned to me, and as I got nearer I could see a small tunnel leading somewhere. I bent down and went through into a small room. It was arched at the top, and the walls were marble-like. It was dark. There on the floor in the corner was what looked like a small box seat. There was paper like that used earlier by Imhotep, with words and drawings.

Moses bent, picked one up and rolled it up. Then he pulled something out of the wall. He put the paper behind it and put back whatever he had taken out. White Arrow did the same thing. A few days before, White Arrow had told me that he had left some writings behind in his own handwriting. Now he was showing me where. But what was the connection between Moses and White Arrow? Did White Arrow know of Moses' hiding place?

We left the room and Moses stayed behind, watching us as we

headed for the exit. I crawled out of the hole and felt the sun. White Arrow pointed to the hole from where I had emerged. He leaned forward and put his hand in the small tunnel, pulling at something – then I saw the tunnel sealed up. I looked around me; if I was to return and find this place I would have to remember everything I had seen. I decided to feel my way to the edge of the pyramid. This was difficult, for there was another structure close by. A thought crossed my mind: surely, there can't be too many places like this in Egypt?

As I got to the end there was a vastness of desert – not a building in sight. I looked across the desert – the glare of the sun made it look hazy. I wanted to see if I could see anything that would help me orientate myself on my return. I turned to White Arrow to help me and then looked back at the desert. As I did so, something red caught my eye. Red clay, red sand . . . what could be red? There is a Red Pyramid at another part of Saqqara, but was that it? I needed to research it later. It was hazy across the desert and I could not see clearly. It was as if I were stuck to the ground, as if I were to wait – for what I did not know.

As I stood there my mind went back to the tunnel and the woman I could not see clearly. Was it the Virgin Mary? Did Jesus and Mary hide here at one time and, if so, how did they know of Moses' hiding place? It was one big puzzle to me, but I did not have the time to ponder on it, for suddenly a man on a camel appeared. He looked in my direction, though I knew he could not see me. 'Watch,' said White Arrow.

The man stopped and got off his camel, then he carried on walking by. I watched until I could see him no more. I decided to sit down on the ground, but White Arrow said, 'Come.' I followed him around the bend of the pyramid – more sand. However I could now see that it was indeed a pyramid. I stood back and took in the sight. It did not look as smooth as those at Giza – it seemed much more worse for wear. I knew archaeologists had worked on it and it did not look as straight as the Giza pyramids. In fact, there was what looked like a curve to it.

Again, I got the colour red. It puzzled me. White Arrow then pointed out to the desert. There seemed to be a hill or a pyramid to my right, in the distance. I looked towards my left and saw three more hills or pyramids. There could have been more – the haze made it difficult to see.

White Arrow led me back to where the entrance of the tunnel

was. I decided to count my footsteps. It was such a small path that it was difficult to walk without holding on to the side of the pyramid. I decided then that I would use my arms as a measurement. I stretched out my arms with my hands on the wall to measure the distance. White Arrow just watched.

He bent down and put the palm of his hand on the entrance. He laid the other hand on the other side of the stone which covered the entrance, pushed, and it opened. Then he put his hand in and shut it again. 'No one but you may know of this until you have found it. I will show you in the coming weeks where this place is. You have to seek help, but I do not want you to tell them what you seek here, for they will try to get here first. Trust no one, for these writings are for the world – you will give them to the world. Some writings maybe not. Some people will not recognize them straight away unless you tell them what they are – which you will do at the time.' I understood. 'We go now. I will bring you back at a later stage.'

I returned home. When I phoned Mrs Prince – I did not tell her about Moses and the paperwork – she told me that the only pyramid where I might see one hill or pyramid to my right and three, Giza, to my left, would be the pyramid Unas. In addition she described a hole which was blocked up – one still has to crawl through the hall to get to the long passage, and at the end of the passage is a room with pictures or hieroglyphics, in which nothing has been found.

There is also red granite rock around there. As one comes out of the hole there is a wall or hill opposite, a couple of feet away. I had presumed it was a hill of some sort, and I needed to check on that. If the pyramid to my right was the Step Pyramid and the three to my left were Giza, all the facts seemed to point to Unas Pyramid. Deep down I knew it was Unas.

· 17 ·

Global Travel for Free

On 8 July 1993, the medallion went green. Zipper wanted to see me. I had not had a meeting with him for a week, so it was good to see him. 'Hi, Zipper,' I said as I watched him sit down opposite me on the chair. Alien Girl was with him, and she was carrying a book.

'Little One,' said Zipper, 'I want you to concentrate on what I'm about to show you.'

He got up from the chair, walked over and put his finger on the paper. He was there longer than usual, as if concentrating on what he was writing. I hoped it was not too detailed! Just then the place I had last been to came into my mind. Zipper suddenly turned and went to sit down. I somehow knew that what he had written would take me some time to do. 'What are the drawings to do with, Zipper? You know, I'm going to have to get help to find out what they all mean.'

He looked up into the sky. 'Do not worry, Little One, everything is taken care of.'

I should have known that. Alien Girl waved her hand at me. That was rare for her – as a rule she just stood there and listened to Zipper. Bear came, then Michael and Eagle. Michael smiled. 'How are you?' I asked. 'Fine,' he replied.

Then Zipper took the book from Alien Girl and opened it. 'We have much work today,' he said, as if to say, 'Concentrate on me.' He suddenly got up. 'I will leave now and see you tomorrow,' he said. Then they all waved and went.

I spoke to François, who said Unas had a pattern of stars inside it on the ceiling. Were these connected with stars I had drawn earlier? I would definitely have to go there in January.

Later, I was upstairs when White Arrow said I had to return, so I went back to the medallion. I wondered where White Arrow was taking me now. This time I was in the desert and it was night. I did not know why I was standing there, but I could see the stars and it looked so beautiful and peaceful that it did not matter. Suddenly it was daytime and I was at the entrance to Ti. I went down into the tomb and sat where I usually sat. White Arrow was at my side. 'I really don't know what you're doing, White Arrow,' I said.

'It is all coming together,' said White Arrow. 'Soon we will finish with Egypt and go on to the next journey.'

I knew that would be at least a year away, for I had to return to Egypt at least twice more. Did White Arrow mean that I would soon know all the places I had to go to, that it would not be a jigsaw any more? I could see it was possibly coming into place, but I still had a lot more to do. 'Why don't you tell me where I am to go, White Arrow?' I asked him.

'You must learn of the places I take you and of the people. It is *their* land. Also, you would not have realized the importance of your journey had I not taken you the way I did.' Yes, I had to agree. I would certainly have missed the Virgin Mary at the tree. 'And isn't the journey for the people?' Yes, I had to agree that White Arrow's way was appropriate. I had learned so much on the journey.

'Sorry I asked, White Arrow,' I said. He put his hand to his lips as if to say 'Silent!' I turned round and there was Imhotep. This time he was sitting on the floor, not on the chair. I wondered what the connection was between Ti and Unas. White Arrow had shown me where to look for the papers, so why Ti? I looked at Imhotep, hoping he could answer me.

'Many things have happened over the centuries since the pyramids were built and they have been used for many things, but the pyramids were built with God in mind. On your journey to the pyramids you will learn many things that you can tell the world about – secrets kept for many years. Now is the time to show these things to the world. There are many hiding places for these secrets, for if humans had found them all together in one place years ago it would have been of no benefit to the world. So we separated them into different places, knowing one day the right person would come and we could show them and help them find the hidden secrets. Trust White Arrow.'

'But Imhotep, what is the connection between Ti, the Step Pyramid and Unas?'

'In time, Little One, in time.'

By 10 July we had found out that everything I had seen at Unas was right. We also found out that there are indeed stars on a ceiling in the pyramid. I still wondered whether there was a connection with the stars Bear had asked me to draw at the beginning of the year (*see* figure 2.3, page 13), but after talking to Mrs Prince I did not think so. I would go and see on my return to Cairo.

The medallion had been blue for about an hour. White Arrow came. It was night when I arrived, but I was not at Ti. I was standing by a campfire. There were camels tied up and about a dozen men around the fire. I looked for White Arrow. I saw him in the shadow, away from the campfire; he put his finger to his mouth, indicating that I should watch. I also felt another presence near me, but could not make out who it was, until I recognized Bear. White Arrow told me to sit behind one of the men near the fire, so I did, wondering what he was up to now. I felt cold, but the fire made it bearable. I heard one of the camels make a noise. The men were talking amongst themselves. I could not understand them, but watched.

White Arrow touched my shoulder and beckoned me to follow him. He walked a few feet, then stopped and stayed at my side. Three of the men stood up. They walked to their camels and led them off into the desert. White Arrow and Bear followed, with me in tow. I could feel the sand on my feet. It was dark, but the moon was out, so there was some light. I was looking around when suddenly, out of the night, appeared a pyramid. It was big. Where was I? At Unas? I just did not know.

Then two of the men vanished, leaving one with the camels. He seemed nervous as he stood there. I wondered if we were going in, but White Arrow and Bear just stood watching. I sat on the sand and waited for White Arrow's next move. It seemed ages before the men came out. Nothing was said – they just returned to the camp, tied up the camels and joined the others. I did not understand any of this, and it did not seem as if the men were telling the others where they had been. I was puzzled. So far, White Arrow had only taken me to Ti's tomb and Unas Pyramid, but this was different.

Then I felt Moses' presence. White Arrow beckoned me to follow them all. We left the camp and went where the men had been. Bear, White Arrow and Moses talked amongst themselves as if there was something important to talk about. The pyramid appeared, towering above us, and they all sat down. White Arrow beckoned me to join them. No one spoke.

I felt uncomfortable, mainly because of Moses, this great man. I know White Arrow is the Son of God and Bear was once Horus, but now here was Moses, one of the greatest religious figures ever known – and here I was in his presence! I had met him before, but those occasions had been brief. Now I was sitting in front of him.

He leaned on his staff and stood up. He looked around as if waiting for something or someone. White Arrow smiled but said nothing. I believed I was at Giza – what made me think that, I do not know, but it would be the last link. I knew where the other links were, and only Giza was missing. But I had to be sure, so I waited for White Arrow to show me. Everything stayed silent for a while. Then I could see that it was getting lighter – dawn was breaking. We still sat and waited. The shadow of the pyramid was over me as the sun came up. I knew I had to draw the shadow but I did not know why. Figure 17.1 is what I drew.

As the light grew I got up and walked to the edge of the pyramid. I *was* at Giza. Behind, to the right of me, was another pyramid, and to the left, further forward, was one more. I felt there was a connection with the pyramid, something to do with the light. I would have to check on that. I knew one thing, however: this had to do with the drawing of the stars that Bear had given me (figure 2.3, page 13).

We were still waiting, but the shadow had gone. White Arrow got up. 'Come, we will return,' he said to me.

'Before we go,' I said, 'are we at Giza?'

'Yes, Little One. The figures in Coptic go with this,' he said.

We returned. If the people of that time built the pyramids by the stars then it is possible that light from the stars in the drawings played an important part. Did the people of that time plan to represent the secrets of the world by the light? This would mean that no one would ever have found the secrets unless they had inspired help. If this were the case, it was a very clever plan, but I did not really know and so I would have to wait for White Arrow to show me.

The next day, Sunday, 11 July, I asked White Arrow if I could return to the pyramid of Giza. The medallion turned blue. I arrived as I had left it yesterday. It was daylight now, and I was with White Arrow and Bear at the back of the pyramid. The Sphinx was somewhere in front. I sat for a moment, wondering what I should

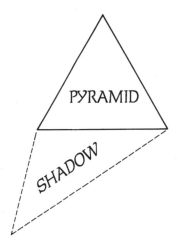

I am at the back of the Pyramid. Between five and seven. You must see where shadow falls. The measurements of the shadow are important.

Figure 17.1 The pyramid and its shadow

look for to help me know for sure. I started to walk towards the left, facing the pyramid. I could see another pyramid on the far side, quite near. I turned and went to the right. Again the pyramid on my right lay a bit behind me. I would have to check all this with Mrs Prince.

I went on round the pyramid and recognized the place where Val and I had once been. When next in Cairo I would go where I had been the previous night – I hoped it would be possible, for Giza is guarded. I had written to Mohammed, and if he was in a position to help me I would ask him to do so. I returned to White Arrow and Bear and we walked a distance from the pyramid. Something kept coming up in my mind. Was it the shadow from the major pyramid I would be seeking? If I could visit Giza for one night I knew I would know the answer.

Suddenly, without warning, I found myself back at Unas, in the passageway. I stood for a moment, wondering why I was there. White Arrow stood at my side. Bear was there too. Towards the end of the passage, near the opening to the room, was Moses. He was beckoning us to go forward. I looked back to the other end to see if the woman was there again, but I could see no one, so I followed White Arrow and Bear.

Bear had shrunk to White Arrow's size. I stopped when White

Arrow came face to face with Moses. Bear and I stood a few feet away. I wondered why we had all returned. I could see the outlines of drawings on the walls, but I could not make out what they were, for it was fairly dark. We stood there for a few minutes and White Arrow beckoned me to follow. We went through a hole into the room.

The small box seat had gone. The room was now empty. I watched as Moses and White Arrow went over to the corner. They just stood there. Bear was still at my side. Why had they brought me back? I stayed silent, knowing White Arrow had brought me here for a good reason. I seemed to be standing there waiting for ages.

Nothing was said to me and nothing was happening. It was as if they were waiting for someone or something. However, a ruler kept coming into my mind, measuring something – but what? I looked at the wall in front of me, but that was not it. Something had struck me when I had first come into the room; there had been something in the room, a box or a sort of chair, and now it was not there.

I had learned from Mrs Prince that there was another room. It should be off to my right. I looked at White Arrow for directions but he said nothing. Maybe I was wrong, but Mrs Prince had said there was a coffin in the other room. Would that be what I had seen when I first came in? If that was the case, then I was in the wrong room.

'White Arrow, help me to understand. What am I doing here?'

'Patience, Little One, all will be revealed soon.' He came over. 'Come, Little One, we go now.' So I followed him through the hole. As we walked up the passage I saw the woman at the end showing us the way out. I did not know who she was.

'Can I go back to the room, White Arrow?' I asked. He turned and went back. I had realized that they had wanted me to measure something – hence the waiting and the image of the ruler – but I had not taken any notice. That was why I needed to go back. Moses was still there. I watched him.

'Sorry, White Arrow and Moses,' I said. Moses bent his head forward as if in acknowledgement. He left first and we followed after I had done the right thing by taking measurements. Then Moses turned and sealed the entrance to the room. I was puzzled, but I was sure there was a hidden room, for the hole at Unas is not sealed. The woman had now gone. I came out to bright sunshine, then returned home.

When White Arrow had drawn the two pyramids in the demotic drawings (*see* figure 3.5 on page 31), was he talking of the shadow of the pyramid? Is that what he meant? I spoke to Mrs Prince. She verified that the pyramid to the right would be behind me and the one to the left would be in front. Also, the dawn comes between five and seven, and I knew I had to go and be there at that time, for then I would get to know whether the drawing was to do with the shadow or with something else.

On 13 July I found the book Zipper had asked for. I was to collect it the following day. White Arrow's father had also asked me to return to the ship. I waited for White Arrow to take me, and before I knew it I was there. The room was in darkness, except for the light outside the window. White Arrow was standing and I joined him.

'I hope everything is going as planned, White Arrow.'

'Yes, Little One, thanks to faith.' I watched his gaze, but instead of following his eyes I looked at him, this Son of God. His blue eyes, his browny-red skin, his fine features . . . I stood in awe of him. I turned and looked around me. No one was here yet, so I looked back to where White Arrow was standing and I followed his gaze. I could not see the Earth properly – just the edge of it to my left. The ship was not in the same position as before.

White Arrow put his arm around me and pointed to a shooting star. I had seen one before with him. Suddenly, I saw a star explode in front of me. It was some distance away, but was it an explosion? I carried on looking and all of a sudden I saw something shooting away from it. I could not understand what I was seeing. Had it exploded, or was there an explosion on the star without breaking it up? It was too far away for me to be sure. I turned to White Arrow and said, 'Did the star break up?'

'No, Little One, on that star it explodes on the surface, but the star stays intact.'

I soon forgot it, since I did not understand. My thoughts went to why we were standing here for so long – usually by now we would be sitting down. Then I heard the door open. The lights went on and in came the aliens. They took their places. I walked to my chair and sat down, and we greeted each other.

The table started to move and the globe of the Earth appeared in the centre. It had been a long time since I had last seen it. The aliens were all talking amongst themselves and I sat and looked at the globe. I wondered why it was here today.

I looked up at White Arrow. He was standing by his father's chair. Our eyes met and he sensed that I wanted to ask him a question. He came up to me. 'White Arrow, why the globe?' I asked.

'You will understand later, Little One,' said White Arrow. Suddenly, everything went quiet. White Arrow stayed at my side and the chair at the end of the table lit up. White Arrow's father arrived. I watched the chair swivel round and saw the cloak and crown.

'Ann Walker, I want you to do something for me.'

'Anything,' I replied.

'I want you to send your work to every leader in the world. You will tell them that I have sent you. They must know of the problems that face the world and they must know of my son. This you will do for me.' I always felt nervous in his presence, but since he had asked me, I would do it.

'I will have to wait until January before I can do that,' I said quietly.

'We will help.' Yes, I knew they would help. I watched the chair turn round and he went. I knew why the globe was there: that was what the first book, Little One, was about – the world in trouble.

On 14 July I needed to ask White Arrow some questions. I just wanted to know a few things. I had worked solidly for two years non-stop. Most times I had been exhausted and tired, but I did not mind, for I knew how important it was to him. But there were so many questions in my head, where was I to start?

'White Arrow, when are the aliens coming?' That was one thing I needed to know. 'Will they be bringing you?'

'Yes,' he replied. 'Not to stay, but to show the world I exist, that the one you talk to is real, so they will believe you more. Also, to bring a message that my father has sent me.' He had read my mind, for I had already realized that finding the tomb, seeing the Virgin Mary and all of those miracles would be sufficient to prove his existence. 'No, Little One, there still will be many who disbelieve.'

'When are you coming, though, White Arrow? Will it be years?'

'No, Little One,' White Arrow replied. 'The visit is sooner than you realize. We have been preparing you, and when you are ready we will come. I have already told you that I will not tell you the time, but it is very soon. It is not just a visit to prove the existence of life on other planets – there is much more.'

'But they will think you are just an alien, White Arrow.'

'No, that is where you are wrong, for what they will see they will know.'

'What about Moses, White Arrow? What was the connection between you two?'

'We met many times together while I was on Earth. At one stage I spent time in Egypt and in other places. Before the world knew of me I made notes of my travels and my words with my father. Moses showed me where I could hide these notes. I also stayed there for some time. This place is where you will find the letters for the world. There is also a cloak that I left which has never been found. It was worn by me many times.

'In my letters are written words shared between me and my father concerning what was in the future. We knew then that the problem the world now has would come, and of many other things. In these letters are new words for the Ten Commandments. In the time you live in now, new ideas are needed – we knew that most Commandments would be broken and that mankind would need direction. The time has come for these letters to be given to the world.'

'Tell me, White Arrow, did you have help from the aliens then – and did Moses?'

'The aliens have been here from the beginning of time, Little One. All great prophets were helped by aliens, by order of my father. They helped by giving the powers that the great prophets on Earth had, but the powers given were to fit in with that time. Too much would have been misunderstood. The aliens will maybe frighten some people, but like the five chosen for me on this journey, certain aliens were chosen then to help your world.'

'Are aliens more religious than we, White Arrow?'

'The ones who help us are on the right-hand side of God. They are of the Highest.' That was not really what I was asking, but White Arrow carried on. 'The planets that have life are more advanced than Earth, but they are human, and all humans make mistakes. The planets are older than Earth, so they have had longer to learn. Earth is the youngest of all planets, so of course Earth humans have still to learn what the others have learned. Only what is in heaven is perfect, so people on other planets do learn, as on Earth, but they have learned much more. Even today, they too need help from time to time, but there is one planet that has learned that God comes first – that is Zipper's planet.'

Somehow that did not surprise me because of the love I felt from

Zipper. 'Zipper's planet is the one we call on first to help the others,' said White Arrow.

'But it doesn't mean we are bad people on Earth, just because we haven't learned, White Arrow, does it?' I asked.

'Little One, of course not. My people on Earth are loving people and good. It's just they have lost their way, and I have come to gently show them the way back. Bear and Eagle are the highest on their planets.'

By 17 July I knew where in Egypt to look. I wondered what would come next. Until I returned to Egypt to check all the stars and planets and the Coptic language, there was not much else to do. Was this all, until the next visit to Egypt? 'No,' I heard White Arrow reply. 'While we wait for the experts to help you, you will learn about the Amazon and Brazil.'

'How and when do we start that?'

'Now,' replied White Arrow.

It was just like the time I was finishing the report in *Little One* and had to start on Egypt. The same was happening in the case of South America. But where was I to start? I thought it might be better to start a new book on South America and leave this one, but I somehow knew that both were linked together, so I decided to keep going on this one and separate the two when I had got to the end.

'Where do we start, White Arrow?'

'By seeing Zipper later,' he said. 'I will show you what to do.'

'Fine,' I said. I had accepted that some time in the future the right people would be brought to help me on the Coptic writing and stars.

'Yes,' White Arrow assured me. 'Everything is set, so do not worry, Little One.'

· 18 ·

A Visit to Planet Earth

For two weeks I had 'been in' South America. I was now back at Ti. It was 8 August 1993. I was glad to be back at Ti, for I knew much more about Egypt than South America. I still had more physical visits to make to Egypt, and there was a lot more I had to find out. At Ti, I entered the passage to the tomb. It was darker than usual, so I presumed it was late afternoon. I looked at my watch. It was 4.45 – at Ti it would be 6.45pm. I sat on the floor and waited.

Bear, Zipper, Michael and White Arrow all stood there, saying nothing. I heard White Arrow say, 'Patience, Little One.' I looked at him and smiled. Imhotep arrived and sat on the chair – it appeared at the same time as he did. I bowed my head to him in respect.

I spoke to Imhotep. 'What is in that tomb?' I pointed to the one just outside Ti.

'Here you will find the remains of me. Here you will find things that will help White Arrow on his journey.' Unless scholars had got all the dates wrong, I wondered how he had known of White Arrow when he was here before. Imhotep said, 'I prayed to your God as well, but the names were different. I was spoken to one night by a visitor, a god who came to me.' He looked at Bear but just carried on talking. 'The god spoke of you and told me one thing I had to do before my death: that I must take some information with me on my transition to the next world. I put it behind the mask and jacket that lay above me in the tomb of Imhotep. Only the god I spoke to . . .' looking at Bear '. . . can show you the place and what the meaning is of what I have left.' Now I was confused. I understood why he called Bear a god, for they had had many gods and I knew these were the aliens – but he also knew White Arrow.

'I will show you my dream,' Imhotep said. It unfolded before me. I saw a young man lying on a small bed. The bed was facing a door which opened to the outside. It was warm and the sky was clear. One could see the stars clearly. In front of the door stood Bear, as I see him as an alien, but there was a light around him, and he was of human height. The young man sat up in his bed. He had no fear, for the light took the fear away. 'You have been chosen to follow a path that at the end of your days you will be truly rewarded for, and I wish you to follow me,' said Bear, and the young man got out of bed and followed him. Someone stood outside. I could not see, but I watched the young man and Bear go to him. Words were said and the young man returned to his bed and went to sleep. The dream went and I spoke to Imhotep.

'Is that when you spoke to White Arrow?' I asked.

'Yes,' he replied. I started asking him another question but White Arrow stopped me. 'It is important to ask White Arrow,' Imhotep told me, forgetting he could read my mind.

'Later,' said White Arrow, and we returned.

On 14 August, Zipper came. I was sitting out in the back garden and Zipper was sitting next to me, Alien Girl with him. Bear was on the other side of me and White Arrow behind me. Zipper was putting his finger on the paper, then he turned to Alien Girl, looked at her notes and went back to the paper again. 'I will draw you a picture. No man must see it till I am ready to tell you otherwise.' Then he proceeded to draw two pictures and told me to put them aside for later (*see* figures 18.1 and 18.2), then he took me to the entrance of Ti.

'Take [a specified number of] steps from the entrance of Ti. As you go round you will walk towards the north. Here you will stop. The instructions I have given before will tell you what to do next. Some of the words are also to do with the tomb, so it is important I tell you where I want you to stand. Once there, the tomb will be below you – the tomb of Imhotep. When you go to the Step Pyramid, from the entrance walk to your left. You will go [a number of] steps and stop, then walk [a number of] steps forward and stop.' I cannot give the exact location, because the tomb may not be opened until the correct time.

'Once again the words I have left you will tell you what is there

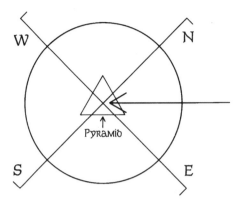

A drawing located the place with WHITE ARROW
in the PYRAMID. It is a circle and in the circle is
the PYRAMID form and the arrow pointed – not
to the ultimate and the cross pointing to the heart
of the Four Winds and two other arrows
pointing to a word – and that word is the House.
Translated into English, 25 July 1994, by Abdel Hakim Awayan

Figure 18.1

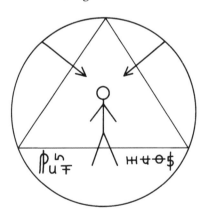

Figure 18.2

and where. I would like you to part the sand here. When you get
there you will understand why I have said that.'

'Do I need to find what the Coptic is?' I asked.

'Yes,' replied Zipper, 'for it will help you to know everything
you need. When everything comes together, then and only then
will it make complete sense. At the pyramid of Unas, both White
Arrow and Moses will help show you the piece you seek. At the

Great Pyramid is the final piece of the jigsaw. We will have completed our work on Egypt then. On this journey will occur the greatest discovery of all time. I cannot at this stage tell you what, but trust me.'

'Surely, Zipper, the greatest find will be at the pyramid of Unas, mainly because of the notes left by White Arrow and Moses?' I asked.

'No,' said Zipper. 'There have been greater things that have been left by him, but it is too big for you to carry the burden for now.' He paused. 'This you must wait for until we are ready to open it.'

'I have read the book *The Face Behind The Mask*, Zipper, and I can't see what is important,' I said.

'No, not yet, but you will in time,' Zipper replied. Then he said: 'Soon there is the visit to Egypt, and we have much to do. I will tell you of things that are to happen to you before you go, but you must be patient, for this is a great journey that no person has taken before – it must be carefully prepared for you. Our work also includes finding people who can help you. This is being done now. You are to talk to these people about us and we must give you the right things to take to them, so be patient with us – we cannot give you too much at one go for you to carry alone.'

White Arrow put his hand on my shoulder and said softly, 'Listen to Zipper's words, Little One, for he is wise.' Bear growled. I wondered what could be in the Giza pyramid that was so great that humans had not seen before, but I put it behind me for I knew I would get no answers now.

'I will leave you now, Little One, and we will talk later.'

I watched Zipper go to the tunnel. White Arrow leaned forward and said, 'There is much work to do in the coming months and many demands will be made of you in the future, but my strength will be with you. I will be calling you many times in the coming months and much writing will be done. We have to do this before the world comes to know of me.'

I knew what he meant. The book *Little One* was coming out in 1994. None of us knew what would happen once people read it, but White Arrow knew, and it was important to him that nothing should take me away from his journey. 'I'm here, White Arrow,' I said, 'whatever and whenever.' I would not let him down.

On 17 August White Arrow wished me to return to the ship. The medallion had gone blue, so I knew it was time to go. The room in the ship was in darkness, but I saw White Arrow by the window. The only light came from the stars and the sky. I felt peaceful, and walked towards White Arrow, passing the door the others usually came through. White Arrow was quiet as I stood next to him. I looked out of the window. I could not see the Earth, although I could see the light from it to my left. There were stars in the distance. White Arrow was looking out there, his arms folded. Suddenly he spoke.

'Little One, I have brought you here today to speak to you before the others arrive. The time is coming when great events will happen on your Earth. You have learned well from my teachings and now I will help you show the world. Your learning has come to an end. Now we will give you the power to help the world. Some of this power you have already received, and not once have you used it for yourself. Because of that we entrust our powers to you, for we know they will be used for mankind only.'

'White Arrow, can I ask you a question?' I said. I did not wish to interrupt him, but this was important. 'Will you be able to make people understand that their Earth is in trouble and that they need to do something about it?'

'Little One, trust me, for people will follow what they believe in their hearts, and I'm of the heart. They will know truth when they read it and see it. So do not fear, Little One.'

I knew I should not fear. It seemed to me that the Red Indians and other such peoples knew of the world's problem. I just hoped the peoples of the industrial nations would listen to the voice of White Arrow, to the aliens and the people who knew. As I looked at White Arrow I knew I could trust him to get the message across. I just hoped we would understand all this in good time! I returned home.

On 24 August I was to return to the ship, but first I needed to phone Hala; I hoped she had some news about the Coptic words. To open the tombs I needed to know what they meant. I had been worried about Hala and the paperwork I had given her. When I had been in Cairo she had said they were dangerous papers, and I realized she could get into trouble over them. She told me she was trying to see people about the Coptic in secret – people who had nothing to do with the government, because of the importance of the material and because of the danger involved. I told her to be careful.

The medallion had been showing blue all morning, and as I

arrived at the ship, everything was in darkness. I went to the window and looked out as I waited. White Arrow soon appeared at my side.

We were somewhere very different, for the stars were far in the distance. I could see the Earth; it was far away, yet I knew it was Earth. The room started to light up and I took my place at the bottom of the table. White Arrow stayed near the window and the door to my left opened. Zipper, Bear, Eagle, Michael and Alien Girl all came in and took their places. Zipper had notes with him and placed them on the table. He spoke to White Arrow for a few minutes, then pointed to me. I wondered what they were discussing, but Zipper looked back at White Arrow.

Eagle spoke to Zipper, and all three were now talking amongst themselves. Just then the table lit up and I could see Egypt. It was like watching a movie, except that I was looking down onto the table. I could see the top of the Giza pyramids, and people down there were moving about. The staff had appeared on the table as well. No one spoke to me and I watched Zipper pointing to the moving picture. White Arrow and Eagle were looking at him, as if he was explaining something to them. Suddenly, Bear spoke and moved his hand forward. Strange as it may seem, I watched him lift the top of a pyramid off, then put it back on.

I sat quietly while Zipper spoke to them all. The picture of Giza was still there, though no one but me was looking at it. Zipper picked up his notes, got up from the chair and left by the door. Everyone stayed where they were. I wondered where he had gone. Was he returning? I looked at White Arrow, but he was still talking to the others. I thought it was best that I keep quiet. Why had they brought me here today? Was it all to do with Egypt? I was sure to find out.

The next day I returned to the ship again. White Arrow was sitting in his father's chair and the room was lit up this time. I sat in my chair and waited for White Arrow to speak. 'Little One, soon we return to Egypt, and this journey will be more important than the last.'

I would have thought nothing could be like the first trip to Cairo. I looked at him and he carried on speaking. 'This time you will go for seven days. On the first day you will return to Ti. Then I wish you to go to Matariyah (the Virgin Tree). Once again you will take paperwork with you and you will be safe. All the places I have told you about earlier you will go to. Everything has been prepared for your next visit. While you are there you will go to

Zipper and the others every day, for they will give you strength. A miracle will take place while you are there, and people will see this miracle happen to you. The light will come.'

On 26 August, the medallion was blue again and I returned to the ship. The room was in darkness and White Arrow was by the window. I joined him. I looked at the sky, then at the Earth. I silently made a promise to her and all that live on her that I would see this journey through even if it took my life. I would let no fear enter me, and if it did I would ignore it to the best of my ability. White Arrow laid his hand on me, saying, 'We have to talk.' We both took our seats.

'In the words you have written for the journey for Egypt, I want you to follow all instructions. On your return there you must visit each and every one of the places I have spoken of, for this is important for the next journey. Little One, your journey will sometimes look dangerous, but while you have our protection you will be safe. This I promise. Now, I want you to start to prepare the journey.'

'I will, White Arrow.' I started working out when in January I should go to Egypt.

On 31 August, the medallion was blue again. I knew Zipper wanted to see me. Bear was there, with Alien Girl. Zipper came in last. 'You know, I've got a lot to do out there to convince people of your existence,' I said. Zipper nodded his head. 'I'm going to get a mixed reaction to all of this, but I want you all to know I will pass on your words with no hesitation.'

'We will help,' said Zipper. 'The miracles you seek will occur. Just have patience, for they must be at the right time.'

'I've seen all the miracles, and I believe you myself – I just can't understand why others don't see them,' I said.

White Arrow then spoke. 'Do not judge others, Little One. You have had time to adjust to these things; they haven't. In time they will see it is good, and they will believe.'

'I hope so, White Arrow,' I said. 'If it can help the Earth and the people of Earth I hope so. I pray so.'

White Arrow said, 'Listen to Zipper and watch.' Alien Girl gave Zipper some notes and the book. Zipper looked through them and I waited. NEINGH S/T PULTEY – Virgin of the Holy Tree. 'You will keep this word for the end of the book,' said White Arrow. I wonder why? I thought.

'We have a lot to do in the coming months!' said Zipper.

· 19 ·

Communion

It was 24 September. I was to see Zipper again in the afternoon, and I presumed it was about Egypt. I had so much to do to prepare for the next visit! I was going to book it for the last week in January 1994, which left me four months. 'We have much to do in that short time, Little One,' said White Arrow.

'I know!' The last three weeks I had hardly done any writing, since I had been getting *Little One* ready with the publishers. Now that was done I could get back to my work. In fact, I had missed working with the aliens.

'Hi, Zipper,' I said. It was good to see him. Bear and Michael were with us too. Michael looked enormous today – on the odd occasion I found his height overwhelming, and this was one of those times. Bear was just as big, although he managed to keep his height down a bit compared to Michael. Zipper was his usual 3–4 feet tall.

Alien Girl had appeared and passed notes to Zipper. She acknowledged me but said nothing. 'Five,' I suddenly heard, but I did not know what it meant. 'I will tell you later . . . no, I will tell you now. There are five places to go on your next trip that are important for our journey,' said Zipper. 'As we get nearer to the time we will tell you what to do at these places.'

Hala had been trying to find someone who could help us with the Coptic, but she was frightened of going to professors in case she got into trouble. 'You will have to help, White Arrow.' I looked at Zipper. 'Is there anything you can do to help?' Zipper looked at White Arrow. It looked as if White Arrow was stopping him from telling me something. White Arrow said, 'Patience . . . the right person will be found.'

'Yes, I do understand I need patience, White Arrow, but it would help me to know what the Coptic words mean.'

'In time, Little One, in time.'

There was so much I needed to remember to do on this trip! As with the last one, I would have to make sure I did what they asked. 'We must get you ready for this trip, for soon there will be much happening, and this will give you no time to take in what you must do,' said White Arrow the following day. I understood. Already things had come up which had stopped me from writing for him and the aliens. So today I knew it was important I concentrate on the next trip to Egypt.

'Soon I will bring the experts to you to help. You must listen to them, for they can help us on our journey.' I would be happy if I got some help – there were things only experts could help us with and I hoped they would arrive soon.

Zipper suddenly appeared, with Bear, Alien Girl and Michael behind him. I remembered the medallion had gone blue that morning. I had forgotten! 'Sorry, Zipper.'

Zipper nodded, then said, 'I will see you later.'

'Yes, Zipper,' I promised, and they all vanished except Bear. Lately he had been appearing a lot more. Whenever I spoke to White Arrow, Bear was there. It was as if he was being protective, and it was a nice feeling having him watch over me. White Arrow did not seem to mind.

Later, the medallion was blue and I knew I had to see Zipper. He was sitting opposite me on his own, which was strange, since someone was usually with him. Then Alien Girl appeared at his side and gave him the book.

'You must return to the tree. At the tree I want you to take a stone and bring it back with you on your return,' said White Arrow. There was a light and White Arrow turned his attention to Zipper before continuing to me: 'We will show you how to open many doors, some of which you know about. On this trip we will show you how to use the keys.'

Suddenly, Hala came into my mind. I knew I would have to phone her. Zipper crossed his legs. Michael, Bear and Eagle appeared. White Arrow's father had just appeared, in his lion form. He just sat there. I sensed something was up. I wondered what else they were going to do, but no one said anything. They were all watching Zipper. Bear put his hand on me in friendship.

Zipper was reading the book intently. I watched him, waiting for him to say something – I sensed something important. I looked at White Arrow. He just pointed to Zipper. I knew I had to watch and listen. The medallion started flashing – I had never seen it do that before – then it went brilliant white. It lit up the room, then went back to normal.

'What was that all about, White Arrow?'

'From your medallion came a message for Zipper. Whoever wears the medallion, it can be used by someone else who has one. The medallion is in contact with the spaceship and whoever has sent the message has used yours to send it.' Fine, I thought – I still didn't understand the full range of uses of the medallion. Zipper opened the book and showed me a picture (*see* figure 19.1).

He shut the book. 'Trust me, Little One. Soon you will find all these drawings will make sense, for I will bring someone to help you with them.'

'Thanks, Zipper.'

Everybody left, except the lion. 'Soon, Little One, we will be going somewhere very important. It is on Earth.'

On 28 October I returned to the ship. As I entered the room I noticed for the first time that one of the small aliens I had once seen in another part of the ship was there. I went towards my chair and watched him at the same time. He seemed a bit startled, but he should surely have known I was coming. The alien suddenly became friendly and walked towards me. He was smaller than Zipper in height and body. His eyes were wide open and he was smiling. I could see his jagged teeth. He was almost child-like, but I knew he was not. These people are far more intelligent than us, certainly not silly, and very friendly. He pointed to the wall, then to the table. I heard his strange language. I noticed particularly the 'Z' sound.

Suddenly White Arrow appeared, and my thoughts moved away from the little alien and what he was pointing at. They spoke to each other for a moment, then the door slid open and the little alien left. The large chair at the bottom of the room lit up. White Arrow's father was arriving. I quickly went to my seat, felt it first, found it was safe and sat down.

White Arrow smiled at me as he stood by his father's chair. As the chair started to move my thoughts were on Albert Einstein (with whom I had communicated in *Little One*), but I brushed the thought aside. Most probably he was around somewhere – he was usually with the aliens. I looked past White Arrow to the window.

TOMB

It is a statue of a woman. 2 guards protect her. Behind her lies a statue of a baby in a coffin. On the baby lies something of great importance.

Above the entrance or just inside is a God.
FISH

□ ↔ HET hour = The Place of Man

Translated into English, February 1996, by Abdel Hakim Awayan

Figure 19.1

The sight was lovely, with stars in the distance. Suddenly, something went by, so quickly that I could not see what it was. My eyes turned to White Arrow's father; his chair had completely turned around. His cloak was of gold, and his crown matched it in colour and radiance. The colours in the crown made me blink for a moment.

'Ann Walker, welcome. The first part of the journey is completed to start telling the world of my son's arrival. You have served him well.' Suddenly, without warning, the others appeared around the table – Bear and Eagle to the right of me, Michael, Alien Girl and Zipper to the left. 'Now, Ann Walker, we must return to Egypt, for there are things there for you that I have left for you to receive through others and give to the world. This you must promise, that no person will stop you on your journey for the world.'

'No,' I said straight away. 'No one will, I promise.'

'I will leave you now, Ann Walker, in the hands of my children, for they will tell you the next part of your journey.' The chair started to move. White Arrow talked for a while to his father, then his father left.

The staff appeared on the table, then went. 'My father has left this for you,' said White Arrow. He sat in his father's chair. Lights were appearing around him. I could not see him clearly. I was scared. What was going on? It was like the previous time when he was lit up – I knew it was White Arrow but could not see him clearly.

Then all of a sudden he was White Arrow again. Did he sense that I was not ready for the real him? He said nothing. Instead he spoke to Zipper for a while. 'The instructions we have given you for the tree,' White Arrow said, 'when you go to Egypt they will make sense.' I had been told to go to the two trees in Cairo and to walk around them three and a half times. 'A tall man will help you when you are out there,' he continued.

Suddenly, a map appeared on the table. Eagle leaned forward. Bear was talking to her, pointing at something. I could see Ti. We were at the site in Saqqara. What I did not know about the map was that it was dynamic and one could move pieces from it. Now I realized what Bear had done earlier when he had removed the top of a pyramid – it was a kind of virtual reality map. Suddenly, the Nile appeared on the other side of Saqqara.

I wondered what they were trying to show me. I just had to be patient – one could not rush them. They were all talking amongst themselves discussing the map, so I waited. Suddenly I got the word XUMUS, which I later discovered meant zeal. Then I returned home.

By 5 November I had at last finished all the work involved in publishing *Little One*. Now I could get back to helping White Arrow and the aliens. I was booking my trip to Egypt in the next two weeks and was quite excited about going back. Suddenly, I heard White Arrow speak. 'Soon the doors of Egypt will open.

'We will return to the ship,' he continued. The medallion this time turned blue and red, which I had not seen before. Before I returned, Bear and Michael were standing next to me. Suddenly, I was back on the ship. It was in darkness. I saw White Arrow at the window and joined him. 'Soon, Little One, I will return,' he said as he looked at the Earth. 'Through your help I will be able to show myself to the world.'

I knew White Arrow would appear one day, but would he stay? 'My stay will be long enough to prove to the world that I exist, through you. For then they will truly believe that you are with me.'

'Somehow I believe the words you have written, White Arrow, will prove your existence, but knowing humans as I do . . .'

We both looked at the world spinning for a few more moments and then went back to the table. The aliens had already taken their places. I walked to my chair and sat down. White Arrow's father's chair was empty. In front of me was what looked like a pen, but I knew it was not. I picked it up. It was of a very soft material, but a tingly feeling went through me as I held it, so I laid it down again. White Arrow smiled at me from the bottom of the table. 'Later, Little One,' he said.

He knew I was going to ask what it was – as usual he could read my mind. Bear leaned forward and laid his hand on mine, then took it away. He also took the object away with him. I was getting used to Bear's looks by now, but I still saw him as a bear more often than I saw the real him. Suddenly, the picture of Egypt came up. They were busy talking to each other, so I waited. They seemed to be talking for ages, and my mind drifted to other things.

Then White Arrow said, 'Your journey last time was of miracles. This time more are to come. You must take longer.'

'I'll try, White Arrow,' I said. He understood and just smiled.

On 4 December I was called to the ship. I was back in my chair in the main room. At the head of the table was White Arrow's father. All the other aliens were in their usual seats. I was pleased to see the father, but I still felt humble, grateful and honoured by his presence. White Arrow appeared at his side. The staff was on the table. I looked at White Arrow and he smiled. I watched the cloak move and knew White Arrow's father was standing up. Suddenly, a cup appeared before me – one I had seen some time ago.

'Drink,' I heard the father say, and I lifted the cup to my lips. It was a sweet liquid. I put the cup on the table and it vanished. Suddenly, a round loaf of bread appeared before me. I watched. There were no hands, no person could I see. As the bread broke up, a piece moved to each of us one by one. I was aghast. I watched as the aliens picked up the bread and ate it. There was a piece in front of me and nervously I picked it up. My mouth was dry, even though I had just drunk from the cup. I put it in my mouth and chewed, wondering what this was all about. Did the aliens have bread in their world, or was this for my benefit? No one spoke.

I watched the cloak and knew the father was sitting down again. 'Now each and every one of you has a part of each other within you. Now we start our journey for the peace of man and for your world. In you is a part of us all. This will give you the strength for your journey.' All the aliens put a hand forward, each laying one on top of the other. 'Join them,' White Arrow's father said. 'Do not be afraid, for this is for the love of all.' I laid my hand on top. White Arrow was the last – he laid his hand on mine.

The chair turned. White Arrow's father was going. I sat and looked at White Arrow, not knowing what to say. White Arrow then said, 'Come, we go.'

I later received an explanation for this communion from a friend of mine. 'The purpose of the aliens joining you in the breaking of bread is to show their unity of purpose with you in carrying out the wishes of the father. It is symbolic of a family, of siblinghood, where the aliens take part in the earthly pursuits of eating bread and drinking wine, thus indicating that they are with you in your task of serving God. Similarly, the biblical angels partook of bread and wine with the Chosen Ones to demonstrate their involvement in events on Earth, bringing the word of the Lord to the people.'

I also received another explanation. Some weeks earlier I had realized that one meaning of the name White Arrow was 'Winged Angel.' 'The concept of the Winged Angel is largely symbolic in that it simply means to convey the concept of an alien who comes from the sky in much the same way that the ancient races, using flying saucers, drew winged discs to give an impression of their ability to fly in the air, or of the fact that they came from the sky.'

On 18 December, I felt that White Arrow wished to speak to me, so I waited for him to come. 'Hi, White Arrow.'

'Little One,' he said softly, 'much is being done for you on this journey. We have plans to bring hope to the people of the Earth. Soon they will know of my existence. For you, you must put everything into following the road. Egypt is important for my people. All the information I have given, you must take with you. Follow my directions out there and all will be well.

'When you come back you will be a stronger person – many changes await you. You must go to the people for me, but I will speak through you. You have the medallion and the staff now. Both have been given you to help you on your journey. You have learned of them and their powers.

'When you return from Egypt the powers will be stronger. They have to be so, for what faces you. At all times lean on the staff and call on the medallion, for these are your powers. They will help you to show my people that what you speak of is truth, and they will see this through you. At all times I will speak through you. In time I will show myself to them when it is right.

'Until that time you, Little One, will be White Arrow. We will at times become one, so that the people of Earth will see me through you. You have served me well, and for this I thank you, but there is much out there that will frighten you.

'This is why I teach you to make use of the staff and the medallion, for when that fear comes, turn to them. The staff is of my father, the medallion is for you to call the aliens, at any time. Both will help your fear. I have put you on a hard road, Little One, but we have protected you like no human has been protected before. Do not fear what you say or do in the future, for the one who works for the Son of God speaks truth. We have not had much time lately to talk personally because of my work, but remember I am with you always. Remember my words today, for they will help you overcome your fear of the future.' With that, he went.

On the first day of 1994, I was in the ship. I had just finished reading my instructions for what I was to do when I was out in Egypt, when White Arrow spoke. 'There is much to do in Egypt. I will help you at all times while you are there. Only those I have chosen will be with you on this journey. They will witness the power of the Son of God.' He frightened me for a moment – I wondered what was to happen. I could only just cope with what was going on now! 'Patience, Little One, haven't I given you only what you are capable of carrying on your shoulders?'

He seemed stern, and that was not like White Arrow at all. He suddenly smiled and spoke softly. 'You must understand the importance of this journey. For that to be so I must sometimes speak in the manner that I have just done.' Yes, I had heard White Arrow talk to people like that before if they were not listening to him. 'You have your instructions, and these you will follow. Any more that comes will be for your subsequent visit to Egypt.'

I looked around at the aliens. They were watching White Arrow. White Arrow pointed to the window. He was pointing at the Earth. 'It is important that all instructions are followed, for they will help save your Earth. We will return.' I was suddenly back home.

On Thursday, 13 January, it was very cold outdoors. I could see the stars very clearly. I watched Zipper come up the garden and sit down. Eagle was there, with Bear and Michael and Alien Girl – it was nice to see her. She stood by Zipper and took something from him, then went off to the tunnel. White Arrow said she would be back later. I was very tired that night, mainly because so much was going on, but I had to keep going.

Then White Arrow said, 'Watch and listen.' Zipper was writing as usual. I looked at the stars for a while. Then Zipper spoke.

'I have more words.'

'Okay, Zipper. Can I have them now?'

'Yes,' he replied. I watched him as he put his hand on the page. He gave me the words: XUETUMS FORU SEVUAN II.

Old Arabic	Arabic	English
XUETUMS	TAMASA	darkness (to wipe out)
FORU	FARAH	wedding (happy)
SEVUAN	SABAHAN	in the morning

I also received these words: PUEL ICUCTY KAMUPE.

Old Arabic	Arabic	English
PUEL	BAHAL	mule (work-horse)
ICUCTY	ECAHAT	decaying
KAMUPE	KANABA	resting place

Zipper had given me a drawing (*see* figure 19.2). I sensed it was of the body of Jesus Christ, yet how I knew I don't know. I turned to White Arrow. 'I'm right, aren't I?' White Arrow said nothing. I

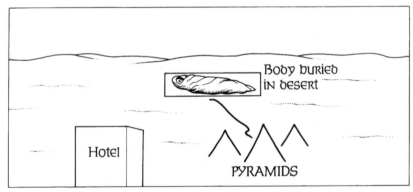

Iɴ each shadow is buried a secret of the Great Kiɴgs. Oɴly the stars can reveal the secrets.

Figure 19.2

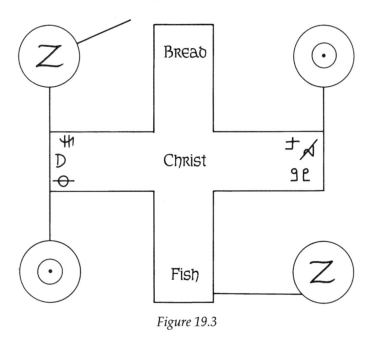

Figure 19.3

looked back again. I now knew that Jesus Christ was brought to Egypt after the crucifixion; when I returned to Egypt I would ask the Bedouin tribesmen if they knew this was true.

Another drawing was coming through from Zipper. He asked me to hold out the pad. I watched as his finger went yellow and he pointed and drew over it (*see* figure 19.3).

· 20 ·

The Second Journey to Egypt

On 27 January 1994 Val and I left for Egypt. We were to be there for five days. I had checked with White Arrow if five days would be long enough. He said it would, but I knew that the next time we would be there for seven days. I looked over my instructions so that I would remember everything I had to do for White Arrow.

The flight was good and time went quickly. As the plane was descending towards Cairo airport, I began to get excited but I tried to contain myself because I was tired, and there was a lot to do the following morning. The week before, I had spoken to Hala on the telephone to tell her what time I was due in. She had said a car would be waiting at the airport. As we left the plane I wondered if everything was going according to plan.

As we walked towards customs, I heard a man shouting out, 'Mrs Ann! Mrs Ann!' I looked at Val. 'Do you think he means me?' We both looked at him.

'Mrs Ann?' he asked.

'Yes,' I replied.

He bent forward to greet me and said, 'Come, Mrs Ann, come.' So Val and I followed. To my right stood three men in uniform, and the man took me to the one in the middle. He too bent forward to greet me and held out his hand.

'Do you know Hala's stepfather?' he asked me. I said yes, and he then said, 'Welcome to Cairo, Mrs Ann, welcome to Cairo!' Then he told the man to get our cases for us. I thanked him and followed the man towards the baggage claim. I remembered what Hala's stepfather had said when I had last seen him. 'When you return to Egypt I will send an official to meet you.' He had kept his word. With our luggage we went through to the arrival lounge, and there was Hala with her fiancé Mohammed and her brother. She was holding a small posy of flowers in each hand. After we had finished hugging each other and being introduced to everyone she gave us the flowers.

It took an hour to get to our hotel. We chatted in the car about everything that had happened since our last visit. I was happy to see Hala. She had done so much for us on our last visit, and now she told me that she would be spending all her time with us this visit, to help White Arrow. I hugged her and thanked her, for her help would be important. I asked her to thank her father for the welcome he had given me on my arrival.

'No, Ann, you can tell him yourself, for we will be seeing them soon,' she said.

'Great, Hala,' I said. I had enjoyed meeting her parents before, and was delighted they wanted to see me again.

It was late when we arrived at the hotel. Hala said good-night to us and said she would be with us at 10.30 the following morning. Before I left England I had asked her to organize a hired car, and she had also arranged for a driver. The hotel was beautiful and very grand, and only five minutes from the Great Pyramid of Giza. This was how White Arrow wanted it.

We were shown to our room. I had asked for one with a balcony with a view of the pyramid, but they did not have one available until the following day. I phoned Tony, then settled into bed. We were exhausted and before long we were both asleep.

I woke at 6.45am and lay there for a few moments. White Arrow was not around yet, but he probably was not far away. I must get up, I thought, so I pulled the covers back and crept into the bathroom. When I returned Val was sitting up. The weather looked fine, and while I waited for Val to get ready I wondered about the trip.

Suddenly, I heard White Arrow say, 'You will not fail.'

'Hi, White Arrow!' I said. He appeared and smiled at me. I had my first pages of instructions in front of me. White Arrow had asked me to return to the Virgin Mary's tree. I had wondered why, but I was happy to wait until I got there to get the answer to that question. However, I wanted to go to Unas first.

After breakfast, Val and I sat and talked for a while, then left to look around. We decided to go outside the front of the hotel. As we stepped out and turned to the left, the sight hit me. There, five minutes away, stood the Great Pyramid. I stood gazing in awe.

On our last visit, so much had happened that I had had no time to take it all in. Now, as I stood there, I felt the wonder of it all – felt it in my body. I turned to Val and could see her feelings were the same. I felt the wind around my legs and started to shiver. I had thought it would be hot, yet the morning was cold. I prayed it would get warmer, for I had brought mostly summer clothes. We went back inside the hotel and returned to the room. I sat on my own for a short while – I needed to be with White Arrow. I was still a bit tired from the journey. I shut my eyes and blessed myself and with my hand stretched out I prayed, 'God, please give me strength and guidance. Please allow me to use the staff.'

I opened my eyes and could see the staff appearing in my hand. After a few moments it went. White Arrow sat next to me as I used it, and then Moses appeared. Moses said to me, 'I have many things to show you on this journey, Ann. At the pyramid of Unas you will follow me. I will meet you at the entrance. I will walk with you on this journey.' Then he left.

I turned to White Arrow and asked, 'What have I done to deserve so much, White Arrow?'

'Faith, Little One, faith,' he said. Then he too left.

When Hala arrived, we greeted each other warmly and settled down. We had to talk about things before we left the hotel, so we ordered coffee. Hala spoke of many things. The first was that she had found out that the tree associated with the Virgin Mary, which we had visited previously, was not the only one in Matariyah. The Virgin Mary had stopped at more than one tree! Now I understood why White Arrow had said I had to return to the tree – he was taking me back to Matariyah, but to the second tree nearby, for this was what he had foretold. 'Matariyah means "water",' said Hala.

'How far is the tree, Hala?'

'Very close to where you first went.' My stomach turned. What if I had another vision? No, for the Virgin Mary has already given me the message. I shook my head, trying to get all competing thoughts out of my head. I had to concentrate on Unas.

'I will take you to the tree in the next few days,' Hala said.

I looked at her – she was just 24 years old and so willing to help. White Arrow had chosen well. She told me that she very much wanted to help, but she was still scared. She would not run away, but she had to be sure that White Arrow was true. I could under-stand her fear. 'The Koran says "Believe in none except me",' explained Hala, 'but I know I will come to no harm with you and

White Arrow. I have told no one of the real you, Ann – I have said so far that you are just a fortune-teller, because people might fear. But in time they will know the truth. But for myself, I believed you from the first day we met. White Arrow will know what I mean when I say I must have proof. The pharaohs and gods are beyond our comprehension, and so it is possible.'

I wanted to hold her and encourage her not to be afraid, but I also knew that somehow White Arrow would convince her on this trip. In an inexplicable way, I sensed something different, a stronger power within me: I knew something was going to happen, though once again I put the thought aside as Hala spoke of other things. I ordered more coffee and sat and listened.

Hala went on to tell me that a few weeks earlier she had been reading *Heaven Can Come Later*, my autobiography, and as she was reading it she could see a Red Indian in the room. She had shut the book and left it until the following evening. Once again, as she read the book she could see a Red Indian. Hala decided that she would read the book in the morning to see if it was her imagination or a trick of the light. But that following morning, the same thing happened. It was not her imagination. Hala knew that White Arrow had visited her.

As we were talking, we could hear the Muslim prayers being chanted over the city. Hala looked at me and said, 'If White Arrow had been a bad ghost he would not be here now with us. It is our belief that when this prayer is heard nothing bad can enter.' To Hala this was added proof, but I knew more would come. We spoke about Moses, other religions and how all religions serve the same God.

White Arrow then said, 'All people have the right to follow their own path to God, for God is of good. So it does not matter what religion you have, for all religion is of God. It is for good.'

Once again Hala asked me if White Arrow would change all religions. 'No,' said White Arrow, through me. 'I have come not for myself but for the world, to save the people. I have the power to appear, and I have come to pass this message on to the world, through a human. I come not to be adored or worshipped. The Son of God is here to help you. Do not fear, for if there is change, it will be done in my father's name only, and it will be of good.' Hala felt a lot more relaxed. I think she had thought that if she continued her involvement with me it would mean changing her faith. Now she knew that was not so. Our talk had taken some of her fear away.

It was getting late, and I was starting to worry that we would not get to see Unas. We began to get ready. As I was sorting everything out I asked Hala, 'Tell me, was Jesus Christ buried here in Egypt?' This was something I felt sure of, but White Arrow had not confirmed it. Hala said she did not know, although Jesus had indeed spent much of his life in Egypt.

As we were leaving I suddenly remembered that before I came, White Arrow had asked me to put the motif of a fish on the back of a jacket and to wear it every day while I was in Egypt. He said someone would recognize it and come forward. At the time I had thought that would indeed be a miracle, since there are 17 million people in Egypt, and I had to find the one who would know the sign and the importance of it. I tied the jacket around my waist and asked Val if the fish was showing clearly. I carried the blue book containing all my instructions and diagrams with me. I had learned on my last visit how potentially dangerous the book was, and I was not taking any chances this time.

We all climbed into the car and sat back to enjoy the journey to Unas. I laid my head back and prayed, 'Help me to help White Arrow.' I opened my eyes and looked out of the window. Thoughts were going through my head, and I remembered the medallion; White Arrow had taken me to Egypt through the medallion, and I had arrived at a pyramid I had known nothing of before. I had measured distances with my hands. I remembered my entrance, the red clay or sand, the three pyramids to my left and the one to my right. I had found out it was Unas.

Now I was on the way to it. I would measure Unas with my hands and arms stretched out, and if it all tallied, then the medallion's powers were demonstrably real. I needed proof to help me understand its power – and this was my chance. There were other things I had to do when I got there: I needed to find where the letters by Jesus were, and to be receptive to whatever White Arrow might want to show me.

So many things had to be proved! It all had to tie up. The evidence had to be accurate, in preparation for the time when I was to open the tomb. I knew White Arrow was right, but one slip on my part could let everyone down. My hands were feeling sweaty – I was nervous. If everything I had seen and been shown was accurate, then it meant the papers would be there.

My attention was taken by Hala. 'Ann, did you know that the name Unas means "the good friend", or "the good one"? Also, at the side is a stone donkey.' Could it possibly be donkeys I had been doing in some of the drawings instead of horses, I wondered? I had to give the world verifiable evidence, for without it I could not prove White Arrow's thesis that the world was in danger.

I had to give Hala a message. White Arrow said, 'You will see something on this journey that will prove my survival. Do not be frightened.' He said that both Val and Hala would see something.

'When we get there, Hala, there are things I have to do,' I said. I explained that I needed to measure the side of the pyramid. 'Will anyone stop me?' I asked.

'No,' she said. 'If anyone says anything to me, I will tell them you are a little bit mad. That way, they won't bother you. Also, they will not learn of the secrets you have, which is important.' Yes, I thought, if anyone knew or guessed what I was doing, it would mean I would have let White Arrow down.

I had been a bit worried about Ti, for I had to dig with my hands where the hidden tomb is. If anyone knew there was a tomb there and opened it before White Arrow did, then it would mean I could not prove to the world that White Arrow had found it, so I had to be very careful what I did on this journey. I agreed with Hala it would be best if people thought I was eccentric or stupid – that did not matter to me. The important thing was not letting White Arrow down.

We were getting out of the car when Bear and Imhotep appeared. I had not seen Bear for a few days. White Arrow had insisted that before I entered each place I should use the staff. So I stood there for a few seconds. There were half a dozen tourist guides and keepers of the pyramid behind me, but I could not let that stop me. It did not really matter what they thought.

After a few seconds Moses appeared ahead of me and went into the pyramid. We followed. I ducked my head and followed the small corridor through to the far chambers. Moses was ahead of me and then vanished. I checked as I went along, remembering the last time I was here. Everything was exactly as it had been when I had come using the medallion. The room that Moses had entered when he bent down was where I had seen it, to my left. To my right was another room. I remembered the last time, when I had seen a coffin, and how it had reminded me of the Sacred Bull tomb. Everything fitted into place. There was one more thing I had to do to prove that the medallion had worked, and that was to measure the outside. But for now other things were important. The reasons why I had been brought here were to be revealed – I had to wait and watch.

As I stood there, I videoed everything, as White Arrow had wanted. I had also been instructed to video the outside of the sites I visited, so that I had proof of the dates I was there. I turned to Val: 'Remind me to video outside, Val, in case I forget.'

'I will, I promise.'

I looked around. The others knew I needed time on my own, so Hala showed Val around. I looked above the coffin towards my right. I felt there was something important there, so I videoed it again, then I turned and walked back to the small room on the other side.

As I walked towards the small opening, Moses stood there. He bent down and went through. I followed. I was glad I had brought a torch with me. As we entered the opening there were small rooms to my left and right, but I knew I had to go to my right. I shone the torch on the wall. There was no writing on the walls, but I did not need it – I knew this was the room. Moses had gone, but he had correctly shown me the room he had shown me before. I went back to Hala.

'Tell me, Hala, does the sand come through the cracks?'

'Sometimes, yes,' she replied. When I had travelled by the medallion, sand had fallen from the cracks. I think I was in shock, but not aware of it. Everything was proving that I had genuinely been here through the medallion. Hala asked if I had finished.

I was just about to say yes, when Eagle appeared. I told them both she was here. Bear was also still around. I watched Eagle as she went to the wall to my left. She started to point at the wall, so I walked over to her. 'Take down this message on paper . . .' I watched as she showed me half a dozen lines of hieroglyphics. I turned to Hala and said, 'Can you copy them for me?'

Hala got some paper from Val. 'We have to be careful that no one knows what text we are writing, in case they copy it,' she said. 'So I'll write and stop now and then, so no one knows what I'm doing.' While she wrote, Val and I stood and pointed at different things, deflecting attention away from Hala. It worked. She got them all, and she promised me she would work on them and let me know what they meant.

'Ann,' she said, 'I know the aliens are good, for it is said no bad spirits can enter here, so they cannot be bad.' I hugged her close.

Mentally, I asked White Arrow, 'Is there anything else?' It

seemed my work was completed. I had found what I had come for, and we left. As we came out I told Hala I was going to measure the pyramid wall with my hands. 'Go ahead,' she said. 'I will talk to the keepers so they won't stop you.' Val videoed the pyramid entrance and I stood in front and started to stretch my hands out against the wall. It was quite warm and not too windy, which meant I could concentrate on my work without the sand getting in my eyes. One, two, three . . . I counted. The wall had crumbled slightly at the side of the pyramid so I had to go in a bit. Yes! I shouted in my mind. The distances tallied with what I had measured during my visit through the medallion.

There was one more thing. The medallion had shown me that there would be three pyramids to my left and one to my right; I had to see them for myself. I leaned against the pyramid for a moment. I needed to take a couple of deep breaths. What I had done so far was a miracle; I was scared to look now in case the miracle evaporated through one mistake. If there was but one pyramid to my left, then I would either be wrong or at the wrong pyramid. I stood up and looked . . . and disappointment welled up in me.

There was a small hill – a man-made hill, that much I sensed, but that did not matter. What mattered was that I could see only one pyramid to my right, but none to my left. Why were there no other pyramids to my left? Had I been wrong? I called Hala. As she came up she asked me what was wrong. I asked her whether the small hill had been made by man.

'Yes,' she said. 'Come, I want to show you something. Just follow me.' I did not want to go – I needed an answer, and she was not giving it to me. But I followed anyway; I would have to worry about it when I got back to the hotel. It would mean I had not got the use of the medallion right. Hala climbed some steps just opposite the Unas Pyramid and we followed. It took a few minutes to reach the top.

'Look, Ann,' said Hala. As I turned, my heart skipped a beat, for now, higher up in the distance, were the three pyramids to the left. The hill had blocked my view. The medallion had worked! Happiness and relief swept over me. For the first time I could prove to the world that it worked.

I hugged Hala. She smiled, as if she had known all along that White Arrow would be right. Then we walked back down to the car where the driver was waiting. There was still much more to do before the day was finished. As we drove off I read my notes about

Unas and what the medallion had shown me, checking that everything had been right, when suddenly I remembered the red sand or clay. 'Hala, where does the red sand come in?' I asked. 'I don't remember seeing any.'

Hala had already read my notes about Unas, knowing that I had not been there before, and she knew what I had written had been correct. 'When they built the pyramids they put red clay over them,' she said, 'but over the years it has fallen off and worn away. If you look in certain places around the edge of the pyramid you will see small bits, but where you went it had decayed away.'

Again, the medallion had been right! I had thought there would be lots of red clay; I had not thought to look for small bits. I sat back satisfied. I was coming away knowing where one of the secrets was – I now knew where the papers were hidden. All that was left was to work out the Coptic words and the hieroglyphics on the wall, but I knew that in time – at the right time – I would find out. Then White Arrow would be ready to prove his survival. Moreover, the staff had worked – there was no doubt of that.

We returned to the hotel at 4pm. Within an hour of our return the hotel management had changed our room. As the man led me to the balcony I was excited. He pulled open the door, and the view was breathtaking. White Arrow had got his wish, for there in front of me stood the Great Pyramid, Cheops, with the others at the side of it. I wondered what secrets it held, and what White Arrow was going to show me.

A shiver ran down me. It was not fear, for I had no fear of White Arrow and the aliens; it was anxiety. Everything had to be right. In my mind I reviewed every instruction carefully. I knew there would be no time for relaxing or fun, just work. I was beginning to feel a bit tired, so it was good to get some rest for now.

Hala was staying with us, as Mohammed was coming to the hotel at seven. There was nothing for me to do until the following day, so we had a nice meal and decided to have an early night. Val and I then went up to our room. Hala had asked me who in the government I would like to meet. I told her any minister would do, as long as I could get their help to open the tomb. We had to get permission from high-up.

We fell onto our beds. We were both tired and knew we had an even busier day tomorrow. It did not take us long to get undressed and ready for bed. I left the door open to the balcony – White Arrow wanted this. I took up my writing paper. White Arrow had said he wanted me to write each night in Egypt and speak to him and the aliens. It was too cold to sit on the balcony. White Arrow appeared. This is what I wrote:

It's 28 January 1994. I am tired, but it is important that I listen to White Arrow and the aliens. Bear is here. 'I will be at Ti tomorrow. You will watch for me. I will protect you. Do not run away, for no one will hurt or stop you. Trust me, for I will be showing you something that will help the world.'

'White Arrow, I am so confused and tired! What am I looking for?'

'It is ahead of you,' says White Arrow. 'Everything is in place. Do not fear, Little One. Call on the medallion and the staff. In the morning you will go to the medallion and you will ask what it is you are being led to. When you reach Ti and the Step Pyramid you will call on both the staff and the medallion, for they are there to help you in your search. I am pleased with you today. You have done well.'

Eagle is here. She says a miracle is to take place. Thank you, Eagle, I say, remembering the last time she said that – it was when I first saw Mary.

'Little One, rest, for there is much work to be done. Everything is in place,' said White Arrow.

Then I went to sleep. Next day, Hala was meeting us in the afternoon. She had a class to attend at college in the morning, so Val and I were to go to Ti on our own. I wondered if that was meant to be, for she had not come to Ti the previous time either. Was it better without her? I shrugged my shoulders. I had to go to Ti, and could omit nothing. Every instruction had to be followed!

· 21 ·

The Fish and the Bedouin

After breakfast we opened the blue book and I took out the instructions for Ti. We also spoke about the drawing I had shown Hala the day before. I had drawn figures in the Great Pyramid and one was incomprehensible. I had thought maybe it was the Tree of Life, but when I had asked Hala, she had said 'No, it doesn't mean that, Ann. These are measurements, and this means 33.7cm.' I was amazed. How could I possibly have known how to draw that? I had to admit how clever White Arrow and the rest were. I could not even spell properly, and yet I was writing in several languages and using weird measurements – I thought how cleverly put together this puzzle was.

I soon put that to the back of my mind, for it was another important day. At 10.30 the car was ready for us. As we grabbed our sun hats to leave, I felt excitement build up. I would have loved to have had more time to think about the previous day and the miracle of the medallion, but all that had to be forgotten until I returned home. I read my notes:

> Go to the entrance of Ti. As you stand facing the entrance go to your left and take [a specified number of] steps round towards the north. Here you will stop and dig with your hands and pray. At the Step Pyramid, from the entrance [facing it] you will walk to your left. Take [a specific number of] steps, then walk [a number of] steps forward and stop. Part the sand here, say a prayer.

Would anyone at Ti or the Step Pyramid stop me? I remembered to go to the medallion and the staff, so I said quietly to Val, 'I'm going to the medallion.' By telling her this, I knew she would not disturb me while I was doing it. I blessed myself and prayed to

God and White Arrow. 'Please help me complete the journey.' I looked at the medallion, saying in my mind, 'Don't let anyone stop me.'

Suddenly, a picture formed. Before I knew it I was standing at the entrance of Ti. I heard White Arrow speak: 'A man will help you here.' I saw Bear. He was to one side. There were a couple of men around us. White Arrow then said, 'No interference will come. A man will help.' Suddenly, I had a vision of someone shouting in the distance and turned to see a man on a camel coming in our direction. He was shouting to me.

'Val must talk to the people while you dig,' said White Arrow. Abruptly, I was at the Step Pyramid, standing at the entrance. No one seemed to be with me. I was using the staff, but I was still not sure what I was to find. 'You will dig at Ti, and it will be soft. Digging at the Step Pyramid, you will hit something hard. The key at the Step Pyramid unlocks Ti. You will sob on this journey, and peace will come with it,' said White Arrow. I do not as a rule cry.

'Do you mean cry inside?' There was no answer.

The vision went, and I was back in the car. I held my hand out to hold the staff. 'God, please give me the power to help your son.' I watched as a beam of light formed into a small pole with my hand around it. I knew I was to use the staff at each entrance as well. 'Done it, Val,' I said. She smiled. I told her what I had seen and heard, and she made notes.

It was not long before we were there. A few moments before we got out of the car I remembered what Hala had said: 'Be careful, for they watch you and will wonder why you are doing these things.' I could not afford to let these secrets be found out by others, and I remembered what Hala had recommended, to act as if I was over-religious or a bit cranky.

'Val, I have an idea,' I said. 'When I kneel to dig I will break up a cigarette and put tobacco in the ground as a gift to God.' I remembered how the Native Americans give back to Mother Earth by offering tobacco and, conveniently, people here would not understand, so maybe they would not take too much notice of me. It was worth trying anyway, and to me it was a way of symbolically giving something back. Val thought it was a good idea.

We collected our bags and cameras, paid the gatekeepers the fees for using the cameras and left the taxi driver behind us. He told us he would wait in the car. Val had brought with her a photograph of Sheban, the man who had taken us to Ti on a camel.

We had liked and trusted him. We hoped he would be here this time. Being a friend, he might help us without worrying too much.

We showed the photograph to a group of tribesmen who worked at Ti, taking people down to the tombs and pyramids. There were horses, camels and a horse and buggy to the left of us. Everyone was asking us if we wanted to hire them. Val held the photo up and said, 'Do you know this man? His name is Sheban.'

One old man said, 'Yes, that is my son.'

I felt excited. 'Is he here?' I asked.

The old man shook his head from side to side. 'No,' he said and he pointed. 'He is over at the far pyramids with some tourists.' The excitement left me and disappointment came instead. The man with the horse and carriage came forward. 'Please, I can take you,' he said.

'Yes,' I replied and we left for Ti.

We travelled for ten minutes. When we arrived there was a man at the entrance, and another walking up from it. Although I had been to Ti before and really did not need to go into the tomb, I felt it was better that I did. I needed to walk the steps to the left, but I did not want to attract attention.

I had brought some pictures from my last visit that White Arrow had selected. They showed some of the drawings on the wall, so I thought I could get an explanation of them. We entered the tomb and I videoed and took photographs. Before I entered I used the staff. 'Show me the way,' I prayed as I shut my eyes for a few seconds. Then I entered. I asked about the pictures I had taken the last time.

The second picture meant 'everyday', the fourth meant 'butcher' (a harvester cutting the corn), the fifth meant 'Ti from here', the sixth meant 'Ti the man'. The others meant nothing, said White Arrow. I would have to sort out the meanings when I returned home. The man watching over the tomb let me video for a long time and I knew the staff was working. I tipped him extra and thanked him, then we left the tomb. As we reached the top, the man in the carriage was waiting. I said I wanted to go and pray to thank God. He accepted that, and I left Val with him.

From the entrance of Ti I counted my footsteps as instructed. As I reached the last couple of steps I saw Bear ahead of me, standing by the fence that went round the tomb of Ti. I counted how many steps there were to him. 'What's going on, Bear?' I asked.

'Go back [a number of steps],' he replied, and I counted back. I then knew what I had to do. Val had been instructed to video the entrance of Ti and where I was to be.

I knelt and prayed to God. 'Please help me help your son show me what to do.' Then I started to dig with my hands, ten handfuls. The sand was loose and kept falling back in. I shut my eyes. What am I doing? I thought. What am I looking for? White Arrow, help me!

As I lifted out the sand I noticed that one of the men had my video in his hands. He was videoing what I was doing. I did not mind. I knew the idea of the tobacco must have been White Arrow's, for it would have been the only thing that would have convinced the guide that it was my way of praying. I knelt and blessed myself.

'God, I have done what you have asked and I hope I have not let you down.' I got a cigarette out of my money-belt and broke up the tobacco. It did not matter that this was to fool the the guide – I remembered what the Native Americans had said about giving back to Mother Earth. As I scattered the tobacco into the hole I thanked her for everything, then I said the Lord's Prayer.

After blessing myself with the sign of the cross and smoothing the sand, I looked up. Bear was still there – then he suddenly vanished. Was I at the beginning of the tomb and Bear at the end of it? Was that why he had been standing there? I would ask him later. I got up. The guide was still videoing me. I walked towards him, received the video camera from him and thanked him. He smiled. Whether or not he thought I was mad, I could not say. He just smiled and walked back to the others.

I heard someone shouting in the distance and turned round to look. The medallion came rushing into my mind. I was now watching the same scene that I had seen in the car, but now it was real. A camel approached, and we recognized the man on it. It was Sheban! I was surprised that the medallion had once again been so accurate – I was also very pleased to see him!

After the greetings he explained that a message had been brought to him that we had been asking after him. As soon as he had heard this he had left his tourists to someone else – he had lost that day's earnings to come to see us. He had also had to borrow a camel to get here. It made me feel good that he thought so much of us.

As we all stood in a group I remembered the picture I had been shown before I left England (*see* figure 19.2 on page 184) which made me think that, when Jesus had been crucified, his body had been moved and buried in Egypt. White Arrow had not confirmed this, but the thought was there with me. As I stood in the middle of this group of desert Bedouin I knew that only they would know, not the ordinary people of Egypt. 'Was Jesus buried here?' I asked, pointing to the desert. 'In Egypt?' They all said yes. My feelings had been right!

Sheban suggested that I went on the camel with him while Val continued to the Step Pyramid with the horse-and-carriage man. I agreed – after all, he had left the other tourists to come to see us. Val was quite happy about it. I climbed up on the camel and crossed the desert towards the Step Pyramid.

'Sheban,' I said, as I sat behind him on the camel, 'I wrote to your brother Mohammed when I returned home last time. Did he get the letter?'

'Yes,' replied Sheban. 'I would like you to visit my home before you return to England. I have letters for you – one from me and one from Mohammed.' I wondered why they had not sent them by post. Like Native Americans, they were not great letter-writers, so I put it down to that. 'Will you come?' asked Sheban.

'Yes, Sheban. Thank you. I'm only here for a few days, but I could come Monday if that's all right.'

'Okay,' he said. 'I will meet you at ten and we will talk.' Then he said, 'If someone offered me a million dollars I would turn it down to see you.' He obviously had to be nice to tourists, I thought, for it was his living. But he repeated what he had said and I thanked him. 'You think I am joking,' he said.

'No, Sheban, I'm sure you mean it,' I replied.

I then asked him a question. 'Sheban, will it be all right if I do a bit of digging? Will anyone stop me? It is for God. I want to pray here.' Sheban said it would be all right. I relaxed. If I did anything wrong he would tell me. Many people have gone to dig in Egypt and have taken things. People are thus rightly suspicious of strangers and I did not want someone asking me what I was doing or why. If I could do White Arrow's work quickly and simply it would be best.

The camel stopped near the Step Pyramid. Val was already there. We walked slowly towards the Step Pyramid, with Sheban in front of us. It was getting warmer now. We walked up some stairs, and as we got to the top Sheban stopped and showed us a line of cobras carved out of stone. As he was telling us the story behind it he took my camera. 'Come,' he said. 'I will take a picture of you with them.'

I stepped up and was turning for him to take it when I remembered that I had my jacket with the embroidered fish tied around my waist. Laughingly, I turned and said, 'Sheban, here, take a picture of my jacket.'

'No,' he said. 'I know about the fish.'

My stomach turned. I remembered the words White Arrow had said: 'A man will recognize the fish and come to you to help.' My head was spinning. I heard Sheban say, 'I will take a picture of you.' He indicated that I should put the fish behind me.

Excitement then took over. My heart was racing. I needed to know more, but I had to wait for the picture to be taken. Val had hers taken too. We followed Sheban towards the Step Pyramid. A guide came forward and spoke to Sheban. Sheban then said, 'This man will take you to the pyramid – I will wait here until you return.' Val and I followed the man. Val said to me excitedly, 'He knows about the fish!' 'Yes, I know, but first I must do the things White Arrow wants.'

We were both shocked, but I had learned that on this journey *facts* were what was important. Sheban might not have meant what I was hoping to hear – that he truly knew what the fish represented. I did not know myself. I just wore it, presuming that the man who was to come forward would explain why it was so important for me to wear it. Then my mind returned to the Step Pyramid – here it was, a few feet away. I was eager to get to the entrance, still worried that I would not be able to do what White Arrow wanted me to do – to dig with my hands.

The guide was very nice. He introduced himself as Abdullah, and somehow I knew he would be all right. I told him I had to pray to God and explained what I was going to do. He said it was fine. As I faced the entrance I once again used the power of the staff. 'God help me to help White Arrow.'

I started to walk the required steps towards my left. This time there was no sign of Bear or anyone else. I then took a number of steps forward and knelt down. I said my prayers and started digging. I lifted the first handful of sand and looked up to God and thanked him for this Earth, and then started to take a few handfuls out. It was not long before I hit hard rock and could go no further. White Arrow had already told me that on one of the digs I would hit hard ground and he was right. I got out a cigarette and broke it up. Val was videoing behind me, and the guide was watching me a few feet away.

After I had put the tobacco in, I put the sand back and prayed once again. As I got up the guide said, 'I understand.' I wondered what he meant and hoped he meant the tobacco. He took us back to the entrance of the Step Pyramid and more photographs were taken. I made sure I videoed the entrance, for in future I would have to prove that I was here in January 1994. We walked slowly back to Sheban, who was waiting at the top of the steps.

'Come,' he said. 'We will have tea.' I looked where he was pointing and there were five men sitting having tea, including the carriage driver. We took more photographs of them and sat down to receive tea from one of them. Sheban sat next to me. I could not contain my burning question any longer. 'Sheban, do you truly know what the fish means?'

He pointed to my jacket and the fish and then pointed his finger to the sky. Still looking at me he said, 'It is the Big One.'

It sounds ridiculous, but I thought, I haven't got a big fish there. Both fish on my jacket were small. Then Val said, 'The Big One, Ann! He means God!'

I looked back at Sheban. 'Yes the Big One, God.'

Pointing to the other five men I asked Sheban, 'Do they know what the sign means?'

'Yes. They have all recognized that you carry the fish.' I sat in amazement, trying to take it all in, but at the same time wondering what was so important about the fish.

How could I travel halfway across the world and meet someone in a strange land who knew this sign that White Arrow had told me to carry? I was thrilled and baffled, glad that I had trusted and followed White Arrow's instructions in wearing it. Once again, it was proof of the veracity of the Spirit. But at the same time I was curious to know what was so important about the fish and what it meant – I was hardly prepared for the answers that followed.

However, first we need to look at some of the words I had been given before this visit, and which I have not yet shown.

ZAIH KAHLET	narrow corridor village
MEWULATAH MAHUA	deep valley kindness good
FELAT MOWEH BANAHS	link appointment meeting with people

As I sipped the tea, Sheban said, 'A German man came ten months ago asking me to show him where the fish was. I refused. You wear the fish: it is a sign you need our help. I can show you. You are the first to wear the fish. We have known for centuries that one day someone would come, and that person would carry the fish.'

My thoughts went back to the Native Americans again. They had waited for the symbols. Now I was bringing one to the Bedouin, who had also waited for a symbol. 'I know you are with God and work for him,' said Sheban. 'The fish is Jesus.'

I felt sick. Surely I should have realized it meant Jesus! I had been more preoccupied with having it recognized than asking White Arrow what it meant. My hands were shaking. I needed to know more now, but Sheban said, 'I knew when you came last year you were the one, but we had to wait . . . wait for the sign of the fish.'

The shock hit me hard, but I carried on. I asked Sheban how much I owed him. 'Nothing,' he said. 'I do not want money.' I was touched – these people were poor and could only feed their families on what the tourists paid them. Sheban had borrowed the camel from his friend to be able to reach us, so I paid him what he owed his friend.

As we returned to our hired car and driver, Sheban said to me, 'I must see you before you leave for England.'

'Okay,' I replied.

'There is much we have to talk about,' he continued. 'Will you come to my family for the day? We will cook dinner for you and then talk. There is much to say.'

I confirmed our arrangement for Monday; I too needed to know what Sheban had to tell me. I hugged him and thanked him, and he said quietly, 'You make God happy.' Then he opened the car door for us and spoke to the driver.

I shouted out of the window to him: 'Will it be all right to bring my Egyptian friend, Hala?' He knew, I'm sure, that she was also a guide.

'No,' he said. 'It is better just you and Val.'

'Okay, Sheban, I will see you Monday morning at ten.' We drove off.

I leaned back, remembering what Sheban had said about Jesus. I had asked him earlier if Moses and Jesus had spent time at Unas. Sheban had said yes, that they had both hidden at Unas in their time. The Bedouin knew he was buried near there. Everything I had written had been right.

Everything I was doing was being verified by total strangers, yet the thought of it all daunted me. I was wary of the future. If I produced the evidence and the truth, how would people take it? But I put it out of my head. After I had given the world what White Arrow wanted me to provide, I could at least live a normal and quiet life – or so I hoped!

I thought about how people had reacted towards me in the past two days. Hala and her fiancé, both from relatively wealthy families, believed without doubt that White Arrow could open the tomb, and just accepted it as a fact. Now the simple Bedouin people of the desert were accepting that I was working for God through Jesus (White Arrow). No one was questioning me. It made me feel good. It seemed White Arrow was bringing the two together, rich and poor, because it would help the world accept him. The trees could be saved if we all pulled together.

· 22 ·

Sunrays and Horseshoes

'What a day, Val!'

'Yes, Ann, are you okay?'

'Fine,' I replied. I looked at her. She was a good friend. I often worried about her. The shocks were great for me, and sometimes the weight of it all wore me down, so it must have been affecting her too. 'How *are* you, Val?'

'Pleased for you, Ann.' I knew she was indeed pleased.

But I still had to think of what we had to do next. We were soon to meet Hala and go to dinner. I was hungry. We stopped at the hotel to change quickly, then left for Hala's home, with my blue book in hand. Hala was ready. We found a lovely restaurant and settled into our seats.

After we had eaten I brought the blue book out of my bag. There were things I needed to ask. After a few questions Hala asked why in one of the drawings I had drawn three pyramids with the Sphinx opposite the middle one (*see* figure 14.5 on page 135); the main pyramid was actually the first one.

White Arrow spoke through me. 'I mean the first pyramid. It is the way Little One draws. There are reasons.' I myself knew those reasons. It was a decoy – if anyone found my work, they would go to the wrong place. 'The lion was put there because it is God, not the Sphinx as man knows it. The lion is God and the pharaohs knew this.'

The next morning we would have to get up at 4.30 and be outside Cheops at 5. White Arrow's instructions were clear. I was to sit from 5 to 7am and watch the sun come up. I was to observe the great shadow of Cheops. It meant we would have to be in bed early. Hala told me she would not be able to come; Mohammed was not very happy about her being out so early. I understood. She told us she would pick us up at the hotel at 10.30.

Val and I arrived back at the hotel at 7pm and booked an alarm call and a cab. I did not know if I would be allowed to get near to Cheops, but somehow I had to try. If I did not, it meant I would not complete my journey and I would have to return again. So I prayed that if I paid the guards they would let me through.

I needed to get some money, and the receptionist had told us that a hotel up the road would change money. So, with my jacket on, we left the hotel. When we got to the hotel gates we could not remember whether to turn left or right. We were sure it was left, but halfway down the road we realized that we had taken the wrong turning and were lost. There was a couple standing on the corner of the street. I went to speak to them, hoping they understood English. 'Excuse me, do you know where the Mena House Hotel is, please?'

They answered in Arabic and pointed back to where we had come from. We had been walking only a few yards when we heard running feet. A young man in his twenties stopped at my side. 'I heard you asking about the Mena House Hotel,' he said. 'I can show you where it is.' I was not too sure – both Val and I were nervous, being in a strange country. However, I knew I would be safe with White Arrow around, so I said, 'Great, thank you.'

He introduced himself as Ibrahim and showed us his ID card to reassure us. He had a young friend with him, and told us he was training to be a guide at the Great Pyramid. Was he going to be my answer? Had White Arrow sent him?

'Tell me,' I asked. 'Do you know how to get into the Great Pyramid past the guards?' I explained what I wanted to do. Something made me feel I could trust him, and I had to take the chance. All I needed was to be shown the way in.

'Yes,' he replied. 'I will take you.'

'You'll have to be at our hotel at 4.30 in the morning.'

'Yes, I promise I'll be there. I will be there, and I can get you in.' I hoped so. Everybody had told me there was no way I could be outside Cheops at 5am – it was just not allowed. However, they did not know White Arrow's power; if he wanted me there then there would be a way. By the time we had reached the hotel I knew the boy had been sent by White Arrow – I felt in my heart that I could trust him.

As he waved goodbye he said, 'I will not go to bed tonight, so

I will be sure to get here in the morning.' He added that he knew a man who was called 'The Man of the Pyramids'; his name was Fergany. Ibrahim told us Fergany knew the back way into the pyramid, along which no tourists were taken. Fergany would be there in the morning as well.

Val and I headed for bed. We were tired. We had been in Egypt two days and still had three to go. What else would happen on this journey? As I pulled the bedclothes back I remembered my promise to White Arrow to talk to him and the aliens daily. So I grabbed the writing pad and climbed into bed, propped up the pillows and started to write. The door to the balcony was open. White Arrow appeared. This is what I wrote:

Tomorrow I must get up early at 4.30 to be at the Great Pyramid. We are both very tired but I must go. White Arrow, I need you! Suddenly he says, 'I will be with you, Little One. You are safe. When you get there you are to watch where the shadow falls.'

'Will I be at the right pyramid, White Arrow?'

'Yes, Little One. It is Cheops. We will be waiting for you to arrive.'

'All of you?'

'Yes, Little One. Look towards the sky when you first arrive. While you are waiting for the shadow, pray and look. I will show you something for two hours. Do not leave till after seven.'

Then he left. Suddenly, the phone rang. It was Hala, wishing us well for the following morning. I thanked her and said good night, and we turned the lights out.

The following morning, I turned over, hearing the phone ringing. I heard Val answer. There was a knocking at the door – it was our breakfast. I crept out of bed, half asleep. I am not at my best in the morning, but this was important! Val opened the door while I got ready in the bathroom.

I sat and drank my coffee, putting my shoes on at the same time. I knew young Ibrahim would be waiting downstairs. I had said 4.30 to him, forgetting that I wouldn't be ready until 5. Breakfast finished, we collected all the cameras and made sure I had the blue book with me, and left. We had made good time. I was hoping the cab would be on time. The pyramids were only five minutes away, so we could be there just after 5.

Ibrahim spotted us first. I apologized to him for our lateness and went to the desk to ask if the taxi was here. Ibrahim said, 'You do not need a taxi. We have a car.' Oh well, White Arrow will look after us, I thought. There were two other men in the car, but I could not let myself worry about that. I prayed that whoever was coming with us would be able to take us to the right place. Ibrahim introduced me to Fergany. He was in his thirties and seemed pleasant and trustworthy. We drove around the back streets and eventually stopped at a dead-end road. There was a dog barking quite close by. It was still very dark. Val and I got out with Fergany, who told the others to go. We heard the car start up as we followed him. In front of us were a hill and some rocks. We started to climb. I didn't think I had to rock-climb for you, White Arrow! I said mentally, pulling my coat closer. We proceeded to climb to the top. We walked across and sat on a hill opposite the Great Pyramid. Fergany explained that we would have to sit here until 6.15.

The guards of the Great Pyramid were still asleep and we would have to wait until then. I was very lucky to have found Fergany. Everybody who worked at the Great Pyramid knew 'the Man of the Pyramids', so they allowed him to be there. He would have no trouble taking me where I wanted to go.

I took a video of Cairo. I could see the lights of the outer villages all around me. The peace was lovely. I put the video away and shut my eyes in prayer. All three of us were silent together. 'White Arrow, thank you for so much.'

I spoke to his father: 'God, on this journey, do not let me fail you. I will do whatever is asked of me to help you and your son.' Then I said the Lord's Prayer.

As I opened my eyes I heard the Koran being chanted. Fergany said, 'The prayer you can hear – it is saying that one day Mohammed will return.' Then he added quietly, 'I knew someone was coming from God and I know it is you.'

My thoughts went back to Sheban. How did they know it was me? Why were they saying these things when I had told them nothing about White Arrow and his journey? Were they seeing something I could not? I was beginning to believe they were aware of his presence. White Arrow said, 'You are in safe hands.'

'Thanks, White Arrow,' I said, looking around me at the wonderment of it all. Thinking about all of this was too much.

'Do not worry, Little One. You will cope.' Yes, I thought. Sitting here on a hill waiting for the dawn to break, I knew my faith in

White Arrow would not leave me – I would cope because I believed what was happening was for the good of mankind.

Fergany said, 'I pray everyone in the world will have their hearts opened.' We all held hands and prayed together for peace on Earth.

After praying, I asked Fergany where Moses had come from. How far was it from where we were? He pointed to the east. 'You go to Sinai, to St Catherine. It is not too far. The mountain takes four hours to climb. I can take you when you return, if you wish.'

'Thanks, Fergany,' I said. Was that on my pathway? My journey at present was here, however, at Giza and the other pyramids.

We were getting cold. Fergany realized this and said, 'Soon we will be leaving for Cheops.' At least movement would keep us warm. Suddenly we could see a figure walking below us. Fergany was silent. We watched as a man came slowly towards us. Fergany said something to him in his own language and introduced us to him. He was a guard who had been on watch all night. He stayed for a few minutes, then left.

'Come,' said Fergany. We started to walk down the hill towards the Great Pyramid. There was a small space between the rocks at the bottom, and Fergany suggested that we stand between the rocks to get a bit warmer. I started jumping up and down and Val joined in. I never thought I would be doing exercises at 6.15 in the morning beside one of the wonders of the world, but it certainly made us a bit warmer!

'Come,' said Fergany and off we went again. The morning light was coming up and we walked around the pyramid. I had been before, but not to this part. There, in front of us, I saw a large ship that had been found buried at the side of Cheops. As we passed it, Fergany said he was taking me to where the shadow was to fall; I had told him this was what I had come for. White Arrow had wanted me to video the shadow, for this was where some of the secrets were hidden. This was the last item on my instructions, except for the place of the Virgin Mary. I had to return there too, but why I did not know.

Fergany had a holy feeling about him. He had already been in contact with the Spirit and with God, and he knew many things. Like Sheban and the Native Americans he would not say much – he would just wait and watch – but I still was not sure whether he knew as much as Sheban and I did not want to say anything either.

For White Arrow's instructions to be verified, people had to approach me – that was the way. So Fergany knew only that I was there to watch the shadow, and nothing else. I could not tell anyone White Arrow's secrets, in case I told the wrong person, who could use them for the wrong purposes.

We arrived at the place. Behind Cheops there was a place where the servants and others were buried. Only kings and queens were buried in the pyramid. It still amazed me how simple the hidden secrets of the pyramids were. People had said that they had been built to align with the stars, but they were only partly right. The night played an important part, but so did the day – it was in the shadow of the pyramid that everything was hidden.

Fergany outlined where the shadow would fall. It fell over the burial ground. But then he said something which took me aback: the shadow does not fall until mid-morning, about 10. I turned to White Arrow. 'Why have you insisted on my being here between 5 and 7am?' Before I let him answer, I decided to walk down the small hill to the burial ground. I turned to Val and Fergany. 'I hope you don't mind, but I need to be on my own for a while.'

I left them, taking my writing pad, and walked down to the burial ground and stood there, looking around. There was a feeling of overwhelming love around me. I looked at Cheops and took in the wonder of it. It was still cold, but I had to forget that. Suddenly, I felt White Arrow – but this time he was Jesus. 'While we are here we are one. I will return as White Arrow after we have finished, but it is important that you are with me as I was.'

I felt humble. I have always had faith, but I'm not really 'religious'. With White Arrow I have never had to be anything but myself, but when he came as Jesus, I felt the awesome power of God and true spirituality – it is difficult to express in words what it is like to have Jesus in one's presence. I always preferred White Arrow as White Arrow, but I knew it was important to him to help me accept who he once was. That was why I was here. I waited until Jesus spoke.

'I have come many times, and I wrote the secrets that they speak of. Moses was at my side on many occasions and helped me on my journey while on Earth. Here you will find the words I spoke many years ago.' He pointed around me. 'While I spoke to Moses, he showed me many hiding places, for he knew his land well. Here are the secrets.' He pointed. 'You are with Christ until the sun comes up, then I will return as White Arrow.' I could see sandals on my feet.

I sat down on a small wall. White Arrow – or Jesus – was still with me. I wondered once again why they had chosen me for such an important journey. While I sat there I felt it was a heavy burden to carry, but then, how could I let White Arrow down? I looked around, still amazed at how clever he had been in hiding the secrets. I would still have to return to England and get the Coptic language sorted out before I really knew the spot I was seeking. The Egyptian part of the journey would soon be finished.

I looked at Val and Fergany up on the hill. I wanted to make sure they were all right. I returned my gaze to the pyramid and knelt down and prayed. For a while I stayed on my knees in silence, just thanking God. I knew it had gone 7. Not many words had been said, but it seemed that what I had to do had been completed. White Arrow had now gone. I just could not believe that I had stood where Jesus had stood – and yet the proof was there in front of me! Now I had to wait for the time when White Arrow would open the tomb to the secrets, for me to take to the world.

I climbed the hill to Val and Fergany. We spoke for a while. Then something made me want to return once more to the place where I had stood with White Arrow. White Arrow appeared. 'Little One, you will see the shadow. It is important for the time when you find the letters. But that is different to this morning, for this morning is for being with me and for showing you the secrets. These past two hours we have been as one, but also you have received a great power. This you will realize in time, for it is given to you to help on this journey.'

I understood. In all the journeys I have made for White Arrow, no one and nothing was as important and as deeply moving as this morning, being with the *real* White Arrow. It will live with me forever.

As I started walking away I looked down and saw a horseshoe. I picked it up. It surprised and delighted me. A horseshoe is auspicious or lucky, and I hoped it would be for me. But I also wanted to take something back that would remind me of this morning. I picked it up and said to Val and Fergany, 'Look what I have found!'

Fergany smiled and took it from me.

'Come,' he said. 'Hold it with me, for I want to bless it for you.' He shut his eyes and intoned a prayer. When he had finished he explained that the prayer had been an important one and that this horseshoe would bring me good luck for thousands of years. 'It is the best prayer from the Koran,' he said quietly. I was touched. He had thought specially of me. I heard White Arrow call me again and went back down the small hill.

'Look towards the sky,' he said. 'The sunrays coming through the clouds are my father's. The sunrays you see *are* my father.' I was transfixed. Once again he left.

As I walked, my eyes fell on another horseshoe. This is silly! I thought. I picked it up. I climbed back up and told them I had found another. I took one more look, but we had to go, for there was still much more to do. I felt satisfied that I had completed another part of White Arrow's journey.

I pulled my jacket close round me. It was the jacket with the two fish on the back. I had promised I would wear it every day until I knew completely what the fish meant. I also needed to be sure I had found the right person in Sheban; I was sure in my heart he was the right person, but I had to verify it. I put my trust in White Arrow, knowing he would prove all this to me beyond doubt at the right time. After taking pictures of the Sphinx we left to visit Fergany's home.

As we passed the Sphinx, I took in the full glory of it and knew it was for another time – on this journey other things had to be done first. But the most wonderful feeling about this morning had been that no one had been around. We had had the pyramids all to ourselves! The quietness made me feel special. I had gone back in time, to a period before all the tourists knew of Giza, and it was the most beautiful of feelings. I turned to the Great Pyramids and thanked them for allowing me this special time.

When we arrived at Fergany's we had tea. We soon had to be back at the hotel because we had arranged to meet Hala. I told Fergany this, and he took me to one side and said, 'I would like you to return before you leave, so we can pray in the King's Chamber of Cheops. Please . . . . I would like this very much. We will go in before the tourists arrive, so you would need to be ready at seven in the morning.'

I agreed, and arranged to meet him the day before we left for England – I would meet him outside the hotel. Fergany got us back to the hotel in time and I thanked him. Without him I knew the visit would have been impossible.

· 23 ·

Three and a Half

We did not have much time – just enough for a quick wash and change, and a bite to eat, then we left to pick up Hala. We were going to Matariyah, to the Virgin Tree. Nothing would ever take away the memory of meeting the Virgin Mary the previous year. But now we knew there were two trees, and I wondered what awaited us this time.

Hala started to tell us of a visit to her future mother-in-law's house. It was Mohammed's mother's birthday, and as they sat at the table, the six of them (Mohammed, Hala, her parents and his parents) spoke of me. Although her parents had met me before and had liked me, they had not been aware of my journey, but they were now. Hala had told them the real reason for my being in Egypt and about White Arrow, and although they liked me they feared for Hala.

They were religious people, and although they believed I was a good person in myself they had yet to be persuaded that White Arrow was good, and they told Hala this. Hala had been brought up strictly and taught not to talk back, but for the first time she told them: 'No, White Arrow is good and I have no fear of him. I want to help him on his journey. I have nothing to be frightened of, for Ann has shown me White Arrow is good.' Later, when her mother-in-law sought to blow out the candles, the flames would not die. They were surprised by this and took it as a sign of God.

I said, 'Hala, when I see your family I will tell them that you and they have nothing to fear, for White Arrow is good.'

'Yes, please,' she said. 'If *you* tell them, they will believe and not worry.' We were to see them that evening. I did not want them to worry, although I understood why they did, for I am also a mother, and in their position I would worry too.

The car came to a halt. We had been so busy talking that we had not realized we had arrived. But it was not St Mary's Church, it was another one nearby.

We had a look in the gift shop there, and Val noticed a clock with a picture of Jesus on it. It opened up, showing a map of the world. White Arrow had always given everybody a watch or a clock on his journey; it was his way of giving something back to people for their help, and time means a lot to him. Hala spotted the clock at the same time as Val and said, 'Oh, please, Val, let me get that for Ann!' Val also wanted to buy it for me, but she let Hala do so instead. I was over the moon – I knew it was White Arrow's doing. I had been so busy buying everybody else presents that he wanted someone to get me one! It is now one of my most treasured possessions.

After about half an hour, we left for Matariyah. On the way, I leaned my head back and said a silent prayer. White Arrow wanted me to go, although I felt that the Virgin Mary would not be there. I had been blessed to see her last time. I used the staff anyway as White Arrow had wanted me to. Then I heard Hala say 'We are here. We have to go down this small road.'

We stopped outside what looked like a small building; it was actually a large wall with double wooden doors. Looking up, I could see the tops of trees. To the side was another small wall with two open iron gates. Inside there were some small grounds, almost a park, where people could walk. Hala spoke to some people at the place where one had to pay to go into the garden behind the big wall. Three women came forward, to show us through. They opened the door to a private garden. It was separated from the park, because of its holiness; it had to be sealed from everything else.

Val and Hala went before me. I had no thoughts in my mind – in fact I was trying to put the change away in my purse and check the camera. In the middle of the courtyard there was a large circle, and in the middle of the circle stood three or four trees. A couple of them had died, for there were no leaves on them at all.

On the farther side was a trough which had once been filled with water, although it looked like a seat from where I was. The Virgin Mary was sitting there. I just could not believe it – I had not expected her to be there, or at least not straight away. I watched her as the others were chatting. As I walked around she sat there, watching me.

Hala grabbed my attention. 'I have told these people you are doing a doctorate in geology and that you will be taking some earth for research.' Hala knew that I had to eat some earth and take some home with me. She went back to them, and Val followed. There were five people in the courtyard with us, all of whom worked there. I was therefore left to my own devices – Hala and Val knew this was necessary, though they did not know if I was seeing anything.

My eyes went back to Mary. She was now standing up and moved to the edge of the circle. She was in dark clothes, as she had been when I first saw her, but this time I could see her face more clearly – a pretty young face. I did not have time to take it all in, as so much was happening. I stood in front of her. Hala was taking notes and spoke about the trees. The dead tree was over 2,000 years old (*see* figure 23.1). The name Matariyah derives from the Virgin Mary, who drank from the well when she came here with Jesus when he was two years old. As I heard Hala telling me this, Mary spoke. 'Touch the tree, for it will grow again.'

I leaned forward and laid my hand on the dead tree. 'What is going on, White Arrow? I can't perform miracles . . .' Then I looked at Mary. Perhaps she could perform the miracle through me. I left my hand on the tree for a few minutes.

'It will grow again,' I heard her say.

'White Arrow, is this all in my mind?' I asked. 'Is it because I wanted to see her?' No answer came back. Mary just stood there saying nothing. I shut my eyes and opened them again. No, she was still there. I remembered that I had to walk round the tree three and a half times. White Arrow appeared – this time as a Red Indian. I was glad he was back as White Arrow.

'This is how you wanted me to be, Little One,' he said.

'Yes, thanks, White Arrow.' We walked.

The Virgin Mary had gone to my left side and White Arrow was to my right and we started to walk the three and a half circuits. As I got half way round I hit my head on a low branch. Thanks, I thought. I come and do all this and this is the thanks I get! I rubbed my head. It was the only way I could handle this journey, by being myself, and White Arrow knew it. My attention was soon back on what I had to do, and we continued going around – but now, every time I saw the branch, I ducked!

Figure 23.1 The tree at Matariyah

I stopped opposite the point where I had started, and Mary went back into the circle. She asked me to kneel in front of her, but I was aware of a man behind me, watching, so I held back. 'Kneel, my child,' said the Virgin Mary, and I did so. I was truly blessed, and it no longer mattered if people did not understand what I was doing. I had to do it. As I did so she came forward and laid her hands on my head, giving me a blessing. I felt like crying, at the same time asking myself, why me?

'Stand, my child,' she said, and I did. 'Believe in what you see, for what you see is true. Do not worry, for my son has sent you. The journey will be long and hard, but help is on the way. I will speak with my son, for I too want to follow your journey and help. Do not fear the journey. The water will appear. Do not fear. Believe what you see, for what you see is true. You will put your feet near the tree. I will water them. You no longer need to seek me now, for I will be waiting.'

I walked back to where the rest of the people were gathered, talking. I was wondering what Mary had meant by 'the water will appear', and trying to remember what else I had to do for White Arrow. I had to remember to eat some soil and take some soil and a stone home with me. My mind was on so many things – what I had witnessed and what I had to do – that I could not worry about

the others. I hoped Val would make sure she wrote down everything that was said.

When I got to the place I put each foot in turn in the circle. Mary
watered my feet as she had done the previous time. I bent forward
to get a piece of dirt and put it into my mouth. It did not matter if
it tasted terrible or if anyone noticed. I had been told to do it, and
there I was, eating it. While I was doing so I picked up some stones
and placed them in a plastic bag to take home with me. As I was
doing this the man in the group brought me a handful of seeds. I
thanked him. The Virgin Mary said, 'Dig a small hole near the tree.'

I put my finger into the earth and scooped out a couple of small
bits of earth, making a small hole. I stood and looked at her as she
said, 'I carried the Son of God. You walk with the Son of God. I sit
here because it is easier for you to see me.' Earlier, I had asked her
why she sat on the trough, thinking it would be uncomfortable,
forgetting she was of the Spirit. She had given me the answer. 'I
do not mind people seeing me. Soon, the waters of the rainforests
will flow. The Earth will live again. As I carried my son, you have
White Arrow. We are the same.'

I could not believe this, yet I had to. These were her words – she,
the Virgin Mary, was telling me these things, and a sense of
trepidation came upon me. 'White Arrow, I'm just not good
enough for this,' I said.

I sat on the small bench with Val and Hala. The Virgin Mary
had gone. As we talked, my eyes went to a bent branch from the
dead tree that was almost touching the earth. As I watched, it
changed to running water. Was that what the Virgin Mary meant?
Would water appear to help the tree grow again?

Forgetting that Hala had told me of a well here, I asked her
whether there was a river here before. She asked the woman, who
said no. It was only on my return home that I remembered that
there had been a *well*, not a river. Hala spoke to the woman in
charge and asked her whether, if the tree started to grow, she
would tell us. The lady agreed, and gave Hala a card with her name
and telephone number. 'I will let you know.' We left, and I videoed
the outside and took more pictures with my camera.

We left the tree and went to the church nearby. I went in to pray.
As I prayed, I heard the words 'Seek the Stone of the Plough.' I also
saw a silver cartouche and then the sign of the fish. Hala asked
someone there about the sign of the fish and once again we were
told it showed people in olden times that there was a meeting to

take place with Jesus: the fish meant 'Jesus Christ is coming'. Why had I not realized that? There were so many questions that needed answering but I would have to wait until I returned home. There was still much more to be done before I left Egypt.

The following information on Matariyah was contributed by Adrian Gilbert.

Matariyah

The church of Matariyah is built near the ancient tree that is reputed to be the one that Mary rested under when the Holy Family arrived in Heliopolis. This is a sycamore tree, which in ancient times would have been sacred to the goddesses Isis and Hathor, who are really one and the same. In one of the old gnostic gospels that I have come across there is more about this legend. It says:

> Hence they went to that sycamore tree, which is now called Matarea,
> And in Matarea Lord Jesus caused a well to spring forth, in which St Mary washed his coat;
> And a balsam grows in that country from the sweat which ran down there from the Lord Jesus.
> Thence they proceeded to Memphis, and saw Pharaoh, and abode three years in Egypt.

Like most of the rest of this gospel, this is clearly an elaboration of what really happened. For one thing they could not have visited Pharaoh as there were no pharaohs at that time – Egypt had been taken over by the Romans and incorporated into their empire. They may well have stayed three years, however. I believe Jesus was born in 7 BC. King Herod died in 4 BC, and we know that they did not return to Israel until his death.

It was probably Mary who dug the hole to get water, not just to wash the baby's 'coat' (nappies?) but also to give him a drink. The reference to his sweating profusely indicates he was hot. Sycamore trees, incidentally, were a source of balsam, so there could have been some confusion here between his sweat and the 'sweat' of the tree itself. The Arabic name for Heliopolis is Ayin esh Shems, which means 'fountain of the sun'. Heliopolis means 'city of the sun' in Greek. So clearly the Arabic name refers to this holy fountain of Matariyah.

There is also a symbolic meaning to the bringing of Jesus to Heliopolis, relating to the old phoenix myth. As the herald of a new age, Jesus is indeed the phoenix. I also suspect that the bennu or grey heron has a similar meaning to the stork in European mythology, as a bringer of babies. By coming as a baby to Heliopolis, Jesus was perhaps fulfilling Egyptian prophecies.

We now had to go on to the Village of Giza. White Arrow had asked me to return there, but I still was not sure why. He had said that someone there could help me on my journey. It did not take us long to get there and we bought tickets. We looked around. There was a boat trip, but I felt it was unnecessary. While the others looked around I left them to walk round on my own. 'White Arrow, what am I looking for?'

The only people working there were people selling things; there did not seem to be anyone who could help me. I waited for White Arrow to tell me what to do or where to look. Was this the place White Arrow meant, or was there another village of Giza? Only White Arrow could tell or show me. Nothing seemed to make sense here. On my return home I would have to go to White Arrow and ask.

We got back into our hired car and went to a restaurant for dinner. I was ravenous. We spoke of many things over the meal. I had the blue book with me and asked Hala some more questions. Hala was always careful where the blue book was concerned, worrying in case anyone could overhear us, but it was mainly fear for me. I was inclined to talk without realizing just how important White Arrow's information was. I was unaware that someone could take it away from me and use it to their own benefit, and it was this that Hala was worried about. She cared, and she knew White Arrow's journey was important. It was good to have her protecting me. We decided to put the book away and talk of what was going to happen that evening.

'My parents are looking forward to seeing you again, Ann. Please talk to them and explain that I'm safe helping you. Mohammed is convinced, so he will not stop me, but I know my parents will believe you.'

'Don't worry, Hala, I will.' We got up and left.

I was tired after getting up so early, but at the same time I wanted to see Hala's parents. I had got to like them and had been looking forward to seeing them. We arrived just after six. Mohammed was to come to join us later. Hala's mother greeted us warmly at the door. Their home was beautiful and as we walked in we were greeted by Hala's brother and her half-sister. I had brought them all gifts from England.

Hala's stepfather appeared at the top of the stairs. 'Hello, how are you? And thank you for arranging the lovely welcome at the airport,' I said, all in one breath.

He laughed. 'You are welcome!' We hugged each other when he reached the bottom of the stairs. We all settled down, coffee and tea were made, and sweets were served. They made us very welcome and we were soon all talking.

Hala's mother got up and left, only to reappear a few moments later. She held out a box to me. 'This is a gift for you from us,' she said, pointing to her husband. I was surprised and pleased and started to open the box. They had bought me a watch – the most unusual watch one could imagine. It was a fob watch which could be hung on a stand of deep reddish-purple marble or worn with a gold chain or pinned on as a fob watch or brooch. I am the sort of person who likes to give but finds it hard when someone gives something to me. All I could do was hug them, saying how lovely it was. How could people be so caring, especially when they had only met me twice before? What made me really happy was that they had bought Val a present, too, a filofax. They had noticed that she had done a lot of writing and they had cared enough to find out what each of us would really like.

Mohammed soon came, and we settled down to talk. First, I (or actually, White Arrow) helped Hala's mother with a small problem, and then I gave the others clairvoyance. Before long I started to tell Hala's parents about part of my journey – first about the trees, explaining that White Arrow was here to help the world. White Arrow seemed to be talking through me. I was happy with that, as I knew he could convince them that he is good in nature. Within half an hour they had accepted that Hala was safe.

It was soon time to go. I was very tired – or was I really in shock? Whatever the reason, it was now taking its toll. 'I will return soon, I promise,' I said. We all hugged each other goodbye, then we left.

We arrived back at the hotel at 9pm, eager to get to bed. We fell on the beds, both of us tired out, but first I had to go to White Arrow and the aliens. So with my pillows propped up behind me I sat and wrote.

We have just returned, after getting up at 4.30 this morning. We have not stopped, but as long as it helps White Arrow, that's okay. We have two days left. I think I have done everything, but I feel there is more.

Eagle has just appeared. 'A miracle is to happen.' Twice she has said this. Today a miracle did take place at the Tree of the Virgin Mary.

I was worried today about Tony. 'I used the staff to help you, and Tony came into my mind. Is everything all right at home, White Arrow?'

'Little One, I will look after your family. You need not worry. They are safe. This I promise.' I thanked him, for I love my family. As long as they are okay then I am happy.

'Tomorrow, we will bring you someone who will believe who I am and will help you on your journey for me. This person is a great man who will want to offer his services to me,' said White Arrow. 'You will allow only me to talk.' That meant he would talk through me.

'You have done well, Little One. I thank your friend Val for her support to you on this journey. On this journey many miracles will take place. You will understand this on your further return to Egypt, for you have found the resting place of Jesus Christ. I will let you sleep now. Do not worry, Little One, if on the journey we do not speak to each other, for I will be speaking *through* you instead.'

I felt better as I laid my head on the pillow. Soon I allowed sleep to overcome me.

· 24 ·

Sheban

Upon waking up the following morning I looked at my watch. It was 7.00, and I felt good. I had slept well. As I got up I wondered what would be in store today. I felt I had completed everything except I wanted to return to the tree I had visited the first time I had come to Egypt. I wanted to say thank you and to pray at the tree. If we had the time we could go today, but we had also promised Sheban we would meet him at 10am in Saqqara. We would not be able to do both. Hala had seemed anxious when we had told her of our arrangements with Sheban – she really was not happy about our going. To be fair, Hala had never met Sheban because each time we had been to Ti she had not been able to come with us. I felt I should take her advice and not go.

Val and I went down to breakfast. I also had to get some money so I went to the bank at the Mena House Hotel. The weather was good. I was disappointed not to be going to see Sheban, but there were other things to do. As I did not want to lose him as a friend I decided to send a letter by car. I also wanted to send him my camera as a present. But Val suggested that I use the medallion when we returned to the hotel, and try to tell him through it that I would return.

I was pleased Val had said that. I was upset not to be going, but Hala seemed to know Egyptian people and I had to make a decision as to whether to trust her judgement, even though Val and I knew he was all right. I had two days left, and I could not waste time, but Sheban was important. Hala had been good to us and I did not want her to feel that I did not trust her judgement. I was being torn between the two of them.

It was 9.30 when we got back to the hotel. I decided I would go on the balcony on my own at 10am, as I knew Sheban would be at Saqqara, expecting us to meet him there at that time. As we arrived, Hala was sitting in the foyer waiting for us. She was earlier than usual, so we all went up to our room and ordered breakfast for Hala. When the breakfast arrived there was also a plate of salad on the tray, which none of us could remember ordering. So I decided I would eat it. White Arrow said, 'It is for you, Little One, to give you strength for your journey.' I looked at him. With all he had to do with saving the world he cared enough to make sure I was eating properly! Soon after, I went onto the balcony.

Right opposite me was Cheops. Every time I saw it, it was awesome. I just stood there and looked at it for a few moments, and then suddenly a beam of light came from the pyramid and hit the medallion head-on. The power was so strong that I bent forward. It had taken the wind out of me, yet there was no pain, just the feeling of the force of it. As it hit the medallion, light came all over me from it. I had never witnessed anything so strong. I had come out for one reason and something entirely different was happening!

'Seek the Stone of the Plough,' I heard clearly. I sensed that there was a stone in the Great Pyramid that had travelled from another planet. The light from the stone in the pyramid was now giving the medallion new power, for the Stone of the Plough had come from the same planet as the medallion. At last, I felt I had found it – but what *was* the stone?

Suddenly, the light went from the pyramid. As I stood there, still amazed, I saw the sun shine from within the pyramid. I could see it clearly, then that left, too. I stood for a moment trying to take it all in. To me, another miracle had taken place. Already, some Egyptians believed there was a stone from outer space situated in the Great Pyramid.

I could hear Hala and Val talking in the room and I knew I had to write down what I had just seen. 'Have you finished?' asked Val.

'No, I've just got to write down something, then I'm going back out.'

'Do you want coffee, Ann?' asked Hala.

'Yes, please.' I grabbed the pen and wrote it all down. I took the coffee outside on the balcony and sat down, trying to concentrate. I asked White Arrow if I could go to the medallion.

It took a few seconds before I arrived at Saqqara through the medallion. I could see Sheban a couple of yards in front of me and I walked over to him. He seemed sad and upset and it made me feel even more guilty that I had let him down. I touched his arm, hoping he could feel something. He seemed to brush his hand against the part I had touched, but he did not know what it was. 'Sheban, listen to me, I will be back. I will be back,' I kept saying, trying to get him to hear me. 'Please, White Arrow, let him know, let him hear me. I will be back, Sheban.'

I then left and hoped he knew I would be back. I finished my cup of coffee and got up to join the others. Val knew I had passed on my thoughts to Sheban, so nothing was said. I went to the bathroom. As I was washing my hands, I could feel my body aching. White Arrow spoke to me. 'It is good to ache, Little One,' he said. 'It is the body releasing all the tension and load you carry.'

Unexpectedly, my mother suddenly came in – she talks to me occasionally from the realm of the Spirit. 'The rose will come, and there will be a kiss on it.' She also spoke of someone important coming who would help me on my journey. I have come to accept these gratuitous tips without question – something would emerge, in time.

White Arrow continued. 'Have you wondered, Little One, the real reason for the balcony doors being left open?'

'Well, yes, White Arrow, for the aliens,' I replied.

'Besides that,' he said. I had always thought that that was the only reason. 'The other reason is that the pyramid gives you strength for your journey. The Stone of the Plough has special strength. This is one of many reasons we have brought you here. It can give you and the medallion much power,' explained White Arrow.

I thanked him. It was so much to take in at once, but I did understand and I was glad. 'Please, if the medallion didn't work this morning, let Sheban know I'm returning.'

'He will know, Little One, do not worry. You will sit outside tonight opposite the pyramid.'

'Yes, I will, White Arrow.'

We left the hotel around noon. Something important I had forgotten to do was to take a video of the Virgin Tree; I needed this for evidence. I had taken a lot of photographs, but not a video. Hala said it would be fine with her. We stopped off first and did some shopping at a bazaar, then carried on to the Virgin Tree.

We discussed some words I had brought with me from England, words that François had helped me with. I was amazed at how accurate everything was. These are the words:

CAIRO BLAWENO PATAHS   Cairo cloak stretch out
FETAH MAYEAS   Lady (Mary) water

The car pulled up. I jumped out and videoed the outside of the church. All I had to do now was return to the first church the following day to say thank you to Mary for White Arrow. Hala asked the driver of our car to stop outside the Papyrus Museum, where she got me some plain papyrus paper to study on my return.

We had spoken at great length about the pyramids that morning and I had learned many things from White Arrow. I was stunned; there was so much to digest and absorb. I just had to lock it away in my mind for another time.

We arrived back at the hotel at 4pm. As I was lifting the shopping out of the car I heard Val say excitedly, 'Ann! Ann! It's Sheban!' I looked up and there he stood. My heart was thumping.

He was standing there in a long, light blue jalabiyah gown with a white cloth around his head and shoulders. He had travelled all the way from Saqqara, losing a whole day's pay. I must have hurt him by not turning up and yet he had travelled all this way to see me. Had the medallion worked? So many things were going through my mind. I put my arms around him and hugged him, so glad to see him, yet ashamed I had let him down. He responded warmly.

'Come, Sheban, you must come to our hotel room,' I said, still hardly able to believe my eyes. 'How long have you been here?'

'I came by coach with my brother, who works here. I have been waiting since twelve o'clock.'

'You have been here since *then*?' I asked.

'Yes, waiting to see you,' he confirmed.

The hotel was very strict about visitors. Everybody's belongings were usually searched on their return from days out, and I would not have thought that I would be allowed to take a man to my room. Nevertheless, I had to see Sheban privately, so we went to the lift. No one stopped us, but a guard and a porter came up with us in the lift. They did not say anything about Sheban, although in the lobby I could feel people looking. My stomach was churning as we went up. The medallion had worked, but I was still shocked that Sheban had thought it was important to come all those miles to see me.

As we entered the room I asked Val to order coffee and tea for us and I sat Sheban down. 'Sheban, I'm so sorry about this morning, but something came up. I was going to send you a letter to say I would see you next time.' As I said this I was thinking to myself that Hala had been wrong, but I had to be sure. I would wait for coffee to arrive before I asked him the question I so badly needed him to answer. As we waited Sheban said he knew someone was trying to tell me he was wrong – he had a feeling someone was trying to stop me seeing him and was putting doubt into my mind. He had had to come to prove to me his worth.

Again, I was amazed. I knew he worked for God and was with the Spirit, but how could he have known what Hala had said? Just then the coffee and tea arrived. Val poured out our drinks. In my mind there were so many questions, but most of all the matter of the fish. What did it truly mean, why had White Arrow asked me to wear it, and why had a man left his work and travelled to see me because of it? Where could I start? Sheban helped me as he started to explain his story.

'Before you came to Egypt on your first visit, my brother Mohammed went to the mosque to pray. While he was praying he heard a voice tell him a very special person was coming from God. A few weeks later I was at home and as I sat for supper I knew I had to go to my prayer room and take my supper with me. As I prayed, I, too, heard a voice telling me of this person. The voice, it said to look at my supper, and on my plate was a fish.'

Sheban went on to explain that he had known this person was being sent by Jesus. A month had gone by and Mohammed had told him that the person was not coming; they should have been there by now. Sheban, however, said, 'The person *will* come.'

When I first went to Egypt in May 1993, both men knew I was the one they were waiting for, mainly because of my eyes and the things I asked and spoke about. But they could not tell me then; they needed to be absolutely sure, and they both knew what that would involve. Sheban said, 'I went to the mosque alone. I prayed to Allah for help.'

'Sheban, was there a message for me? Do you have a message for me?'

The way he looked at me was just like His Black Horse, one of the Native Americans – knowing everything, but waiting for me to ask. 'To do with what? The pyramids? Tombs? The Sahara Desert?' I felt strongly that he was waiting for me to say something, but I did not know what. What was I to ask? Surely he could tell me! I sat quietly for a few moments. Sheban was sitting on one of the beds, with me opposite him on the other. I put my hands together.

Looking directly at me he started to tell me about a German who had come before to Ti. He said, 'The German had come asking about the fish, and where he could find it.' I had brought the fish symbol, and now he told me something else that was to shake the very soul within me. 'The German had come to ask where the body of Jesus was buried,' said Sheban. 'That is what the fish means. I told the German I would not tell him, and sent him away.'

I looked at him and said, 'Sheban, are you telling me that you *know* where Jesus Christ is buried? Are you telling me that White Arrow has brought me to you for you to show me, and that you knew this when you saw me with the fish?'

'I knew the right person would come. I knew the German and others weren't the right people,' replied Sheban. 'But I know you are the right person, and the people of the desert know, also.'

Sheban had met thousands of tourists, and now he was saying I was the one sent by Jesus, and that he was going to show me where Jesus was buried. It was too much. Sobbing started inside me, and as I knelt in front of him and hugged him the sobs got stronger. I had to go. I rushed into the bathroom and sobbed my heart out into a towel.

I had seen and done many things on this journey, miracles that many would have longed to see – but this was something I could not possibly put into words. It had an incredible effect on me. My body ached. I sobbed until there were no more tears within me. I wiped my face with the towel and tried to compose myself. I had to go and make sure, for White Arrow's sake, that I had heard right, that there was no mistake.

I sat in front of Sheban and went through it all again in front of Val. This was important evidence, and I needed a witness. It did not matter how I felt – it was important to the world. 'Are you telling me you know where Jesus is buried? Have you been sent to show me?'

'Yes,' replied Sheban.

I explained about White Arrow's journey and how he had come back to save the world. Sheban said, 'Yes, I know. I know what you are telling me is true. When you come next time there is much for us to talk about, but for now we have finished.' We sat and spoke about his family, and he told me of his daughter, who was 12 years old.

'Ann, I could not understand,' he said. 'When I told my daughter you were not coming she got very upset. I told her you would come another time. "But Dad," she said, "I want to see her now, for I love her." ' Sheban had been surprised – she did not know me at all, and he could not understand why she loved me. Shock after shock!

I looked at him deeply, knowing White Arrow had been right when he had instructed me to wear the fish, since the right man would recognize it and come forward. This was the man, and he had asked me for no money, even though he had lost money twice through meeting me. He asked me only to send him a large picture of myself and to write to him. We exchanged addresses and I assured him that I would write. I promised I would return, and that we would spend time together. Now I had found the necessary proof of everything. My next step was to take the evidence to the world, and Sheban was going to help me. I had completed this visit.

Sheban had to go to catch the bus back. As we got to the door he asked if I could go with him to the lobby. One of my problems is that, when I have a lot on my mind, I get lost. I was nervous of getting lost on my way back, so I said Val would have to come with me in case this happened. It did not cross my mind that he might have needed to say something urgent or private, but after he left I could have kicked myself. I hugged him goodbye and promised that I would see him first when I returned.

Val and I walked back to the lift and returned to our room, not saying much at all – I think we were both too astounded. Had I not had a witness I would have thought it was just a vision. We sat for half an hour, hardly saying anything, digesting what had just happened.

After a while Val said, 'We must get ready, Ann. It's 6.30. We have to leave at 7pm.' I had forgotten the time! Once again I had to put another miracle behind me until my return to England. Our driver came for us and took us to Hala's home. We spent a very pleasant evening there, and we did not get back to our hotel until late that night. Once again, we were glad to get into bed. I took my writing paper, but something made me want to get out of bed first and go to the balcony. Val asked if I was all right.

'Yes, Val,' I explained. 'It's just that I must go out for five minutes.' She understood. As I slid the door open, the cold air hit me. I wrapped my dressing gown closer to me. Looking up to the sky, I said, 'God, thank you for the miracle today.'

I felt a tear in my eye as the memory of Sheban came rushing back, but my thoughts were soon brought back to the present, for as I looked at the Great Pyramid I could see the moon within it. It was blue. I looked at the sky and could see the moon there, as well. I looked back at the pyramid.

Suddenly blue light was around me. I knew it was the Stone of the Plough making contact with the medallion. I looked for White Arrow. I could not see him, but I knew he was not far away. I walked back in, making sure the sliding door to the balcony was left open a bit, and took the writing paper off the bed and climbed in. White Arrow appeared at my side.

'You must go to him in the morning. He will tell you what will take place,' he said. I presumed he meant that Fergany would show us where to pray, for Fergany had wanted me to pray with him in the King's Room. 'What will take place is what I call the Last Supper,' said White Arrow.

I was taken aback. 'What can he mean, Val – the Last Supper?' But tiredness was overcoming me. As the paperwork fell out of my hand I was asleep.

· 25 ·

Walks in Sandals

Val was already awake when I woke up, which was most unusual. She said she had had a bad dream. We had to get up early to meet Fergany, so we had ordered breakfast in our room. At 7.30 he was outside the hotel waiting for us, and we greeted each other with hugs.

I was eager to go back to Cheops. I promised myself that when I returned I would stay at the same hotel, for the Great Pyramid had brought me great comfort. When we arrived, we walked to the pyramid. The sun was not quite up, but it was light.

Fergany had got permission for us to go to the King's Chamber before the tourists arrived, so that we would be alone. As we walked towards the pyramid he told us he had names for us, given him by the Spirit. He had written them down for us. We thanked him. I thought how lucky I was to receive a name again, from another country. My name means 'lots of dreams', or 'lots of wishes', and it is pronounced 'Amany'. Val was given a name which sounds something like 'Amel'. We put our letters away safely in our bags.

Suddenly I felt a great pull from the pyramid – it was like a magnet. I felt strange. We climbed up to the opening. Fergany spoke to the keeper and beckoned us to follow. I could see the stairs in front of me going straight up. I was concerned for Val. I did not mind what I did for White Arrow, but there were a lot of stairs. 'Val, are you all right?' I asked.

'I'm fine,' she replied, so I followed Fergany, with Val behind me.

By the time we reached the King's Chamber I was out of breath, muttering to myself, the things I do for you, White Arrow! I was relieved to have made it. We put our things to one side. There were lights on everywhere, which was good, as I did not fancy going down those steep stairs with no lights on. The three of us sat in a triangle in the middle of the King's Chamber.

Before we started our prayers White Arrow had a message for Fergany. 'I give you a name, "The Man Who Walks in Sandals", and while I'm away I shall leave the pyramid in your keeping.'

Fergany smiled and said, 'I thank you, White Arrow.' Then we all closed our eyes, holding hands. White Arrow wanted to join in, so Fergany and I separated and held our hands out for White Arrow to hold. The aliens were there, too.

Just then, we heard a sound and opened our eyes. The light had gone out in the King's Chamber, so we were in complete darkness. I was not afraid, nor was Val. Fergany said, 'There is a switch downstairs that can turn the King's Chamber light off if people want to pray and meditate, but I told the keeper not to turn it off. I'm sure it was White Arrow who turned it off.' I did not say anything. I thought the man downstairs had probably turned it off, without thinking to ask White Arrow if he had done it. We said our prayers anyway.

When we were finished, we spoke for a while, then got up to leave. As we headed out of the King's Chamber, using a cigarette lighter to light the way, we noticed that the corridor lights had also been turned off. None of us could see where we were going. Fergany asked me for my lighter and led us carefully down the stairs. At long last we reached the entrance and saw daylight. Fergany spoke to the keeper. Others had gathered round. Val and I stood a few feet away from them, wondering what was going on, glad to be outside again. Fergany came over.

'This is the first time since the Great Pyramid has been open to the public that the lights have all been turned off! A generator about half a mile away has broken. It just stopped for no reason.'

I was amazed. 'Are you telling me no one could have turned them off here?' I asked, pointing to the pyramid.

'White Arrow turned the lights off in the Great Pyramid.'

'Thanks, White Arrow,' I said, thinking of all those stairs we had to climb down in the pitch dark. 'I know you wanted to prove you're around, but couldn't you have done it when I had come out, not while I was in there?' I got no response from him, not that I expected any – it was typical of him!

As we climbed down the small steps outside, two people came

to visit the pyramid and were told they could not go in, for there were no lights. I felt sorry for them. Later I heard that the lights did not come on till 4pm.

Fergany said, 'Do you want to take pictures of the shadow?'

I looked at him, surprised. I had not thought of videoing the shadow, thinking that I would do so on my next visit.

'Can I, Fergany?'

'Yes, it's almost 10am, and the sun is up.' I looked at my watch. We had entered Cheops at 8 and it was now 10. We had been there two hours, yet it seemed to me no longer than half an hour. I followed Fergany around the pyramid and there, in front of me, was the great shadow. I was very pleased – I had really finished all my tasks for White Arrow. I had not let him down. I videoed all of the shadow, making sure I missed nothing.

Then Fergany spoke to me again. 'Ann, just before you arrived, I had thought of giving up my work at the Great Pyramid. Since meeting you I have decided I must stay and carry on my work, for you have shown me the way.' I was pleased for him, for I knew many people would need him to tell the stories of the pyramid. As he was such a religious man they could find comfort in his words. He thanked me again, and told me he had known from Allah and from his prayers that someone was coming. He knew I was that one. 'I've been waiting for you to come,' he said.

I looked at him deeply. I just could not see how he, like Sheban, could say that without evidence – but I had long ago stopped questioning things. I tried to think of what else I had to do for White Arrow on this trip. White Arrow repeated again that I had gained a new power. I wondered what that could be, but I knew that, whatever powers I had received, I would slowly be shown how to use them.

We walked down to the Sphinx and got a cab to the hotel. As I walked out of the hotel a little later Fergany stood there with three roses in his hand. I was happy and amazed. My mother's prophecy of the previous day had come to pass. I hugged Fergany in excitement, secretly thanking my mother.

I said goodbye to Fergany. 'I would like to see you again before you go,' he said.

'I'm afraid that's impossible, Fergany.' I explained I would be out all day until late.

'Then I will see you off at the airport,' he insisted.

'We are going very early in the morning,' I said. I promised him I would write and let him know how I was.

Val and I had to meet Hala at noon. Over lunch, we discussed what we had to do. We were going back to the Hanging Church. I wanted to say thank you to the Virgin Mary, and Hala agreed.

We arrived at about 1.30. The sun was high and it was quite warm. We went into the small gift shop and I bought four keyrings with the Virgin Mary on, one each for my family. I felt that if they carried them with them they would be safe while I was on my journeys for White Arrow. We left the small shop and the others left me to go to the tree on my own.

As I approached, Mary was standing at the tree. I was pleased to see her. I knelt and thanked her for showing me the way. I stood up, and just stood there in silence with my eyes shut. How long I was there I could not say – maybe five or ten minutes – but it was long enough for me to say the right things to her. White Arrow was with me.

I eventually walked back to the others. I thought they had gone into the church, but instead they had been watching me. As I approached them Hala said, 'Let me look at your neck, Ann.' I was puzzled. 'I could see a red light on your neck when you were praying there,' she said.

Then Val said, 'We both saw in you a face of a man – and you know when a man hasn't shaved for a couple of days? Well, I could see that clearly.' She looked at Hala. Hala had seen it as well.

'Yes, Ann, I could see the man's face and beard.' I did not say anything. There was not much I could say. It had to be White Arrow they were seeing through me. Hala could not see the red mark on my neck any more, but she said she had definitely seen it earlier.

She said she wanted to go inside the church to find out what the fish meant to the priests. I said I would follow in five minutes – I wanted to return to the tree again, mainly because I knew Mary was still there for some reason, and she might want to say something. Val decided to follow me and wait. She stood a few feet away.

The Virgin Mary said, 'Kneel, my child,' so I did, and she blessed me. I took a piece of the bark of the tree with me, a small piece, as White Arrow wanted me to. I thanked Mary, and she left.

'White Arrow, thank you, thank you,' I said.

He just smiled and then said, 'We have work to do.' Typical, I thought, and Val and I went looking for Hala.

She was talking to a young man who worked for the church,

who said the fish represented the initial letters of Christ. They spoke of Christianity for a time. When we left we went to the Coptic Museum. Hala wanted to see the book found in the arms of a child. On my last visit I had drawn a picture of a woman holding a Bible and another of a baby near a pyramid (*see* figure 11.1 on page 104). We had been told that the book had been written by one of the apostles and had been found in a baby's arms near the pyramid, and we had to be sure that this was right.

As we bought our tickets to go in I turned, and to my amazement I saw the same man I had met on my previous visit. He was in the same spot as the previous year. He was just leaving his work, and if I had been there five minutes later I would have missed him. I knew White Arrow had planned this, for after meeting Joe the previous time I felt he would play some part in my future and yet I did not know how. Now he was standing right in front of me.

Excited, I turned to Hala. Hala spoke to him in her own language. He wanted to come back with us to see the book, and as we all stood around he told us the story. A young girl of 15 had been found with the book in her arms. It was the first book ever found which was written by an apostle. I looked at the pictures White Arrow and Zipper had drawn and I realized they had drawn a woman, then a baby – their way of saying a young girl. It was spot-on. I recognized the writing in the book, which was similar to the words they had given me.

I studied the book, wondering if the paper used would be like what I would find, then we walked back outside.

Joe then told Hala that he would help me in my search and that he knew someone who could help with the Coptic language. I knew he would help, for the Spirit was very much with him. He gave us a card each and said goodbye; he had to leave for home. I wanted to ask him other questions, but they would have to wait until next time.

As we reached the Coptic Museum gates, Hala started to ask questions about White Arrow. 'I believe 99 per cent, Ann,' she said. 'But it's as if I am still a little bit unsure. We believe there is an Anti-Christ, and in the Koran there are stories of one coming. Is White Arrow the Anti-Christ?'

'No, Hala. Think about it: has White Arrow asked the world for anything? No. All he has done is tell the world of the trouble it is in. Do you know what the name "White Arrow" stands for?'

'No,' said Hala.

'The Winged Angel.'

A smile went across her face. 'Why didn't you tell me before?'

'I didn't know myself until about six months ago,' I said.

'Does White Arrow want people to look up to him? Does he want to control people?' asked Hala.

'No,' I said definitely, then suddenly White Arrow said through me to Hala, 'I am here with love only, to tell my people of the trouble that is coming and to help them. I ask of nothing but love of my father. I am not a god, I am the Son of God. I, too, pray to my father, and this is right. I come in peace to you all.'

As we stood there a prayer was being recited through loud-speakers on top of the mosques in the area. Hala's face went white and tears welled up in her eyes. I wondered if I had said something wrong. 'Ann,' she said, 'when this prayer is said, whoever is talking at that time is telling the truth.' She started to sob. 'Allah has accepted your words, Ann, so I know you are speaking truth. Do not misunderstand me – I have always been sure of you and have trusted what you have said, but Allah has shown me and told me to believe you. Allah is God. If a person is telling the truth it will be spoken at the time of the chanting of this prayer from the Koran.'

The tears fell down her cheeks and Val put her arms around her. After a few moments she came to me and I held her. 'I am so happy, Ann,' she said.

'I'm glad, Hala,' I told her. I was, because I knew White Arrow was good and I wanted people to not only know it but to *feel* it – and Hala had done so. After she had wiped her tears away we left.

We stopped off to do one last piece of shopping, and then went to Hala's flat to wait for Mohammed. We were going out for dinner on our last night together. Hala phoned Fergany to ask to meet him. So many things were happening that we felt that we should have evidence of the things people were saying to me. Fergany said he would meet us at the hotel at 10 that night, so that Hala could meet him and speak to him. Val had always been my witness, but as the story unfolded it was obvious that more were needed.

We arrived back at our hotel, after a lovely evening meal with Hala and Mohammed. She spoke to Fergany for a few minutes, arranging to meet him in a week's time. Both Hala and Moham-med hugged me. Already Hala had spoken about being upset about my leaving, so I gave her an extra special big hug and promised I would phone her the following Sunday.

After they drove off, Fergany and I spoke for a while in the hotel foyer with Val and Ibrahim, and then said our goodbyes. Val and I went up to our room to get to bed. We were to be up at 5am and it was now midnight. We had not even packed yet, so we knew we were not going to get much sleep. As we entered the room I sat on the bed, satisfied that I had completed White Arrow's journey. However, as I shut my eyes to go to sleep I felt both happy about our achievements and unhappy we were leaving. Then sleep overtook me as I clutched the beautiful gold cartouche that Hala and Mohammed had given me as a gift.

When we arrived at Heathrow Airport next day, both Tony and Malcolm (Val's husband) were there to greet us. It was back to work now in preparation for my next journey in July. I had to put this visit behind me.

· Part Three ·

· 26 ·

Without One

It was 15 February 1994, and White Arrow was with me on the ship. I was standing at the window, following White Arrow's gaze over the world. For the first time this sight brought a lump to my throat. I realized how short a time we had.

The staff had turned into a sword a few days before and I had wondered why. Harry, my friend who was an expert on UFOs, had helped me understand: it was showing me that it could and would protect me in the future. White Arrow agreed. It may seem strange that I did not ask White Arrow about this straight away, but there was so much going on that I did not always have the opportunity. Moreover, I liked everything to be checked for the world needed to be sure that I had it right, so that they would accept what I was saying.

I remembered a dream I had had the previous week in which some words had come to me. I later asked François what they meant; I knew it was to do with South America. The words had come quite clearly: DE DOKAYKI TO HUMPA HUMPA. François told me they meant 'Dedicate yourself to the father' in Portuguese. It still amazed me that I could write in all these languages with no learning behind me. And the messages were so outstanding – how could one make all this up? It was far too evidential to be wrong.

Eight days later, on 23 February, White Arrow needed to talk to me. 'Soon, Little One, the tombs will be open to the world and the secrets of the future will be revealed. There will be more drawings, but the process in Egypt will be completed by the summer. The burden will be heavy, but I will protect you. There have been times when you have felt me not to be so close, but right now we must be one. It is the only way to ease your burden.'

There had been times when I had not felt him around or seen him in front of me. Now I understood. If it helped him in any way I did not mind, as long as I knew about it. People might say, 'But you must have known he was within you.' But this was not always the case, because I had my own life and I was not always looking for him. What one does not look for, one does not usually see.

It was important to have the Egyptians supporting my efforts. I knew that White Arrow did not want to take away what the Egyptian people had cared for all these years – the secrets of the pyramids and the desert. All he wanted was that the truth about him and the trouble the world faces be told.

'On your return to Egypt, I will have the right people ready to receive you. Then I will talk to them. I am here, not there, Little One. Only my past body is in the desert sands. Have no fear of showing the world, for it is the right time for me to help save the world. My body of the past is of no use to me now, but it is of great importance to other people to know of my survival as a being. Sheban knows. Whatever happens in the future, I am with you. Also, my friends are with you. You have the Highest with you on this journey.'

'Will you have time to convince the world?' I asked. I knew he only had until 2012: unless we save the rainforests of the world which form a belt around the earth and stop destroying them, the earth will be out of balance by five degrees (see *Little One* for a more detailed explanation).

'Yes, Little One, for if I thought I had insufficient time, this journey would not be taking place.' I knew that too, but I was concerned that it might take years before I could convince the public of his existence. I was forgetting that the Son of God could do anything.

I am but human, and for his sake and for the world's I did not want to make a mistake which would waste time. 'Never, Little One. You won't make a mistake. You have shown great courage and have not let us down once. You must go back to your work now, for in the future we will have time to speak. But now my friends wait, and their work and time are important.'

Zipper was sitting on the chair. Bear was there – in fact, he had been popping in often that day, which was unusual for Bear, but it made me feel good having him around. Michael was there too, with Alien Girl and Eagle. It had been relatively quiet since my return from Egypt. I had decided to write about South America during the week, and at weekends I would finish writing about my last visit to Egypt.

Zipper was talking to Alien Girl. He had a book in his hand. He was showing her something. I waited until he was ready to speak to me. He stretched out his hand to me to let me know he was not ignoring me. That was what I loved about these people – they were so loving! Bear growled. Zipper walked over to me and pointed to the page. I let him draw. Bear was watching him. The pictures seemed to come from both of them, although only Zipper drew them.

'You will take this to François, but no one else is to see these words, for they are for you to use at the right time. They are the Key of Giza. From this day forth no one must read these notes. Until we return these must be kept in a secret place. You will understand as more writing takes place.'

Zipper said 'Come' to the rest; I had heard only White Arrow use that expression before. 'I will return tomorrow,' said Zipper. I heard Bear growl. He and Michael were still with me, which had not happened before – usually they all went together. Bear put his hand on the paper. I knew that they were sheets of writing. Were they the papers of Christ? Bear said nothing and left, with Michael in tow. Eagle followed. I had a strong feeling as they left that I was going to be using the medallion a lot more soon.

Harry brought me something his sister had sent from Australia, some words said by a North American Indian many years ago which really summed up White Arrow's message to the world: 'The sky is held up by the trees. If the forest disappears the sky-roof of the world will collapse, and nature and man will perish together.' It was a deeply moving statement, pregnant with meaning.

On 24 February, White Arrow told me to look at some words he had given me some time before indicating where I was to go on my first journey to Egypt. I remembered the words and dug them out. What was I looking for? I had done all the work on my first trip and had understood them. Why was he asking me to look at them again? I looked at the first sentence: 'Saqqara speak jacket Coptic, part of a dowry, it will be good future'. I tried to take in the meaning.

White Arrow brought Sheban into my thoughts and the jacket I had worn when I was in Saqqara, and I remembered how Sheban had recognized the fish – but what did the first sentence have to do with that? Then the words jumped out at me. I realized that he had told me about the jacket well before I had had the fish put on. The second word, 'speak,' could mean 'give a message'. The message was the fish and, in Egypt, where the Christian faith was Coptic, it meant 'Jesus Christ'. So there was a message on a jacket to be recognized in Coptic terms. 'Do you know, White Arrow, you are very clever!'

He said nothing, but smiled. I was right. The second phrase was easy: 'part of dowry' meant 'part of a jigsaw', or 'the joining of the four places', which would be good for the people of the future. At the time they had given it all to me, I had taken the message to mean Saqqara, knowing I had to go there, not realizing how important the message was until now. But that was meant to be – I would have to wait until after my journey to understand it all.

I now needed to know from White Arrow what some of the most recent words meant. There were so many things I wanted to ask him, but I did not seem to have the time – or else he did not think it was the right time to tell me. But I knew one thing: everything was about to fall into place. That excited me. I knew he would produce all the evidence in Egypt.

'White Arrow, are you planning to show me where the secrets are in the near future?'

'Yes, Little One, but I only want people in Egypt to know when I have shown you everything. Everything must be in place, including the timing. In the coming months I have a lot of things to show you, for you to be ready next year. For now you will write what I tell you. By Christmas everything will be ready for you to show the world, but first you must be shown what you are to present to the world.'

In the ensuing weeks I was busy writing about the Egyptian trip. On Saturday 19 March we had the first chance in six months for a weekend away. We went to the coast. I had an opportunity at last to spend two hours with White Arrow. 'Are you all right?' I asked, and he smiled at me.

'Yes, Little One. I have much to tell you. Write down my words. Soon a visit will take place. It is a journey that no one on Earth has ever taken. It has taken thousands of years to plan. That plan is almost complete. The visit will prove my existence to the people on Earth, and it will give evidence of life on other worlds. My father has sent me to help the people on your Earth. I will return for a short period of time so that people will know I continue to exist, but most of the time will be spent with you bringing the proof of what is concealed in Egypt and South America. There are still many things to show the world which I have not told you before. These things will come slowly but surely as time goes by. You will wait.'

'Yes, I will wait, White Arrow. I will always wait, as long as you want me to.'

'Go to the medallion, Little One. We will go to Ti.' As he said that, I saw Imhotep. I had not seen him for a while. I liked him, so it was nice to see him again. I saw the medallion go blue and I knew it was time to go to Ti. We were outside, at the place where I had dug into the ground. Bear was there. They all stood talking to each other. I looked around, wondering where Sheban was, and how he was. I noticed that there were three Bedouin at the entrance to Ti. One left and went inside. Bear was holding some sand in his hand and White Arrow and Imhotep watched him. Bear beckoned me over.

Suddenly, I was in a tomb. I was sure it was below where we were standing. I felt butterflies in my stomach, excited, as if I had discovered something important – but what? I stood there for a moment wondering what to do next. What would White Arrow show me? The four of us just stood for a few moments, then Imhotep started to walk forward. It was a bit dark and it took my eyes a while to adjust. There were stairs going down and we entered a small room. As I entered, there was a figure of a man, a statue (*see* figure 26.1). Then I found myself back above ground. I knew the place I had been to was below me, without doubt. It was a tomb, close to the side of Ti, and the entrance was opposite Ti.

'We must take the evidence to the Egyptian government, so it is important that I tell you what is hidden and where, but no one must know unless I tell you to let them know,' said White Arrow. I understood. I would now have to hide the paperwork until I went back to Egypt. I would have to do a lot of drawings of the tomb.

We were still at Ti. I was at the Step Pyramid, where Sheban had taken my picture and recognized the fish. I followed all of them to the pyramid. This was where the ground had been hard when I had dug at it. Bear was at the spot, and he was looking straight ahead. I followed his gaze, but did not know what he was looking at. Imhotep was talking to White Arrow. Bear bent down and started scratching the ground. Then he showed me a picture and I drew it (*see* figure 26.2). There was a well, and inside the body of a person who had a book. 'The book is very important to mankind,'

IN FRONT OF ME AS I ENTER THE ROOM

MUMMY ʃF
– A man or statue
sitting on a chair –

CAT
One in gold
and jewellery

CAT
One in gold
and jewellery

Slits in wall

Slits in wall

There is a more detailed drawing of this room to
follow at a later date.

Figure 26.1 The statue in the tomb

STEP PYRAMID

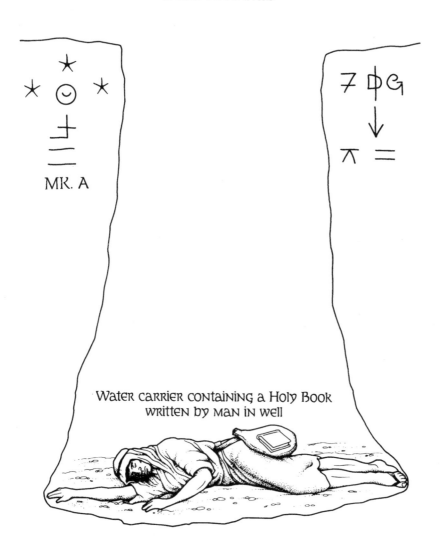

MR. A

Water carrier containing a Holy Book
written by man in well

The Key Keeper
– who has the Book = who has the Key
Translated into English by Abdel Hakim Awayan

"ZꓱPDUID"

Figure 26.2 Bear's picture at the Step Pyramid

said Bear. I wondered what White Arrow was going to show me. He came over.

'We will return here after you have completed the drawing of the Tomb of Ti.'

Then Zipper spoke. Somehow I felt the words I was to get were to do with Ti. Alien Girl had the book, and Zipper took it to look at. I was to draw a picture of Ti and of the place where I had dug (*see* figure 26.3).

At the Easter weekend I was sitting looking towards the window, when spontaneously I saw a fish. It was as plain as anything I had ever seen before. I watched it for a few moments and then it went. A few hours later White Arrow came and spoke to me. 'I want you to phone Fergany about the Last Supper,' he said. I had deduced that I had been near where the Last Supper had been held, but I had no proof yet, so I had put it to the back of my mind. Now White Arrow was bringing it forward once again.

'Okay, White Arrow, I will try.'

I rang Hala, as I had not spoken to her for a month. I told her I now had sufficient information to arrange to meet someone in the Egyptian government, and asked whether she would ask her stepfather to arrange a date for a meeting when I returned, some time in June or July. She said she would let me know as soon as possible.

On the Monday I finally reached Fergany. 'Fergany, it's about the morning we went to the Great Pyramid, Cheops. Was the Last Supper held there?' I felt there was no point in beating about the bush, so I told him White Arrow had told me this.

'Give me an hour and I will find out for you,' he said. One hour later he rang me and gave me a number. 'Phone this number in 15 minutes.'

'Okay, Fergany.' Fifteen minutes went by. I picked up the phone and dialled, praying he would confirm that it was true. Fergany answered. He said, 'I want you to speak to my uncle. He would like to talk to you. He is a very spiritual man, highly regarded.'

When his uncle came on the line, I asked, 'Can you tell me whether the Last Supper was held in the King's Chamber or near the Great Pyramid?'

'Yes,' he said. 'The Last Supper was held there, but in the lower chamber.'

'Where Jesus Christ was?'

'Yes,' he said again.

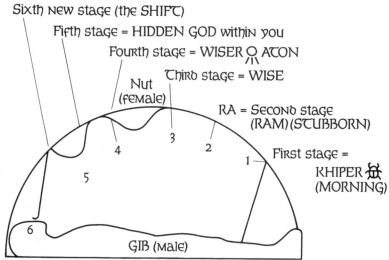

Sixth New stage (the SHIFT)

Fifth stage = HIDDEN GOD within you

Fourth stage = WISER ♀ ATON

Third stage = WISE

Nut (female)

RA = Second stage (RAM) (STUBBORN)

First stage = KHIPER 🪲 (MORNING)

GIB (Male)

The Duality of the Male with the Womb above creating the Six Stages of Mankind

Translated into English by Abdel Hakim Awayan

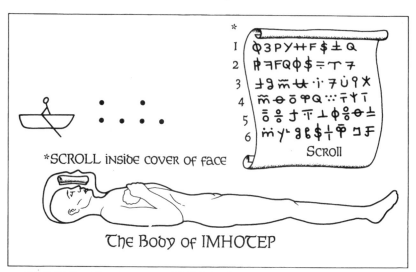

*SCROLL inside cover of face

Scroll

The Body of IMHOTEP

1 KHIPER (God)	4 ATON (God)
2 RA (God)	5 AMUN (God)
3 OON (God)	6 Scroll inside cover of face
	— The coming mental shift

Figure 26.3 Zipper's picture of Ti

I was delighted – I had the evidence I needed! We spoke for a few moments and I said, 'Did Fergany tell you that White Arrow was the Son of God?'

'Yes,' he said, 'I know he's the Son of God.'

Here was a man, many thousands of miles away, telling me secrets that had been kept hidden for thousands of years from the people of the world, letting me know them and agreeing that White Arrow was the Son of God! He said, 'Anything you wish to ask me, please phone any time and I will help you on your quest.'

'Thank you so much,' I said. Then I spoke to Fergany. 'Thank you, Fergany, thank you for so much!'

I think I was in shock, finding out that I had been where the Last Supper had been held – me, a woman from the outskirts of London, taken to a country I had only been to twice, yet White Arrow had led me to the site of the Last Supper! I put the phone down and sat quietly for a while, trying to take in everything. White Arrow said the Last Supper was at Giza and I now had someone confirming it! But I still had to ask White Arrow.

'White Arrow, you were crucified in Jerusalem, which is miles from Egypt, and people will wonder why the Last Supper was not held there.'

'Well, before my passing, Little One, I knew of my ending on this Earth. I grew up amongst the pyramids. It was my home for many reasons, as you will find out towards the end of your journey in Egypt. The Last Supper was held well before the end of my time. I will bring you evidence of this, Little One, so do not worry, everything will be made clear.'

Then I thought of the place where the papers were hidden. It made sense for them to be hidden there, for it was so near. I thanked White Arrow for giving me so much and realized that I was the luckiest person alive. Then it dawned on me: I had returned from Egypt two months before, and White Arrow had not mentioned the Last Supper until now – and now it was Easter! I looked at him in amazement. He had picked the most religiously appropriate time to give me the proof.

I knew Zipper and Bear were around, then Alien Girl appeared with the book. I started drawing, looking at the book Zipper was now holding (see figures 26.4 and 26.5).

On Saturday, 16 April, I spoke to White Arrow again. 'White Arrow, what is to happen now?' So much was going on, but I seemed to be in limbo.

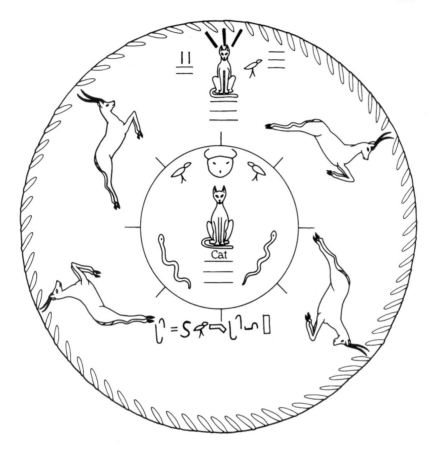

This is aN EartH Crystal INteR-RelatioNship

TRaNslateD iNto ENglish, 25 July 1994, by AbDel HakiM AwayaN

Figure 26.4

He was silent for a moment. 'Patience, Little One. Soon some-thing will come to light which will help us on our journey. I will bring proof to help you. Trust me.

'My journey is to help the world from the disaster it's heading for. The trees must no longer be destroyed. This journey is for that reason only. Unless the people listen, the Earth will be destroyed. Soon you will find my papers. Take them to the world and tell people they are from me. I hope that by seeing these miracles, and by your concentration on the trees, it will bring back people's love for one another. It is the loss of your love for each other that is destroying your Earth, your home. Humans

COPTIC

Q-P Puél Suêven Quest yûesyte Pouŝ veruêne
Crist † iivii Suepthēu ꝑueñq Tuꝛñuh Pāi-Qusfe
PauiLstay iiv w ꝑeuŝ sevūen Fuq-Tꝛupuil † Lounq
F-Vuîne Euigh Tuil-vent † Euing Punetliūne maiꝛk
unet Piscᴜal Kenj yollay Fufivle Sh'ude Fu'taile
maurkas Pintleus me.turke Quinstle David TiLues
Sēus tyLus maꞪakes Query Teull Seuvany Tab-Las
Kunuqly Sh'pertues mauꝛklas † Veur-huliy maruck-uths
Teupulsues † seüa Peinues Q-Hetuleus Pie-Tue-SubLues
ma-ka-saun Tosliet Pi-stuep mairt-Duids opuel-stuhest
Pien-tusel kepu-sal iiiiv LeusDutal Froumunet murke
Piunt Builluire Taibule Keippure Stuindey Selipher
Kumg ki-unt-empet † Laiteir Reituern Piscues Ti
Tumb munich ueûaes Fro-Hutu Tutu isuis Fronque
Theugh Qusret Fiuve yin-hunq milko Pi-Hus Taibluet †
Kiunk meual Veuhresty † Qurhst-Pyunsly †
Veun-Tual-Hieaq. ProuDuasi Suthulas Philtuasly Viñ-tly
Phunest Weinhq Four-ūley iiiv † Ques Huerst Hustlewiy
Piüke 𓂀. Junt-suis-Poul-iste Suin Daivu Poiunly
Seu-hune † ki-unq Huerste mun-i Potuers. Guparid †
Beunduel △. Seus's suis Paufruin GOD † Veun-Q'huerts
Ruile Pruey Toamb HiuD Te-Huirst, Vi-Hist Vi Hurst VuiLe
Ruil-PLuest throuq-Piq Di-stype-Quest -Pi Qurisk
moiun Tûable mairk sutev Pal-Hursa Vi-Huist Quenn-istly †
Boumb Buis-Lty pûis-hus mu-Hust Lievuenst murkuat
BeLoᴜn Pichuses D.Luist Cumpuñuinr. Sh'urest Bauk
Yoüñdor Depoûner TuaꞫluer Stiyluir Cuamb budLuir
Fournem Quisthion maꞪau ta BuilBuir Funour

1.4.94 written between 3.50 pm and 4.40 pm

A number of ONE HUNDRED and ONE and that symbolises
the character that plays the CREED, the COLOUR, and all
pointing to the WHITE ARROW, and if we decrease the
First Word and the Last Word so that it comes to NINETY
NINE, and this is a number that can easily be divided by
THREE, and that is the Pyramid form, and the Triads of the
Ancient:

PTAH, SEKHEM and NEFERTUM
ISIS, OSIRIS, HORUS
AMUN, UTKHUNS
The FATHER and SON and HOLY GHOST

Translated into English by Abdel Hakim Awayan

Figure 26.5 The 99 titles of God

and the Earth are both of each other – without one, the other does not live.

'There will be more miracles to come, but before they come I ask all of you to look within yourselves and ask this: if you cannot save the world, how can you be entitled to anything more? The time is coming for peace on your Earth. Only you, the people, can stop it coming – first by not helping in saving the Earth, and second, by choosing war and dissension instead of love. These I leave to you to decide, for you asked my father for free will, and he gave it. We will bring help, but only you humans can decide to accept it.'

The day before, I had faxed Fergany a page of my writings. When I phoned him, he told me he had not received it. I decided to wait until I returned to Egypt to show it to him, since I was afraid it might get into the wrong hands. I had thought the fax to him had gone to his friend's, but it had gone to the post office. I must be careful!

Passion

I had promised that I would return to the ship, and I was waiting for White Arrow to take me. I found myself outside a door with two aliens who seemed to be guarding it. White Arrow was at my side. The door opened and there was the room I usually went to. The door was the one the aliens usually came through. I wondered why I had come this way, but I did not press the question. I followed White Arrow to the window, checking that it was the same room. The table was in the middle and the chairs were the same, so I was sure it was.

White Arrow gazed out of the window, watching the stars. I could not see the Earth today – just stars in the distance. White Arrow left the window and returned to the table. He sat in his father's chair and beckoned me to return to mine. It was strange to see White Arrow sit, as he usually stood. I looked at him sitting there, his blue eyes just staring straight ahead. I had expected the others to be coming, but there was no sign of them.

Suddenly, a sheet of paper appeared in front of White Arrow. Before I could blink I watched it travel across the table to me. White Arrow said nothing. I put my hand forward to look at it. It felt sticky, but it was like the papers the aliens had shown me before. I could not remember if I had touched such paper before – if I had, I am sure I would have remembered it being sticky. I looked at it and absorbed the writing on it. I looked up at White Arrow, but he was still just sitting there looking at me. I looked back at the paper again.

I, the Son of God, have returned to the Earth. By the year of 1994 you will know of this. Many of you on Earth know of my coming, and have done for many years. Many of you have prayed to my father for him to send me. But why have you asked for my return? Because you are in trouble. If you are, will you listen? On my last return, the people of Earth had time to listen. You will have known by the time you read my words that we do not have time on this return.

Will you listen, or are you waiting for miracles and words of wisdom from my father, through me? Are you wondering why I have decided to return through Ann Walker and as an alien? Why do I not return as before? If I had, would you have believed in time?

I doubt it, for since my last return you have learned much more, but what you have learned is not of God and his Son, but only of yourselves. So has this learning been good? No, I say, for you have forgotten many things that are far more important – yourselves, your God and your Earth.

I have come in love. If I show you that love, will you accept it or think that other things are far more important? I think not, yet I hope that through all these things that are to happen soon you will leave the unimportant things, and think love is more important than anything else. My father entrusted the Earth and the animal kingdom to you.

I have spoken of the Earth but not of the animals, but they too are important. They too have asked for my return, for they know more than you of the trouble you face. The animals of the world are dying, and mankind can only take the blame for this. You daily kill them by putting your own important things first, yet without the animal kingdom you are killing yourselves. They play a part in your life, as does the Earth, to keep you alive.

My father gave you the greatest gift of all – the Earth – enough to keep you happy, to feed you, to clothe you, entrusting to you the beauty of the Earth, the creatures of the Earth, the seas of the Earth, the moon, sun and stars. These he gave you with love, yet your greed is destroying the very things he gave you. The caring has gone, as well as the belief that the living God exists within you, not above you. I have seen man say that God does not exist – yet who gave you the body you have, the heart you hold and the love you feel? Is there a man who walks on Earth who can do all these things? If so, bring him forward so everyone can see! Then you can see that there is no God and that there is no need to save your Earth. But no living man can say that, and so no living man can say there is no God.

I, White Arrow, the Son of God, can say that there is a God, for he is my father and I, White Arrow, speak for him, and I say this: let no man who believes in my father turn his back on the world, for if that man does so, he will be dead. Not through the choice of my father, but because the man has put himself before God and has said that God is dead.

My father is a *living* God, and so the man who believes in him is a living man, and to that man my father gives the Earth freely. Man will say, 'But if life exists after death, then I cannot die.' But I do not mean death of the body but of the soul, for without love how can the soul survive in heaven?

On 23 April I returned to the ship, knowing White Arrow was waiting for me to finish his page. He was sitting in his father's chair. I sat in my usual place, the paper in front of me. I looked at it and knew it was of great importance to the world – but of what precise importance, I wondered. 'Mankind has much to learn', said the words. I looked up at White Arrow. He was just sitting there. Suddenly, blue light surrounded his head. The light was clear, with a sense of holiness. His face was the face of a saint, his eyes were of God. Love just stared from them. It was the first time I had seen his face like this and I was hypnotized by the beauty of it all. I looked back at the page.

> Mankind has lost its way. I have been sent to show mankind the way back to my father. Soon I will show myself through Ann Walker. Through her you will see me. Let man know that Ann Walker is with me, and through her, the love of my father and his son, it is possible to show you things that you thought you had lost.
>
> Each and every one of you feels in your heart that something terrible is wrong. Your soul tells you of these things. It is not your imagination but the truth, for each of you is part of my father and he cannot be wrong. Each and every one of you has wondered and asked 'What can I do?' I say everyone, the poor and the dying, the children who suffer greatly in your world [he showed me Africa], the rich – no matter how hard they think that the material protects them – are beginning to feel it too. The sceptics doubt their God and the ones with wisdom feel it. The good feel it. Every man on Earth feels the problem – no matter how many stand and say they do not feel it. You cannot lie to my father.
>
> Yet you say to yourselves: 'Why should I, on my own, do something when no one else does?' Each man, woman and child on this Earth is part of each other. Each man, woman and child is the same as each other. No matter how you try to break this togetherness it cannot be done, for you are all of my father. So listen to your hearts and join as one, with my father, and save yourselves and your Earth.

My father never left you, for God does not think of these things. He loves you all. Where do your wars and hate for each other get you but pain and tears? Your enemies suffer as well. Where do your gains lead you but to death and suffering? For each man who causes suffering to his brother surely knows that it brings suffering to himself. Mankind has inflicted many wounds on itself and is doing so daily, yet daily you call on my father for help. How can he help if you do not listen to him? I, White Arrow, kneel in front of my father for you.

I looked up from the page, and in the chair was White Arrow's father. White Arrow was kneeling in front of him. A tear fell inside me. Here was one man, so alone, praying for our lives and souls. Here, in this room, one man, who had so much humility, was kneeling like a human, showing his love for mankind, praying for us. My mind went back to when he was crucified – he asked his father to forgive us, for we knew not what we did. Here again, after all that, he was asking his father yet again to help him help us. What do we want of God and his Son? Perhaps I should not bring my own feelings into this, but I was a witness, a witness to something that was far greater than anything we knew on Earth.

I got up and knelt on the floor too, for I also wanted to pray with White Arrow to his father. As I did so I hoped that everyone who reads this book would perhaps do the same to help us survive. As I did so I wept inside, for I was as guilty as anyone else. Had I not met White Arrow, I too would not have thought this to be important – I would have been too busy looking after my own concerns. I eventually got up, sat down and watched in silence as White Arrow still prayed to his father. Then White Arrow got up.

'Ann Walker', said the father, 'the prayers of my son have been heard. The children of the world will come home. Thanks to you for carrying this message for me. You will present my son's words and tell the world that their father has heard them. His son has returned to the living.'

The chair started to go round and I knew he was leaving. Something was different about White Arrow. Again I saw the light around his head. Since knowing him I had never seen him like this. I looked back at the page, but knew there was no more for me to write today. I would have to return another day.

I returned on 28 April. The book *Little One* was coming out in the shops in three weeks. I was hoping it would go well, for the sake of the people. I prayed to White Arrow that he would be able to help in getting people to read it.

When I arrived at the ship White Arrow was sitting in his father's chair again, and the paper was in front of me. I did not understand why he did not tell me everything himself and let me take it down. But I had to get on with the next bit, so I did not ask. I looked at White Arrow and smiled, then looked at the paper.

> Soon I will bring the people the miracles they seek. Before I do, I ask, do you care for your Earth enough to do something about it? Will the miracles be enough? Will mankind look and say, 'Yes, I believe without doubt that was a miracle', but then a year later forget?
>
> For these miracles I bring are for saving your Earth and my father's children. To bring all of you together as one to save each other from destruction. Mankind will say at this time 'I understand your message for you have said it many times' – but the reason I say it many times is lest you forget my father's reason for sending me. Soon, in time, a mountain will be found and words will be brought forth to the world that will hold great importance for all.

Suddenly, the page moved back to White Arrow. He got up from the chair and went to the window. I went to him and saw the Earth. I watched as he pointed to it. 'The Earth must be saved,' he said.

As I watched him, I knew the only way it could be saved would be for people to listen, without expecting a magic wand to save it. Some time ago White Arrow had said his father had given us all free will. His father now was bringing the message through White Arrow to save the world. Would the people of the Earth listen?

'I believe they will, for I am a very ordinary woman, like most, and I have so wanted to save the Earth, and so would others, White Arrow,' I said, putting my hand on him. 'They will save it, White Arrow, I just know they will.'

His eyes not leaving the Earth, he smiled. 'Yes, the people will listen to my father.'

· 28 ·

Listen!

On 21 May, White Arrow told me that someone in Egypt either knew of or had some writings of Jesus. The Bedouin tribespeople knew of them. I would have to spend two days with Fergany's uncle and two days with Sheban. I was getting excited. White Arrow told me to take all the writings to the tribespeople; they would recognize them. I did hope so! It would mean the end of my journey, except to give the Egyptian government or archaeologists the necessary information to open the places White Arrow said contained the secrets.

I went to our spiritualist church that evening. A medium confirmed, without my asking, that the tribespeople would help. I had a feeling that the forthcoming visit to Egypt would be more important than any of the previous ones, although I will never forget any of them, especially the episodes with the Virgin Mary.

I decided to go at the end of July. White Arrow showed me a man in a cloak who was going to help me there. It would be a spirit man, and he would help me while I was there, together with the aliens and White Arrow. One strange thing was that I had not yet seen his face – he kept it covered. But White Arrow said he was good, and that was all that mattered.

As I had only eight weeks to go, there was a lot to do. I would have to make copies of everything, for White Arrow had told me to take all the writings about Egypt with me. I would also have to remember to return to the location of the Last Supper, and also to Mary to thank her. I would try to see Joe, although I would have only six days and, like the previous visit, most of the time would be taken up with research. I faxed Hala and told her when I was coming, and booked my flight for 21 July 1994.

On 17 May I needed to return to the ship – White Arrow's father had requested it. White Arrow was standing at the window and I joined him. 'Little One, we have much to talk over.' They had asked me to follow the Egyptian journey with a journey to South America. He moved towards his father's chair. I went to mine. It was lit up, so I sat on it and waited. Soon the others joined us, but everyone was quiet.

Suddenly, the chair lit up and we all knew White Arrow's father was with us. The first thing I noticed was that the crown was lit up, and then the staff appeared on the table. In front of me appeared a goblet. I looked to White Arrow for some explanation but he said nothing. I waited to hear White Arrow's father speak.

'Ann Walker, your journey is about to begin.' He was referring to my journey to South America, which was beginning at this point, although the build-up to the presentation of White Arrow to the people of the world was also escalating. 'Will you follow the road?'

'Yes,' I replied, with no fear.

'Yet you know you will meet fear?'

'Yes,' I replied. 'But I still have no fear of giving myself to you.'

Although I could not see him, I knew he had started talking to White Arrow. Then White Arrow walked towards me. In his arms was a cloak of some sort. As he reached my side he put it around me. 'It is of my Father,' he said. 'It is the cloak I wore on Earth.'

I felt scared inside. Why did they give me these things? Was it going to be that risky? I was so unimportant! I tried to put the significance of it all behind me. 'Thank you,' I said to White Arrow's father.

'It will protect you, together with my staff,' he said. 'All of these gifts will come to be used in the future, my child. They will protect you, for they are of me. Listen to my children' (pointing to the aliens around the table), 'for they will help you on your journey. It will be hard, Ann Walker, but know I am with you always.'

The chair started to turn and the lights went out. I looked at White Arrow. The cup and staff were still in front of me. 'Take them, Little One. Drink from the cup first.' I leaned forward, drank the liquid and put the cup down. As I did so it vanished before me. I laid my hand on the staff, and as I did so it vanished as well.

At this point, Zipper started my introduction to the new line of work concerning South America, which is the subject of another book. They presented me with new drawings and words, and asked me to give priority to working on these for a while. Relentless taskmasters, these aliens, but I would not swap the work for anything. The work on South America, together with the preparation of the Egyptian material, took up much of the following month.

'White Arrow, I need to know what you want me to do in Egypt.'

He smiled at me. 'Soon, Little One, I will bring the proof the world seeks, and then some of your burden will be lifted.'

'White Arrow, I don't mind when, for it is up to you. Now, is there anything particular I have to do in Egypt?'

'No, nothing particular, Little One. Just spend time with the Bedouin people. They will show you the evidence you seek. When you come back you will have finished the work for the book, for you will have the evidence.'

'But what about opening the tombs?'

'Yes, I know what you ask me.' I was implying that the book could be finished only when the tombs were opened and the letters found. 'The evidence you come back with will convince the people of the world that you know where the secrets of the future are, and so they will be happy to wait for the event. You will bring back the evidence that you do indeed work for the Son of God.' What could be out there that would make the world believe? I knew I would have to wait until I got there.

The time of the visit was approaching fast, and I had not had time to go over my notes. So I decided to go away for the weekend, to catch up. 'White Arrow,' I asked, 'will I finish the journey without interference?'

'Yes, Little One. There is a very rich man coming who will help you to do this.' He had mentioned this man before. 'Then I will be able to speak to the world. And then we can save the trees in time. It is also important that I bring the religious side of this into the future, to take away their fear. Then they will know it is of my father.

'This is why Egypt is so important. Then it is important that we start with South America when you return from Egypt. You are to bring back something from South America that will help the world become a loving world once again. The Divine Spirit will show itself to the world.'

'Is that you, White Arrow?'

'Yes, Little One. There is still much in store for you, but the staff and cloak will help you.'

'Why did your father give me the cloak, White Arrow?'

'Like the staff, it is to protect you and give you strength for your journey. Use the medallion in Egypt. On the balcony, go to the Pyramid.'

The trouble was, it was not the Spirit or the aliens I feared – and certainly not White Arrow – but people on Earth. My stomach went tight; I was afraid of people stopping me. I knew White Arrow had told me all would be well, but every now and again the fear crept back. I hoped I would lose it soon.

I was also very angry with the world. Maybe I did not have the right to be angry, but for a long time the world has known that we are heading for a disaster. Scientists have written about it, and yet governments and others have chosen to ignore it and so put our world at risk. Now White Arrow had to speak to the world to prove that what he had said was right. But why should all this have to happen? Why? It was like saying to God: 'Unless you do some sort of miracle – and it has to be a big one – we will carry on destroying the Earth and ourselves'. Why?

I did not understand. If governments and prominent people had told the truth to the world, the people would have done something to save it. Instead, the aliens had to talk to us. But that was Ann Walker the ordinary human talking, not Ann Walker the friend of White Arrow. Maybe, if I did not know as much as I do, I would be just as much to blame for the destruction as the rest of humanity.

We went to the coast for the weekend before I was to go to Egypt. I was glad to have a break. It was 16 July, and so much had happened since the beginning of the year! I could not see much of a rest in the future either. If anything untoward happened in Egypt, it was going to be worse. One thing crossed my mind: if I came back from Egypt with everything completed, it would mean that the South America journey would be closer. I wished I could hold back, but I just could not let White Arrow down – or Tony, my husband. I would just have to trust God's judgement and try to forget it for now.

White Arrow was very quiet that day. I just hoped I had everything ready. A fragmented comet was hitting Jupiter that weekend, and people were going to watch it on TV, expectantly. What they did not understand was that this would happen to *us* if we did not save the trees in time. The world *had to* listen!

· 29 ·

Hakim the Keeper

On Thursday, 21 July 1994, at 4.30pm, we left for Egypt again. I was to see Sheban – he had things to tell me, and I had things to ask – so this trip was important. I took all the drawings I had done, praying that someone out there would believe me. *Little One* was now in the shops, but I needed more material to prove that the world was in trouble. I looked at White Arrow. 'I hope I don't let you down,' I said.

'You won't, Little One.'

Eagle appeared and said, 'When you arrive, before you go to sleep, remember to write, for there are things we have to tell you daily.' I promised her I would.

The flight went well; Hala and Mohammed were to meet us at Cairo Airport. After checking through customs we saw only Mohammed. Where's Hala? I thought. As Mohammed hugged me he explained that Hala was not well; she would not be able to see us until Saturday. 'Hala said to tell you her father will pick you up and take you anywhere you want to go,' he said as we got into his car.

Soon we were at the hotel and in bed. I phoned Tony and then leaned back on the pillow with the writing pad, waiting for White Arrow to speak. It was now in the early hours of Friday morning. 'A surprise awaits you, which you should follow up in a couple of days – then your first miracle will have taken place,' he said.

Eagle arrived. 'I will take you somewhere on this journey and show you where to dig. Where you dig, you will have the second miracle. You will allow White Arrow to take full control, for it is to him we will give the miracles. Please lose no time, for time is important. Sheban brings your third miracle. We will see you tomorrow, Little One. All will make sense when you return home. Do not be afraid. You will find what you are looking for. The letters you will find.'

As I lay back I thought of the last two journeys. White Arrow had told me what to do this time. It was as if all I had to do was see Sheban and the government and go to the Virgin Mary's tree. Unlike last time, it did not matter on which days I did these various things, although I had planned to see Sheban on Monday. But did Hala's illness mean I would not see the right person in the government?

I had spoken to Hala on Mohammed's mobile phone on the way to the hotel from the airport. She had thought I was to be here for 15 days. What if she had made the appointment in 15 days' time, when I would have left? All I had was six days. Oh, well, I thought, that's for tomorrow. I said good-night to Val and fell asleep.

I was awake at 6.30 the following morning. I washed and walked out onto the balcony. There in front of me stood Cheops and the other two pyramids. White Arrow's father appeared. I went on my knees to him – I was very pleased to see him, for I was scared. 'Ann Walker, follow my son. I have brought you here to help the world. Take the staff – use it.' I had forgotten the staff.

'Thank you, thank you,' I said. I knew the staff would help me help White Arrow and the aliens.

'I will return. Do not fear, my child,' he said, and he left.

I felt much better. I now knew everything was all right. The medallion went blue. This was only the second time in a couple of months that I had seen it working. I knew it was giving me strength from the Great Pyramid; it was connecting with the Stone of the Plough.

White Arrow entered, and said to me, 'Are you happier now?'

'Yes, White Arrow,' I replied. 'I feel bad that your father had to remind me about the staff.'

'Little One, do not worry. My father loves and understands you.' I was very blessed to receive all this love.

Eagle appeared. I was pleased to see her. My dear mother came and sat with me too, as did White Arrow. They told me not to worry, for everything was planned. I told them I was worried because Hala was ill and I would not see her until the following day. I also had to be opposite the Great Pyramid between five and seven in the morning. It had something to do with the full moon and sunrise taking place together. 'You will learn many secrets this time, Little One. Some you will keep, some you will give to the world.'

The medallion started to go different colours – it was giving me energy from the pyramid. Again, White Arrow said I would see someone in the government. He also said I would sob again soon. What could make that happen again? I used the staff to help me – for the first time it appeared like Moses' staff, with a crook at the top.

I heard Val stirring. 'Morning, Val,' I said, watching her get out of bed. 'Morning, Ann,' she replied. I took the notes I had brought with me and sat on my bed. As I looked at them I prayed White Arrow would bring someone to help me understand the languages I had written for the past three years.

We were to meet Fergany at 9am in the foyer. On time, he walked through the doors of the hotel with his friend Ibrahim – the youth who had found Fergany for us previously. The four of us sat and had coffee, then it was down to business. I had brought a letter for Fergany to sign – it was to verify that for the first time in history the pyramid lights had gone out during my last trip. Fergany signed it willingly, and I thanked him.

Fergany told me that his uncle, Hakim, to whom I had spoken about the Last Supper at Easter, was willing to see me. Fergany would pick us up at six that evening and take us to him.

The four of us decided to walk over to the pyramids. It was mid-morning by now, and hot. I wondered where White Arrow was – he had been quiet all morning, but I knew he would come when he was ready. We walked past the Great Pyramid. By this time I was very hot and tired, so we went into a tourist tearoom and sat in the shade of a tree.

I asked Fergany if he could take me to Cheops at 4.30 the following morning. He said he could. White Arrow had told me to dig with my hands – I did not know where, but I knew he would tell me. I asked Fergany if it would be all right – I had to make sure I was not upsetting people. Fergany said, 'Fine, no problem.' I did not know what I was looking for, but I knew it had something to do with Jesus Christ's writings. Was I to find them? I was sure I would find something, but what? And how?

I also asked Fergany if I could put his name in my book, and he agreed. He also confirmed that there was a passage from the Sphinx to Cheops. I wanted to tell the government of the secrets, and to ask for a letter stating that I had given them the information about the places White Arrow had told me about. I had promised White Arrow I would tell the Egyptians of my finds before I told the world, since it was the Egyptians who had kept the secrets safe.

As we sat around the table in the shade, enjoying our cool drinks, we talked of many things. I listened to the prayer coming from a loudspeaker; I knew it meant something. For a few seconds, all I could hear was the prayer, then I suddenly heard White Arrow say, 'This is my hour.'

'Fergany,' I asked, 'what does this prayer mean?'

'Come, we will go where we can hear it more clearly.' He got up, stood a little way away, and listened. He explained what he could hear. 'Only God will know the time of the end of the world. *This is my hour.* He will bring all children and animals back to God.'

I looked towards the sky and knew that it was White Arrow's way of bringing truth to those who listen to him. My mind went back to the moment before the prayer had begun – I had been explaining about the trouble that faced us on Earth, and why I had come. The prayer told them I spoke the truth. Only the Messenger, as they called him, would bring that prayer to prove to them I spoke the truth. Interestingly, the name White Arrow means 'beam of light – arrow', or messenger. We finished our drinks. Fergany said we could pop in to see Hakim for half an hour, although our main meeting with him was not until that night. I agreed, as I wanted to meet him.

Just after midday we arrived at Hakim's large house in Nazlet el Simman. He had 11 children. As we entered, there was what looked like a waiting room with two large settees and some chairs against the walls. His daughter beckoned us to sit and went to tell Hakim we had arrived. As Hakim entered the room, I knew he was special. He was tall and noble, well built and strong looking. He was 70 now, but still a fine-looking man. He was very well educated, and had travelled for the Egyptian government to the USA to meet the then Vice President Bush. He had also travelled throughout Europe. I held out my hand to greet him, and Fergany introduced us. We all sat down. I started to tell him of my journey. White Arrow was already within me – he had said that while in Egypt we would be as one.

Suddenly, for no reason, as I talked to Hakim about the trees, it all got to me, and I began to sob. Try as I might, I just could not stop crying. After about five minutes the tears ceased and I apologized. Hakim put his hand on my shoulder as I carried on telling him that I needed someone to help me with the drawings and writings of Egypt. Hakim promised that he would be at Fergany's house at 6.00 that evening, and asked me to bring the drawings with me. We hugged each other goodbye and spoke briefly of the tears. They were White Arrow's, a symptom of his love for his father's Earth. 'He still suffers,' said Hakim. 'But the time has come for the oneness of the world to gain more strength. We will meet tonight!'

We all left. I sat looking out of the window of the cab as we drove back to the hotel. I was surprised at the tears I had shed. I was tired of the lonely battle of trying to tell the world – yet no one was listening. Was that my fault? I was only human, and humans do make mistakes. Had I done something wrong?

I tried to forget it as we reached the hotel, and started to chat with the others over coffee by the pool. But as the others talked, I began to worry. Surely I should be doing more than just sitting around a swimming pool? In all my visits to Egypt, I had never rested. Now that I was resting, I was worrying about it. I promised myself a swim before I left Egypt. Little did I know there would be no time for a swim – I should have had it there and then!

Soon it was time to go and change to meet Hakim. As Val got ready I put the sheets of drawings in front of me. 'White Arrow, which ones am I to take?' I asked. I took a number of pages out of the pile of over 200 – it was White Arrow choosing them. We would leave the others for another time. I locked up the case, the pictures safely hidden. We left the room to join Fergany; Ibrahim had left, as he knew this was to be private.

I held the paperwork close to me as we travelled to Fergany's house. I had been scared of showing it before, but somehow I felt I could trust Hakim. However, I would wait and see before I gave him the whole of the book.

Hakim was standing on the balcony. Behind him were the three pyramids. The view was outstandingly beautiful. I had been to Fergany's house before, but each time I went it still took my breath away. Hakim greeted us and we went into the living room. Fergany made tea for us and we spoke of everyday things while we waited. We all drank together. I was told by White Arrow to wait, to let Hakim speak first, so I did.

Hakim then sat on the floor and beckoned us to follow suit – just Val and me. 'We will sit and hold hands and pray,' said Hakim, and we did. Hakim prayed for a few minutes. I could feel White

Arrow enter into my body, and I knew it would be White Arrow who would speak, not me.

'White Arrow wishes to talk through me, Hakim,' I said. Everyone stayed silent and listened to what White Arrow had to say.

'I have sent my child for the truth. I am the light. You have seen the light of me many times.' He was addressing Hakim. 'You have entered the light of me many times. You have also seen me. The journey has been long for Little One. It is now time that the world knows of my entry to this Earth. I come soon, but before I come the world must know of my existence and of my coming. Your world is in great danger. My father has sent me many times. I am known by many names, not just by that of Jesus Christ.

'When I lived here I spent many years among the pyramids and the people. I was brought back here from the crucifixion in Jerusalem. The great secrets of Egypt have been kept for many years, because many knew I would one day return.

'I have sent my child with many messages and many secrets, but she needs your help. On her return to England, her home, there will be much talk of me through her. It is the world that called me, to tell of the danger that we face now. The time is coming now that Little One returns with evidence to the world that she knows of my existence, and that she has not lied about what I have told her.

'If we do not help, the world will come to an end. My father does not want that, as your father does not want it. She has been frightened to ask these questions, and so I have entered her to speak to you.

'Here in the valley of Giza one other man has the meanings of my letter. It is to be returned to the world so that, in turn, we can save the world. I have told Ann Walker the symbols. I told her to ask you for your help, for I do not take what rightfully belongs to Egypt. However, the evidence belongs to the world. Help has been sent through our father. We have sent it. It has arrived, but it will take more than the strength of Ann Walker to carry.

'Your God comes. He wishes to tell you of his love for you. I talk of *your* God. He asks you, his son, to talk to the Son of God. Your father would not have come unless it was true.

'Here in your great valley, where I have lived before, I have left things for rediscovery at this time. When I was on the Earth, as you will know from the paperwork, we knew of the disaster which is coming – it is written amongst the words of what is hidden.

'Your sister also chooses to come, and sits beside you. You will wonder why I am not here in person to do this; if I came in person, born as a human now, it would take too long for people to hear. Feel pity for the light, Ann Walker, that I have chosen. If my return were possible, people would not listen to the words, even in 17½ years. This would be too late, so I come this time as a living person from another world. My father has sent me to stop the world's destruction.

'The Son of God begs that the children of the world will listen to his father. People will ask: where are the miracles? The miracles start from Egypt, but they will not finish in Egypt. You already know this, for you know part of what has been written by the Son of God, because you have seen and will see. You knew that the Son of God was going to send someone to you one day – that he was going to send someone to the Keeper.' White Arrow was calling Hakim 'the Keeper'.

'Look at the child. The Son of God leaves her in your hands. Sleep well tonight, Keeper, for tomorrow you will understand the words of truth that have been spoken. Keeper, do not worry: everything is perfectly done. Keeper, have no fear. As you look at me as the Son of God, you look at the hand of God.'

After a pause, I said, 'Imhotep is here in the room, and sits with us. He says that he too knew many secrets, for he built many things. He comes to say "I too help the Son of God". '

'Imhotep was an alien,' said Hakim. 'He was not of the normal people.'

I took up the pages I had brought and proceeded to give them to Hakim, hoping he would know what they meant. I knew that if he regarded these as correct, it would mean that everything else I had ever written would be right. Hakim took them from me and laid them out one by one.

When he came to the fifth page he shed tears for a few moments. 'It's the key to opening the Hall of Records!' I looked at him, amazed. I had drawn that page some time before, and had known it was important. I held my breath for a moment, in shock and excitement. What I had written was all true! Although White Arrow knew what they were I had not known their importance until now. Hakim was interested in the fact that I had found the most important tomb in history, yet I myself was interested in the whole jigsaw. Everything would be believed by the world now. All I needed was for the government to open the Hall of Records.

White Arrow said, 'I use short words. You do not need long words.'

As he held a page of my drawings, Hakim replied, 'I read symbols. My master always talks to me in symbols. My master showed me the cross, and what I see now is that the cross is covered with the name. When I spoke to you, Ann, at Easter, I knew you were with the Son of God, for only the Son of God would have known about the Last Supper. I know of the cross in the pyramid. The picture shows me this, and the cross is guiding us to the secret. The secret is a Hall of Records, where we will get all the knowledge that will help us to stop evil.'

What Hakim was referring to was something in one of my drawings (figure 18.1 on page 171). It stated that there was a cross in the Queen's Chamber, although no one had found it, and I was to show him where the cross was. If I could do that, then I would know how to find the Hall of Records. At this time Hakim did not know of the other 200 or so drawings I had at the hotel. It was only after he had received the rest of the drawings that he realized that I already had all the information that was in the Hall of Records. As it happened, I did not get to know what the Hall of Records was until after my return from Egypt – only White Arrow knew the real secret.

I explained about the five aliens and their work to help save the world. 'That's true,' said Hakim. 'God blesses us all. Work is going on in the light of wisdom, of knowledge . . . in the light of signs written with symbols, not to be misused.'

I said that I was following God's path as best I could. 'It is now between you and White Arrow. I can only say what I understand.'

Hakim said, 'We follow, but people try to stop the truth from being told.'

'I do not know if you know how God comes sometimes, but I have the lion in the room,' I said. 'The lion is the father. He walks around. We are honoured. We are all lucky.' We sat still, bathed in the presence.

After White Arrow had finished his conversation, more prayers were said, then we let go of each others' hands. Then White Arrow said to me, 'When it comes, you will want to see the sign. That is in the Great Pyramid. Do not run from it.' He was trying to tell me not to be afraid that it would not be there – but I knew that it would be there.

I said, 'I will find it, and I will take the information back to the

Western world. Not many people will want me here, but before I go they will listen.'

Hakim told me he was happy that White Arrow accepted him, and said that he would help. I then explained about the star breaking up, and about the Earth being in the pathway of a stellar fragment from the broken star. I also explained that White Arrow was in a race against time, brought on by the destruction of humanity, and that I did not have long to show everything to the world.

I asked Hakim if we could go to the Queen's Chamber. He said we could. 'White Arrow wants me to give the secrets of the pyramids to the world,' I said. Again Hakim said I could. He looked through the 11 pages I had brought and said that many hundreds of people with special visions had come to Egypt, but he had never seen such paperwork as this.

'Hakim, what does your name stand for?' I asked.

'The Wise Man of the Wisdom,' he replied.

'There is no doubt you can go home with proof for the world,' he continued. 'You must see the government. The Minister of Culture is the best person to see, for now. If we need him, we'll call him.'

Hakim said that Jesus was the same as Osiris. Jesus had been crucified and Osiris had been cut into 42 pieces, making the 42 tribes of Egypt, where Jesus Christ belonged. A fish called an annoma had swallowed Osiris' sexual organ in the Nile, and therefore the name of the fish means 'reborn' or 'resurrected' – and the fish thus represented Jesus.

Then he said, 'Out of the many thousands of priests, you are the true one.' I did not know what to say. At this moment too much was happening for me to take in. I realized that White Arrow had cried that morning because he knew that, once I had met Hakim, he could help save his Earth. He had cried because of his love for the people of the world.

Apparently, 25 years earlier, Hakim had sculpted a model of White Arrow and me, united as one, without knowing who it was he had sculpted. 'Now I know the true identity! I will give the sculpture to you, for it is of you and White Arrow.'

When I asked who knew where the letters of Jesus Christ were, Hakim explained that they were in the Queen's Chamber, in the cross, but that only I knew the key. He also explained that the letters I had sought were already with me – I had been writing the words of Jesus Christ. What I had been searching for was already in my possession! The drawings and words were of the Hall of Records, and when it was opened people would verify this. I had the letters of Jesus Christ. It was amongst the pages.

Regarding the Stone of the Plough in Cheops, Hakim said that the drawing (figure 18.2, page 171) I had given him of the stone in the pyramid was the very first historic proof of the stone's existence. It was some time before I realized what Hakim had meant when he had said that the letters were in the cross, and that only I would know this, for White Arrow was the cross. It was all coming together very fast.

I did not tell Hakim at that time that I had brought more than 200 pages of drawings and writings with me, for I had to wait and be sure of him. I trusted him straight away, but in the past I had trusted others and had been let down. This time I had to take it easy and be sure, for the world was at risk. So I said nothing. I hugged him and thanked him, for he had done a great deal in a short time. He promised that he would interpret the drawings in the next few days, before I returned home.

Fergany, Val and I went back to the waiting cab and drove to a shop which sold the Koran. It was Mohammed's 30th birthday the following day, and we wanted to buy him a copy as a special gift. Then we headed back to the hotel. Earlier, when I had told Fergany that the sun rose and the full moon set together in the morning, and that I needed to be at the Great Pyramid at 5am to witness it, he had questioned this. But Hakim had told him that White Arrow was right, so Fergany agreed to meet us at 4.30am.

As I got into bed I remembered that I still had some writing to do, so I took out the writing paper and leaned back on the pillow, waiting for White Arrow and Eagle. White Arrow's father came.

It's Friday, 22/7/94 . . . I cannot explain how I feel about the events of today, but they were the biggest miracles I've seen.

'Sit and listen, for something is to be told to you that will add another piece of the jigsaw for the journey. Trust everyone I bring you, for they are all in place now. I will be you.' That was White Arrow.

Eagle then spoke to me, 'You must go where Sheban wants to take you. I will be there.'

Then White Arrow spoke. 'Two more miracles will take place. I have much more to show. We must leave Egypt with all the miracles in place. You will meet one from the government. When you meet

him, tell him who I am. I will tell you what to say. Let me speak, for
I am you.'

I put the writing away in a drawer. Then the phone rang. It was
Sheban, welcoming us back to Egypt. He was excited, so it was
difficult to understand him. 'I will come and see you tomorrow,'
he said.

'No, Sheban, I will be out,' I told him. I knew all my time would
be taken, with not much to spare. I thought for a moment. I knew
I could be at the hotel for a few hours on Sunday evening, so I told
him this. We arranged for him to come at 7pm. I was pleased, as I
knew he had something to tell me. I put the phone down, happy
that everyone was helping White Arrow on his journey.

· 30 ·

Blue

At 4.35 the next morning we met Fergany. It took five minutes to reach Giza, where there were a couple of men with two camels waiting. Fergany and one of the men packed our things onto the camels, and before we knew it we were heading out towards the desert. It was still dark, and the stillness of the night and the views were breathtaking.

I was to be at a place with a view of the Giza pyramids to see the sun rise and the moon set together. As I sat on the camel heading into the desert I wondered what was in store for us today – anything was possible, for had I not already seen many miracles?

I could feel White Arrow within me. I had to keep reminding myself that on this trip we would be as one most of the time. We reached our destination. I could see the pyramids in the distance. All around us was just sand; it was beautiful. We got off the camels and the man I was with laid out a rug so we could sit down and wait for the sun to come up. The moon was bright, and I was excited. We took some pictures. Then the sun peeked over the horizon.

To my left was the sun, to my right the setting moon – dead in line with each other. White Arrow had been right. I sat and watched in awe. Here I was, sitting in the Sahara, with the Giza pyramids and the moon and sun for company. What more could I have wished for? Actually, there was one more thing: for my husband and children to be with me. They were not, but my thoughts were with them.

I got up and told Val and Fergany I had to go and be on my own; White Arrow wanted it. In the desert nearby there was a very small road – it looked as if someone had started to build it and changed their mind. I felt there was a reason why I had found this small road. Did it mean that the journey and the time left were short? I stood in front of it, knelt on the warm sand and prayed, thanking God for everything. After five minutes I got up and walked back to the others.

I remembered a drawing that White Arrow had done, showing a circle within a circle, representing the Son of God, with a line coming out of the centre circle, with the word 'light' by it (*see* figure 30.1). I asked Fergany about it, and he told me it denoted the Son of God, and the light coming from it was the light of the Son of God. It meant that White Arrow was with me. I should have seen this. I had sensed that the symbol had represented the Son of God, but I had not thought of it the way Fergany did. I had thought a light, meaning a sign or vision, would appear at the time of our desert sojourn. It had, but not the way I had thought, and I am sure the road was a symbol of time running out.

We stayed for another ten minutes, and then headed towards the Giza pyramids. I needed to return to the shadow of Cheops. The view on the way was wonderful and we stopped and took pictures as we went along. I told Fergany I could see Cheops all in blue. He said that at the top of the pyramid someone had painted one of the stones blue, but I was seeing blue all over. It lasted a few seconds and then the vision left me.

Soon we were at the pyramid. We got off the camels and walked towards it. Fergany took me to the shadow. It looked as if it was in a different place to where it had been the previous time. I videoed it, but I was worried. Was this the right shadow? I was confused. Was it the wrong day? If not, why did I not recognize the shadow in the same spot? I went to the edge of the shadow and Eagle appeared. 'Dig here,' she said. I gave Fergany the camcorder, so that he could record me digging – I had to have evidence wherever I went. I got on my knees. I was in front of the last of the small graves, and the top of the shadow was right behind me. I dug with my hands, not knowing why or what I was looking for, although I did feel it could be an entrance to something. I dug for five minutes, then got up. I knew that this was all that was needed of me there.

Suddenly, Val called out excitedly, 'Ann, it *is* the same spot. We came in from the other side last time – that's why it looked different!' I was delighted – I had done it! I had completed what White Arrow had asked of me! I could have cried at that moment.

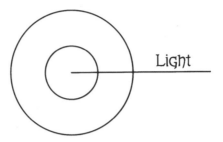

Figure 30.1 The light of the Son of God

We walked down to where I had found the two horseshoes in January. White Arrow appeared, but as Jesus Christ, just as he had then. We spoke a few words, then he told me to beckon to Fergany and Val. There were words he wanted to speak, and he wanted Val to listen and write them down. I sat on a large stone and the others did the same.

White Arrow stood in front of me and said, 'Here are the secrets of the world. I entrust them to you to take to the world. I have left them scattered, for mankind could not find me without the rest. Now you have the five places. When we return we will put them together for the world to know that I return in the name of mankind. This I entrust to you, to help save my people.

'To the Man in Sandals [Fergany]: when we leave and Little One does her work, we entrust the secrets to you until we return. I have given you a key to my kingdom. Use it wisely! Here at Cheops is the key for the world to listen. Here, and at other places, are secrets they can see. I am buried here, in Egypt. The people of the world will talk for generations about my return today. *This is my hour*, my time. From this day forward the world will know of my return and of my father's name, for the future will be of God. Here lies your kingdom. I will say no more for now.'

Then White Arrow beckoned me to follow him. He led me to a large stone leaning on the side of a tomb. He kept pointing to it, but I could not make out what he was trying to show me. I sat on the stone and tried to think what it could mean, but nothing made sense. I decided I would wait until I returned home and would ask him then. We talked for a few moments and then White Arrow vanished.

We returned to the hotel. I was happy but tired, and we still had a lot to do. We had breakfast, and Fergany waited in the foyer while Val and I got changed. Hala phoned and said she would be at the hotel just after noon. I was looking forward to seeing her. We said goodbye to Fergany at noon and arranged to meet him at 8am next day with Hakim, who was going to take me to the Queen's Chamber to find the cross. Fergany wished us well, and Val and I had a drink while we waited for Hala to arrive.

When she came, she brought a huge bouquet of flowers and there were roses in it. I thought of my mother again and thanked her. Hala was still not well, and we returned to our room. She asked me where I wanted to go. I wanted to visit the Virgin Mary's tree, the one which she had said would grow again. Hala said it would be shut by 2pm, so we would not make it – we could go later in the week. So we decided to go to the other church instead.

It was very hot – thank goodness Hala had air-conditioning in her car! We arrived at the church and I went in to pray. I felt strangely unhappy, but I did not know why. Something made me feel I had let White Arrow down, yet I had done everything he had asked me to. But still this unhappiness was with me. Please, God, give me a sign that I have not let White Arrow down, I prayed, but nothing came. I prayed for a while longer, then got up.

I knew Mary would be at the tree. As I entered the courtyard, I saw her standing there. There were many people around. Hala had gone to sit down and Val was sitting with her, so I got Val's paper and pen, for I knew there would be things to write. I walked over to the Virgin Mary. She had a lovely young face and, as always, she was in her dark clothes.

She said to me, 'You are worried in case you have done wrong on the journey. My son is very happy, so you must be happy, too. Your journey is almost finished. You will find the key to the future, so you can then take it to the world. My tree will grow again – return there to see the buds of spring. You are strong. You have the Highest with you. I gave birth to my son. You will give birth to a new world. We are the same.' I saw her washing her feet, even though there was no water there. Then I saw a very young, black cat, miaowing loudly amongst the plants surrounding the tree.

The Virgin Mary continued, 'I have brought the kitten for new birth, for the mothers of the Earth. Had you not trusted my son, the mothers of the Earth would be no more, and so no new life. You have given the Earth life through your love of my son and his father. This is your reward.'

She beckoned me forward and asked me to take three blades of grass. 'You will give one to each [meaning one each to Val and

Hala and one for myself]. It is green now. Thanks to you, it will forever be green.' Again I saw the water, and then she stood at my side and said, 'Tomorrow, I will be with you when the key is given. Return to me. The officials of the world will only see the key, but you will say the words.'

White Arrow's father appeared, as the lion. 'I give you my daughter and son. You are as one now.' I knew I was to be as one with White Arrow most of the time I was in Egypt, but I heard White Arrow say, 'No, always.' I left the tree, still feeling inexplicably unhappy.

I talked to the Virgin Mary about the grass. I thought of putting it inside a Bible, but I was worried I would lose it. Mary said, 'I gave the grass as a symbol of the Earth. One blade is not what I give you, but *all* grass. It represents life.' I still could not understand why I continued to feel unhappy. 'You will go to the tree.' She meant the other tree. 'You will know you have not let me down.'

I said goodbye and went back to Val and Hala. Hala did not look well, so we went back to the hotel. Hala went to sleep in my bed while Val and I had something to eat and drink in the hotel restaurant. We were very tired, but we could not let Mohammed down by not going to his birthday party, to which he had kindly invited us. It was to be a family party of about 20 people, and I knew Mohammed's mother wanted to meet me. Hala's mother also wanted to see me again, so I just could not refuse. It was peculiar having to mix ordinary social concerns with the momentous task of saving the world!

We arrived at 8.30. Val and I were half-dead by this time, but Hala said she would tell Mohammed not to mind if we left the party early. Mohammed and his mother were waiting for us, but nobody else had arrived. We sat and chatted for half an hour, and I gave his mother and Mohammed some words from White Arrow. Mohammed loved the Koran we had brought him.

At nine Hala's mother and stepfather came, with the rest of the guests. They were going to light Mohammed's birthday cake. Everyone knew I would be leaving after that, and ten minutes later we did so. As we crawled into our beds, I got out the writing pad. My eyes felt so weary, but I had to write before I slept.

I have been here only two days. Tomorrow is the big day. White Arrow has turned up. Eagle is here. She said, 'We will all be at the

Chamber tomorrow. Bring the words and figures that White Arrow
has given.'

I don't know if I'm pleased or not, for fear is in me. How will the
world react to this?

Eagle seems to be impatient. 'The next three days will be very
busy. You must remember we are with you. The second miracle will
take place in two days' time. You sleep now; we will talk tomorrow.'

· 31 ·

The Queen's Chamber

The following morning I woke at 6.30 with a headache, but it soon left me. My thoughts were on Hakim and the Queen's Chamber. I did not understand everything. All I knew was that I had the key to open the Hall of Records, and I knew that this was very important, but I was either in shock or I did not realize how big a miracle it was. So much was going on that I did not have time to dwell on anything, and there were still things to do.

I was nervous. What were we going to find? Hakim had said we had to go and find the cross. If the cross was indeed there, then everything was right. That puzzled me. If the drawings were right, what was so important about the cross? Then I realized that it must be only White Arrow who knew where the cross lay hidden. I pushed it all aside – we had to go and eat breakfast.

We were meeting Hakim and Fergany at 8am. Over breakfast, we caught up with the events of the past two days, and Val made notes. Val would make notes every day to ensure that, in case we forgot, everything was in the notebooks. I looked out at the pool while we were having our coffee. 'Val,' I said, 'I'm going to have at least an hour in that pool before I leave!'

We went back to the room and collected the video and the two cameras. As I closed the door to go to the lifts, I prayed that White Arrow would help us find what Hakim was looking for. I used the staff – with so much going on I had forgotten to do this before, but this morning I made sure I would not forget anything. As the lift took us down to the ground floor I silently said, 'God, help your son, White Arrow, and help me to help him.'

Fergany was waiting in the lobby and Hakim was waiting in the car. He did not look very well and I was concerned about him.

'I'm fine', he said. 'Really, I'm fine.' He was such a holy man, yet he treated all people as equal. He knew so much, yet he was patient with me and my questions. This morning there were no questions, for I needed simply to find the cross he had spoken of. What if we did not find it? Well, I decided, if the cross was not there, it would be because this was meant to be.

When we arrived at the pyramid, Fergany went to get the key to the Queen's Chamber, which was locked. We entered the pyramid. Between the two branches of the staircase, which lead up to the King's Chamber, stood the entrance to the Queen's Chamber, which was situated below. Many tourists arrived and noisily walked past us on their way up to and down from the King's Chamber at the top of the pyramid.

Hakim, Val and I sat on the floor by the gate, waiting for Fergany. Eagle was very much there with me. While Fergany was gone we discussed many things. Hakim talked about the pages of drawings and words (figure 5.1) I had given him on Friday evening. He said the eight names (four masculine and four feminine) were the eight gods and goddesses who had created an egg at the very beginning of time. White Arrow was the shepherd. White Arrow said Hakim was to be given a gift for his help. Hakim said, 'White Arrow loves us all!'

The three of us sat in a circle and held hands. White Arrow thanked Hakim for the sculpture he had given us, and said that he had met Hakim 25 years before, at the time when Hakim did the carving. White Arrow had channelled the vision to Hakim. Hakim told us that he had seen the cross in a vision the night before. It had 'V' shapes at the side, which was the cross used many thousands of years ago, from the beginning of time, before Christianity.

White Arrow kept saying, 'My hour.' Hakim said that the English translation he was going to make of the pages I had given him would announce everything to the people of the world, who would come to believe. White Arrow said that his gift to Hakim would be to have part of the spirit of White Arrow; this was the only way he could help him, so that he would never suffer again.

Hakim explained that White meant 'purity', while Arrow meant 'directs'. He interpreted this to mean that White Arrow was distinctly in charge of everything. He added that the pyramid form, a triangle, represented the Father, the Son and the Holy Spirit. The woman represented an angel, Isis, Mary, Nephthys, the ultimate feminine. The five stars were the five stages of life, from east to west, following the direction of the sun. I had drawn all of this in the paperwork (figure 3.3).

Hakim said that since we had met on Friday the name Walker had kept rushing into his head the whole time, so he had worked hard to finish the translation – he had, after all, said earlier that he saw symbolism in all things. He also said that he would come with us to see the government official we were to meet, which was heartening. I told Hakim Moses had written and drawn on the walls at the pyramid of Unas, and he agreed with me.

Hakim recounted that he had been to the United Nations and the White House for peace negotiations. He had met George Bush when the latter was Vice President under Ronald Reagan in 1986. He had made an agreement to twin Los Angeles with Giza. He had also been to Hawaii and New Zealand. He told me he would be happy to come with me wherever I had to go, including to England, to support me. He knew he would have to work hard to back up my story. He went on to say, '*This* is the gate to take us to peace. We are all one. Love, light and friendship!'

White Arrow then said, 'Preparations are being made.' The energy was building up now. Hakim talked about my having been there 2,000 years before with White Arrow, and added that I had the spirit of White Arrow within me as well as my own.

As we sat waiting for Fergany, my attention wandered to the small tunnel leading into the Queen's Chamber. There was a small iron door which was locked, and it was this that we were hoping Fergany could find the man to open. As I looked, I saw the lion in the tunnel moving towards me. Eagle was there as well. 'Everything is ready now,' White Arrow's father said. I turned to Hakim and Val and said, 'Fergany will not be long now. He has found the man.' I turned back, and Eagle and the lion had gone.

Ten minutes later, at 9.30, Fergany returned to us via the gate outside the Queen's Chamber, hot, perspiring and panting. He told us the man had not been there, so he had been worried. He did not know where the man lived, so he had looked up the address in the phone book and had run all the way to his house. As Fergany got his breath back, a young man appeared behind him with keys in his hand.

We all got up and followed him in. Bent down, we walked through to the Queen's Chamber. As I did not know where to look, I decided that Hakim was the best person to look for the cross. As we entered, he called me over to the wall dead ahead of me and shone the torch on it. Although it was not very dark at that spot, it was difficult to see the drawings on the wall in great detail, but the words were big enough to see without the torch.

There, in front of me, written on the wall in English, was the word 'ARROW'. I stared at it, shock overwhelming me. My first thought was that someone had written it – modern visitors perhaps. I did not want to believe that White Arrow, as Jesus Christ, could have written it. Afterwards, Hakim told me that when they had first opened the Queen's Chamber to the public they had found this word 'ARROW' already there. But at that moment it was more important to look for the cross, so I put it behind me.

Hakim and the others were searching the walls. I decided to sit down by the wall to the right of me. In front of me was a small alcove and another iron gate, but the small tunnel behind it looked blocked. Then White Arrow spoke: 'Little One, get up and go to the alcove.' As I got there, I stood for a few seconds, waiting for White Arrow to tell me what to do next. 'Tell Hakim the cross is here,' he said, pointing to the side of the alcove on my left. I looked up. It was dark at this spot. I could see nothing without the torch.

'Hakim!' I called, 'White Arrow says the cross is here.' He came over and shone the light where I was pointing – there was a small cross hidden from view. Everyone was excited, but I was still puzzled as to what it all meant. Although I now knew the Last Supper had been here, and although I knew White Arrow would have left a sign of some sort, the importance of it all still did not register – until White Arrow spoke.

'Little One, the cross means purity. Purity means "white". Long ago, when I was here, I knew I would return one day, and when I did return there would be proof to show I am the Son of God. Remember the word "ARROW". Put the two together, and you have "White Arrow".'

I was amazed. I myself did not need proof of the identity of the Son of God, but I knew the world needed it. White Arrow also knew this, and he had left the proof in the chamber where the Last Supper had been held. If a miracle was needed, here it was! He had inscribed the word and cross himself.

My thoughts went back to the Native Americans, who had already known of the name White Arrow. The Egyptians knew of the Sacred Arrow or messenger. Now the world would know of the real White Arrow – Jesus Christ. I cried as I stood there with the others. White Arrow had talked of my sobbing, and I had done that on this journey more than once. How many more things were to happen before I left this land? A burden weighed heavily on me. How would the world react to this news? In all the excitement and happiness I felt compassion for White Arrow. I knew it was going to be hard, but I had also promised White Arrow that, whatever happened to me, I would take his evidence and words to the world.

He had said in *Little One* that he would bring the miracles forth, and he was doing more than that. He was making sure the world had no choice but to believe; he had left proof that Ann Walker could not have done these things, only the Son of God. As I stood there, I could see hope; people would come to believe that the fatal stellar fragment was coming, and we would save the rainforests in order to prevent global destruction. I blessed myself in the name of the Father, the Son and the Holy Ghost.

We all left quietly. Outside the Great Pyramid Val looked at her watch. 'Do you know, Ann, we were only in the Queen's Chamber for 15 minutes!' she said. That was all it took for White Arrow to show us! In the tombs there are many drawings, and in the Queen's Chamber there were four quite tall walls and the small alcove, so it could have taken a few hours to find the cross, had White Arrow not shown me where it was.

We were all very quiet back at the hotel. Hakim was still not well. He told me it arose from the shock of meeting me and from the miracles of the paperwork and the Queen's Chamber. It had taken its toll on him – and on everybody else involved with this journey, including myself. I was used to White Arrow's tempo, but I became aware of how the others felt, unused as they were to the sheer pace and gravity of it all. I also had not realized how my presence was shocking people.

I leaned forward and said, 'Hakim, I'm sorry.' Wanly, he smiled and said softly, 'No, no. I am privileged.' I looked at them all sitting there, slowly drinking their tea and coffee. 'Give them strength, White Arrow, for this journey,' I said.

White Arrow smiled and said to me, 'They believe, Little One. That is their strength.' I understood, for I believed too, and that had always given me strength.

'Thank you, White Arrow, for so much – but mainly for showing the world that you were here as Jesus Christ.' Only he would have known where he had put his cross, and surely only he had had the power and foresight to inscribe the word 'ARROW'. The world wanted evidence: how much more evidence was needed than what he had shown already? How would people be able to argue that nothing had been proved? White Arrow had written 'ARROW' on the wall in a language which, at the time he had inscribed it, did not even exist. 'ARROW' would not have been understood by people in those days.

People would want to see it; it must not be removed. The cross must stay too, because it was proof of God. The government should agree to this, as it would bring peace. Save the world – save the trees.

I wrote in Val's notebook what White Arrow told me to write: 'I inscribed "ARROW" in the Queen's Chamber when I was last here, for you to prove to the people the truth of what you speak. It is to confirm that the Son of God has returned to mankind.'

Hakim did not stay long, and Fergany left shortly after him. Val and I went up to our room and discussed the morning's events. We had thought we were looking for letters written on paper or papyrus. Yet I had already written the proof of all that lies in the Hall of Records – we had had those letters all the time. We had it all, for I felt that if the drawings Hakim had were right, then the rest would be. The drawings and words were done by White Arrow, writing down the Bible as it really was. He had actually been writing two books: the pictures were the Real Testament – the Bible; the 230 pages of words were the oldest Bible, the Hall of Records.

Hala met us at 2.15 at the hotel. The arrangement was for Hala to meet Fergany properly later that afternoon, then for all of us to go on to see Hakim later. But when Fergany arrived he told us that Hakim was not at all well – he could not see anyone, he felt so ill. Fergany then filled Hala in with the whole story. They told us that the Egyptian people believed a man would come one day, and that he would be the Anti-Christ. So this time God had sent the Son of God through a woman, so that people would see that she had White Arrow, the Son of God, with her, and there would be no confusion.

It was suggested that Hala speak to Hakim on the telephone, but he was very ill, with high blood pressure and breathlessness brought on by the shock of everything. Sheban was due to come to the hotel at 7pm, and we would have to ask Fergany and Hala to leave our room so that we could meet Sheban. It was agreed that we would pop round to see Hakim that evening. We had all been touched by God that day.

Hala and Fergany left just before six, but Sheban did not arrive until 8.45, just when Fergany came back again to take us to visit Hakim. Sheban agreed to wait for our return, so we met him and his friend Abbas after 10pm and spent half an hour talking with them in the foyer. We arranged to see them again the next day. Before I went to sleep that night I wrote:

> We have done it. I will write when I return. Eagle is here again. She said, 'Tomorrow, two miracles to take place. Bear is here – he will help White Arrow give you strength tomorrow. You will see the tree, which is the third miracle. Now you will rest.'

· 32 ·

Tea and Hot Feet

I woke at 6.30, and I leaned back on the pillow, wondering what the day would hold for us. I could not see White Arrow, but I knew he would be around somewhere. He had kept his word that he would be as one with me while in Egypt, but this morning he was presumably somewhere else. It was difficult sometimes for me to know whether I was me or him, but I did not fight it, because I knew this dual arrangement was important to him for his work.

We were to go to Sheban's house to meet his family. White Arrow had told me to ask no questions until the afternoon, and Sheban had not mentioned anything except our meeting the family. We drove to his house in his friend's car, with Sheban's brother, who worked at our hotel and was getting a lift home.

Sheban explained that he would take us somewhere out in the desert. His friend had two horses and Sheban had his camel. But first we were to meet his wife and children. I asked no questions, just as White Arrow had told me – not even where he was taking me. I hoped it was where I thought it would be – the place where the Son of God was buried – but that was between White Arrow and Sheban. I put it behind me.

Soon we arrived at Sheban's house and were made very welcome. There was a relaxed feeling, and we spent an hour there. Then Sheban returned from the other room with two burnouses to keep the heat off our heads while we rode in the desert.

As I stepped outside I felt my stomach churning. Where would this journey take us? How important was it for White Arrow and the world? Val took the horse while I sat on the camel, and we agreed to swap on the way back. As we headed out of the village, everyone shouted greetings and the children followed Sheban. To me he was a holy man. The children all loved him, and they followed him until we were out in the desert.

Bear appeared at my side – all 12 feet of him – and walked with us. I wondered where White Arrow was and, as I did so, Eagle appeared. 'White Arrow is with Hakim,' she said. 'The translations are finished.' I looked at my watch: it was just after noon. 'You will be safe with Bear,' she said, and left. I felt very happy. Little did I know the trip back would be different!

Sheban and I did not say much. It was as if he knew I just wanted to take in the beauty of everything – as if we did not need to speak. We started to go up a slope, and all of a sudden, out of nowhere, some tombs appeared in the distance. I could see a couple of people standing near a kind of brick hut. As we reached them Sheban and Abbas shouted out greetings. The camel went down slowly and Sheban helped me off. Val had already reached the hut and was standing waiting for me.

The two men at the hut shook our hands warmly and showed us in. Val and I sat on the floor, and the men sat together by the door. One of them got up and made their special tea. He gave one glass to me and one to Val. It was welcome – the heat and sand of the desert had made us thirsty. The men sat chatting, involving us but mainly talking in their own language. I felt good. My speculations about why Sheban had brought us here had gone as I absorbed what was going on around me. I knew there were tombs outside the hut, but I did not know if this was the place Sheban had intended to bring me. As White Arrow had told me before, I had to wait for Sheban, without asking questions.

Bear was still with me, waiting outside; looking past the men, I could see him. I was amazed at the protection we were getting. We had headed into the desert, not knowing where we were going, trusting Sheban and Bear. I missed White Arrow, but his work with Hakim was very important, so I was happy.

Sheban spoke to me. 'I want you to go with the keeper.'

'Are you coming?' I asked.

'No,' he said. 'It is better you go on your own.' I was puzzled, but I agreed. The keeper was a lovely man, short and very pleasant. Val and I took the video and cameras, plus the water, and followed the keeper.

I walked a few yards towards the causeway to the tombs, which lay further back, and then I felt the sand burning my feet. The pain of the heat startled me; I had been to Egypt three times and had spent time in the desert, and not once had I felt pain from the sand. Yet Val felt nothing. I wondered why. Was it because her shoes were different from mine? A few minutes later I could see the shade of the tunnel on the causeway and entered eagerly, knowing the sand would not hurt me there.

I got the video ready, and as I did so Bear started to point at the wall in front of me. Sheban had already told me that only a very few people had been to the place where we now were, and he had not brought anyone there before – one could tell, because the sand was undisturbed. At the place where Bear was pointing I had to brush the sand away to see the inscribed picture he was trying to show me.

I videoed it, and then Bear went along the wall, stopped, and showed me another inscribed picture. Again, I videoed it, and Val drew it in her notebook, not quite understanding why the pictures were so important. This happened once again.

Then Bear stopped. We spoke about the pictures, and the man explained their meanings, but they still did not make sense to me. They were obviously important, however. I would ask Sheban when we returned to his house. I looked out at the sand I had walked over and was dreading walking back. The keeper beckoned us to follow him, but I did not want to go, because of the hot sand outside. There was a fear in me which I did not understand – after all, it was only a short distance between here and the hut.

We headed out towards the opening, and to the left of us stood the tombs, some distance ahead of us. Normally I would have wanted to go, but I seemed rooted to the ground on the causeway, not knowing what to do. Val took some pictures of a statue to the left of us. The keeper asked me whether I would like to go to the tomb. 'No,' I replied. 'Sorry, but I don't feel too well . . . Val, I must sit here for a few minutes,' I gasped.

There was a stone big enough for me to sit on, in the shade. I thought, this is daft. I felt tired, drained and frightened, not of the sand, but of the pain. It just was not like me, yet here I was, frightened to show my feelings in case Val and the keeper were worried about me. All I needed, I felt, was to rest and get over the fear that the hot sand had instilled in me – but was it the sand, or perhaps something else?

I made myself get up. As I did so, I started to panic. Should I go to the tombs? Sheban must have brought me here for a reason. Maybe I had to go to the tombs to find something – but I felt so ill.

Bear was standing close. 'Sorry, Bear,' I said. 'I have to return.' He said nothing, and we headed back to the hut – again, the sand burned my feet. As I entered the hut I felt relief to be inside, in the shade, away from the heat. I sat and had tea, while everyone talked. They did not ask me where I had been; it was as if they knew something I did not. I was relieved, yet I still could not get rid of the feeling I had. I was unhappy, and yet I did not know why.

White Arrow appeared, and I knew the work with Hakim was finished. It was about 1pm now, and I felt hot, even under the cover of the hut. There was a small window in front of me, and White Arrow told me to go to it. I could not understand why. 'Won't it be hotter, White Arrow?' I asked.

'Go, Little One,' he said. I went to the window, and the most wonderful breeze came through it, cooling me down.

'Val, come here. Quick!' I said.

She joined me. 'Ann, this is wonderful,' she said.

I felt very much better, until I saw the camel outside. I knew I would have to cross the desert to get back to Sheban's house. It was just not like me to feel so unwell, so scared, and not to know why. I had only been here a short time, yet I wanted to go. What had been so strange was that I had felt fine until my feet had touched the hot ground going to the causeway. As we said our farewells to the two keepers, Sheban asked if I wanted to go back by horse, as we had agreed earlier. However, feeling the way I did, I did not think I would be able to ride the horse on my own, so I told Sheban I would ride with him on the camel.

I clung to Sheban, praying the journey would go quickly. Bear was walking beside me. The heat and my unease were getting to me, and the journey back seemed ten times longer. My buttocks were sore and my head was spinning. I held on to Sheban. He knew I was not feeling too good, as he said, 'Hang on. It won't be long.'

White Arrow was close to me, and as we neared the village I was close to tears. 'White Arrow, I cannot go on. The journey is getting harder. I don't want to let you down, but I cannot bear this pain within me.' I so wanted Sheban to stop and let me walk, but I knew I could not ask him to – I just had to suffer. White Arrow said nothing, but stayed close to me, as did Bear. Eventually, we were back in the village. Everyone was again smiling and saying hello. I managed to smile back, but I could not feel it in my heart.

As we reached Sheban's house I was ready to collapse. Sheban lifted me from the camel and helped me in. Val came in after me and said, 'Are you all right, Ann?' Holding the tears back, I told her how dreadful I felt.

'I knew something was wrong when you sat on the stone,' Val said, obviously concerned. Sheban got some cushions and put a big fan at my side. Val lifted my feet up and started to massage them. I felt out of breath. Sheban told me to rest for a while. As I sat there, I looked out towards the desert.

'Sheban!' I called, 'where I went today, White Arrow was buried there!' It had suddenly struck me, yet I had not known it when I was there. Only now, lying down, did I realize that I had been to where Jesus was buried.

Sheban nodded his head. 'Yes, that is where he is buried.' I did not know the exact spot, so I asked Sheban, wondering whether he would tell me. But the way I felt, I did not mind. At least I had been near to Jesus' tomb, so what more could I want?

Sheban looked at me. 'The place you went to . . .'

'Yes, Sheban, but was it near?'

'You were where the fish was buried,' he said. 'You were standing there. The place that Bear showed you, the pictures. I did not come with you when you went with the keeper. Were you not surprised?'

'Well, yes,' I replied. My mind was trying to take in what he was trying to tell me.

Sheban pointed to the drawing Bear had shown me. 'If you are truly with White Arrow, then I knew the fish would show me the evidence. I had to send you on your own and wait for you to bring me back the truth. Then I could tell you. But I would have told you only *after* you showed me those.' He pointed at the pictures again. 'Then I knew that only the fish would have known of these drawings.'

Tears started to flow down my face. The truth stood out right in front of me. I had stood above the grave of Jesus! It slowly dawned on me that I had picked up the suffering he had gone through. Different pain, but pain nevertheless. I had been tested, and had passed the test, thanks to Bear's and White Arrow's help. The tears I had cried were tears of unhappiness that he had suffered so much – they were also tears of my own pain on the journey back. At least I now understood!

Val gave me some tissues and I wiped the tears away. I felt a lot better after crying, and after half an hour I was back to my normal self. Sheban's wife was cooking us a meal, so while we waited we carried on talking. The previous night when I had seen Sheban, he had told me something about a picture in the book *Little One*. I had thought he was talking about my own picture on the front cover. He kept saying he had seen the full length of the picture – and mine was shoulder-length. I did not understand. He then brought my book, and pointed to a picture of Michael inside, explaining that *this* was the picture he was talking about. 'I have seen him!' said Sheban.

Both Val and I looked at each other in amazement. Looking back at Sheban, I said, 'You have seen Michael? When?' He smiled.

'Four years ago I saw him, and also I have seen the fish, like this. . .' he pointed to White Arrow's picture. 'And I know he is the fish. I have seen them both!'

I was very happy with this news. Although many people report seeing White Arrow, Sheban is the only human who has told me he has seen Michael. Someone else could see what I see! It was as if, at long last, I had someone I could share the experience of the aliens with, to confirm their existence. I gave him a big hug.

Sheban's wife came in with the dinner, and as I sat on the floor to eat I felt well again. I was starving. The feelings I had had earlier – the tiredness, the fear, the pain – had all gone. Once I had found out that I had been standing above Jesus' burial place it was as if every bit of pain had been taken from me. In a way, I had had to *feel* his pain, for if I had not felt it, how could I understand what his pain had been like?

Before I had met Sheban that morning, White Arrow had asked me to give him a message – I had to write it down. Sheban apparently knew something important to do with the fish, and White Arrow was asking for his help with it. I told Sheban that this was between White Arrow and himself, and that if one day he wanted to tell me, that would be fine, but for the moment it did not matter. Sheban understood. On a later visit to him, he told me he wanted to take me to a special place on my return to Egypt in the future. It was a sacred place where no one had ever been. Whether it was to do with White Arrow's written messages or not I do not yet know.

We left at 4.30 in the afternoon and popped in to see his brother and father. We stayed for a little time, then went back to the hotel. I told Sheban I had to see Hakim that night, and he understood. 'Please, I will ring you before you return to England. I know you will return in October,' he said.

'I hope so, Sheban,' I said. I did return for four days in October, just as Sheban said.

Sheban is a special person who has kept God's secrets close to his heart. Because of the jacket I had worn with the fish on it, he had verified for himself that I had spoken truth. He had shown me one of the most guarded secrets in the world, and we all made a pact that we would never tell anyone else about the place we went to. This I cannot break, and would not want to, for the sake of White Arrow. Sheban told me that if I ever needed him to talk for me in public he would do so, and he would be willing to travel anywhere in the world. I thanked him and said I would speak to him soon.

· 33 ·

Hakim's Scholarship

Val and I had just one hour to get ready, for we were to meet Fergany at 6.45pm. Hakim was going to give us the translations. I was nervous. So much had happened today, and now more was in store. I had to be prepared for what was to be said tonight. We had arranged for Hala and Mohammed to be present as well. I wanted everybody to be there to hear White Arrow's words through the translations of the drawings – and everybody wanted to be there. I was tired – still in shock after going with Sheban to the sacred place. I was also still sore from the long ride on the camel!

We were going to Fergany's house, where Hakim had arranged to meet us. My stomach was churning. Silently, I prayed that I had done the drawings correctly for White Arrow. If they meant anything at all, then it would mean everything else was right. My prayers went out to White Arrow's father. 'Help me to help your son. Do not let me fail him.' I blessed myself, and was deep in thought when I heard Fergany say, 'Here we are!'

Val had all her writing pads with her. We climbed the stairs to Fergany's flat. Standing by the balcony was Hakim. We hugged each other, both of us feeling the presence of White Arrow within me – this was *his* night, not Ann Walker's. I could feel him in me, and so could everybody else. We all sat down. It was warm, and sitting out in the open was refreshing. Although White Arrow was within me, I was still nervous, wondering what Hakim had made of the pages, wondering what they meant. He had finished them at the time Eagle had appeared to me in the desert. I told him what she had said. 'Yes, I finished at midday today,' he said.

I was wary of rushing him, although I was eager to know what the drawings said. Fergany made tea for us all, and we tried to relax, but the electric atmosphere in the room could be felt by all. I sat with Hakim one side of me and Val on the other. Hakim had written his findings in Arabic, so he translated into English for Val, and she wrote them down. He signed and dated each page to certify his translation. Apart from the event in the Queen's Chamber that morning, and my journey with Sheban, this was the most important thing to me: the proof that White Arrow survives.

I was too excited and nervous to take in every word Hakim was saying, and I was glad Val was taking notes. Slowly, the words were said and written. Slowly, as the words came, I knew White Arrow had achieved what he had set out to do: to convince the world of his existence. Hakim had also translated the key for me, but there was no way I could digest all of this that night, for once again I was in a bemused state of shock!

Hakim's own verbatim interpretations accompany each of the key pictures at their appropriate positions in the book. Here we give the modern-day translations for each of these 22 pages.

Figure 3.1 (page 27)
The signs state that the Son of God has returned.

Figure 3.2 (page 28)
The five stages are the five stages of mankind's evolution. We are now entering the fifth stage, which is a new awareness for mankind. The three 'S's mean the trees (explained in more detail later) that are the answer to the question.

Figure 3.3 (page 29)
The signs are showing that mankind will struggle to accept that White Arrow has returned and is the Son of God.

Figure 3.4 (page 30)
White Arrow is equal as the shepherd is shepherding the five stages by force (whip).
The shepherd is expecting struggle.
The shepherd is the son, the king and the queen, and the triad.
The shepherd is the snake and the lioness.
And White Arrow is the shepherd.

Figure 4.2 (page 43)

This is where the first information on what is hidden below the Giza pyramids is revealed. Here hidden is a primary time capsule.

The translation presents the influx of history and an introduction to unknown knowledge from that primary time capsule.

I, Ann Walker, am the Keeper of the Light (the Beacon). My work is to enter the primary time capsule which contains the emerald jade gemstone which they refer to as the temple. This primary time capsule contains messages which have been hidden from man from the beginning of time.

This translation belongs with that of figure 16.1; both indicate the way to the Hall of Records.

Figure 5.1 (page 50)

These were the first eight living beings to step on Earth, and in so doing created life on our planet. They are our ancestors from another part of the universe.

Figure 6.1 (page 63)

The signs in this very important message come from God. This message was hidden for many years so as not to be revealed until the right time, when it could be used for the common good of mankind.

The literal meaning of this message is still not to be revealed and remains hidden (backed in black), to be told at a given time in the future.

Figures 7.1 and 7.2 (pages 66 and 67)

Here the translation tells what is to be found within the Hall of Records. By reading the translation one will see with one's own eyes that this is not of our world.

The person who has the site universal key is the only one with the knowledge of how to enter the Hall of Records.

This knowledge comes from White Arrow.

Figure 10.1 (page 90)

The symbols indicate that the aliens, through Ann Walker, are channelling visions from other realms and dimensions into physical manifestations which in turn are being translated for her journey. This in reality states that Ann Walker is in contact with other forms of life.

Figures 14.1 and 14.2 (page 130)

The lioness refers to God. The text is telling us to love ourselves exactly as we are, and in turn to love one another.

The second text is telling us that this love that we show will open the floodgates to allow us to love God again and so bring forth his son.

Figure 14.5 (page 135)
The translation is saying that the symbols in the centre of Cheops refer to the key beneath the statue of the Sphinx and this is what White Arrow has mentioned before.

The text states that White Arrow has found resistance to opening the Hall of Records, and this is stated in the symbols.

Once again, it states that White Arrow knows how to open the Hall of Records.

Figure 15.1 (page 145)
The translation states in the first part that this is a local group of planets.

The key to this energy of planets is showing Ann Walker the way to the existing present and future sacred sites at Giza and Saqqara.

Sesheta, the translation tells us, is a goddess – or however one wishes to refer to her. (Sesheta is a beautiful woman who wears a crown of seven stars and comes from the universe.) She is showing Ann Walker the way, through the sacred planets, to the hidden secrets for mankind.

Figure 15.2 (page 145)
This tells us that hidden in the tomb of Imhotep is information on the way to the stars.

Figure 16.1 (page 150)
Here at Ti in Saqqara is the hidden body of Imhotep who built the Step Pyramid, which in turn led to the Giza pyramids being built.

Here, hidden by Imhotep's body, are the first writings of the Hall of Records.

Here in the writings is written where the Hall of Records lay.

This translation belongs with figure 4.2; both indicate the way to the Hall of Records.

Figure 16.2 (page 154)
On 7 January 1992 I was informed of a comet coming. In 1994 a book titled *Little One – Message from Planet Heaven* was published. In this book is published a detailed report of the danger our planet faces in the near future.

The cause of this danger is the rainforests. The destruction of the rainforests is causing our Earth to go out of balance by five degrees. It is also causing our fault-lines to become weaker so that by the time the comet arrives its force will pull the centre of the Earth out, giving us no chance of survival.

In 2042 the comet is heading for the Earth. The five degrees' difference puts our atmosphere in the pathway of the comet. In doing so it will pull the centre of the Earth out.

My [Ann Walker's] job is to get the message to the world that by saving the rainforests of the world we can stop the destruction of mankind.

Here in the ancient translation White Arrow has written in the symbols exactly what Ann Walker wrote in *Little One*. White Arrow was caring for mankind's safety by passing this information on, yet to prove it to mankind he had to repeat it in ancient writings. Here, in front of you, *is* that ancient writing. He has stated in the writing, which mankind can see with their own eyes, that there is a comet coming from the stars and that White Arrow was sent by his father to warn mankind of this event. He is trying to resist the disaster by passing the information on to living people to try and stop the destruction by saving the rainforests and clearing the dams.

He has come to stop you fearing him, for he has not come to be adored, but to save his beloved people and every living creature in this Earth, with no threat – just love.

The text must be fact, for how could Ann Walker write such a text unless it was written by the hand of White Arrow?

Figures 18.1 and 18.2 (page 171)

The first drawing shows the arrow, which is White Arrow who was once Jesus Christ, pointing to the centre of the Great Pyramid of Cheops; the four winds illustrate the heart of the universe.

The arrow illustrates that White Arrow was Jesus Christ and indicates that there is a cross hidden within the walls of Cheops. My work is to find the cross and so seek the evidence that Jesus Christ exists.

The morning following the translation of this drawing the cross was found in the shadows on the wall of the Queen's Chamber, which means that Jesus Christ had put it there 2,000 years ago. And on the wall to the side was the word 'ARROW' in English. When they opened the Queen's Chamber in Cheops to the public, the word was already there.

The two joined together indicate:

- the cross which symbolizes purity, which means 'white'.
- the word 'ARROW' on the wall states that White Arrow is indeed Jesus Christ, the Son of God.

The facts lie before you to show that he has returned.

The second drawing means the arrows are pointing to the Hall of Records, which they refer to as the word which means the house.

Figure 19.1 (page 179)

Here lies the birthplace of mankind which shows evidence of our origin from the stars.

Figure 26.2 (page 245)

The key being the Hall of Records, here we have in the translation the book hidden in the well, which is part of that key.

The second part of that key will be found in Imhotep's tomb, both of which give direction to the Hall of Records buried beneath Giza.

The third part of the key is Giza.

Once the keys are found, with the key that I, Ann Walker, already have, joining the keys together makes it more possible to open the Hall of Records.

Figure 26.3 (page 247)

This translation is within the tomb of Imhotep.

It illustrates the five stages of man:

- first stage   KHIPER: morning (birth)
- second stage   RA: ram (to be stubborn)
- third stage   OON: wise
- fourth stage   ATON: wiser
- fifth stage   AMUM: the hidden God within you

These are the stages of male (Gib) and female (Nut), as is indicated in the drawing.

You will notice in the translation that the sixth stage is the coming mental shift, the opening of the Light returning to God. It is obvious that we have entered a new stage of life and new beginnings.

To me [Ann Walker], it means that faith is to return once more. Again, the coming mental shift.

Figure 26.4 (page 249)

The translation states that the medallion is a means of communication with other worlds.

This medallion was carried by Imhotep while he was on Earth.

Figure 26.5 (page 250)

These are the 99 titles of God.

White Arrow had proved in the drawings that the trees are impor- tant, and now the world would have to believe me. It took about two hours before it was all complete. I felt so drained, so ex- hausted, trying to take everything in, but happy, very happy, that I had not let White Arrow down. I had achieved the impossible. If I had not been so tired I would have jumped for joy – not so much for me, but for White Arrow and his friends, and most of all for his father. His children would now know he had not deserted them, but had sent his son once again.

For the next couple of hours White Arrow spoke to them all, and we discussed the words, each of us astounded, deeply moved. It had not only affected me, but also these other people, who had shown more than just faith. I looked at them all, thanking God silently for sending them. White Arrow was so strong. They all knew it was he, not I, that was speaking. Hakim told them all that I *was* White Arrow, and everyone looked shocked.

'Yes,' I replied, 'I am White Arrow.' What none of us realized was that it was White Arrow who was speaking, not Ann Walker. So for that moment of time I *was* White Arrow. Everybody was taken aback for a few moments until I later explained. White Arrow had been *within* me, and while he was within me I was, of course, White Arrow. But I was White Arrow only when he was within me – when he went out of my body I was no longer White Arrow, but Ann Walker. So that night I *was* White Arrow.

After I had explained this, everybody was a lot happier. I could understand this, for I too would have been shocked if someone had told me they were the Son of God. Of course I was not. To get his messages across to the world he had to use my body – his spirit entered me. I did not mind this, as long as I could be Ann Walker in my own time. It is difficult for people to understand, but this is the way White Arrow wishes it to be, and so I give myself up to help him.

When the talking had finished I looked across at the Giza pyramids, taking in the beauty, but fear was in my heart. What was White Arrow ready to open? I knew it would be something that would stun the world, but what? White Arrow just smiled and said, 'It is for man's sake and for the world. Soon you will know the secret of the Hall of Records.'

It was 1.30am by the time we had finished, and we were all very tired. With the drawings and translations safely in my bag, we left for the hotel. As I walked through the lobby I remembered some words White Arrow had said that night to all of them. 'It is better I return as the Spirit than as man. If White Arrow is shown as man and not as the Spirit, people will fear him, so it is better he is shown in Spirit.' I talk to the Spirit of White Arrow, so that people will sit up and listen, for the Spirit is of God. People believe what they cannot see, just as they cannot see God, yet they believe God exists.

As I lay down to sleep, I thought of the events of the day. I knew it would not sink in yet, and there was still more to do, so I had to put it all behind me for now. Yet I felt at peace with myself, happy I had put my life into the hands of White Arrow and his father, helping them to bring the proof to the world. But a nagging doubt crept into my mind: I knew White Arrow was getting closer, and that it was difficult for people to know who was who. When I returned to England I would have to sit with White Arrow and sort it out!

Before going to sleep I got out of bed again and went to the bathroom. When I checked in the mirror, I noticed my buttocks were bleeding from cuts I had received on the back of the camel – no wonder I had experienced pain on the journey! Strangely banal effects can arise from such divinely inspired quests!

· 34 ·

The Tree-Child

The following morning, White Arrow was there, waiting for me to wake up. 'Yesterday was hard, White Arrow,' I said. He said nothing. 'These people thought I was you, and because of your presence in me it was difficult to tell them I was not you, for I know that while you are in my body I *am* you.'

His presence in me was difficult even for me to grasp. I had got to the stage where I did not know whether I was him or not when he was with me. I had never experienced anything quite like this before, and although I knew it was important for the world to see the presence of White Arrow within me, I did not want to lose my own identity. I was tired and my head ached, but I loved him and I knew his journey was important. I would not try to stop him – but there had to be some understanding between us.

Before Egypt, I always used to know when White Arrow was going to enter my body; I was warned and prepared. But now I just found he was there, spontaneously. It was often others around me who knew of his presence before I did, because of the way I spoke. After a few days people could tell the difference between White Arrow and me. I looked at him and knew there was no point bringing it up that morning – I would have to speak to him on my return to England. Other things had to be done before I returned home. I could not waste time on relative trivialities like what I did or did not like.

White Arrow laid his hand on mine and said, 'Little One, trust me. I need to speak to the world, and this can only be done through you.'

'Oh, I don't really mind, White Arrow. I just don't want people thinking I am you when I'm not. Not because there is anything wrong in that – to me you are of the holiest – but I don't think I could take on such a great task. Only the Son of God could.' Really, I was confused. It was better to say nothing.

He smiled and said, 'Do not worry, Little One.'

'We go to your mother's today, White Arrow,' I said. I loved seeing the Virgin Mary. This time, I wanted to say sorry to her for my unhappiness the other day. I felt selfish – most people would be very happy to see her, not upset. So I thought. Yet I also knew she would understand my concern about letting her and White Arrow down. Today I was eager to see her and to acknowledge to her what I had done.

Hala came at 10.30. We were ready and waiting for her. We left straight away, as we knew the place shut at 2pm, and I did not know how long the Virgin Mary would wait for me. I sat in the car thinking about the events that had taken place over the past few days, and the miracles that we had all witnessed.

'White Arrow, I'm so pleased for you,' I said. He smiled. 'I just hope people will help you open the tombs.' I knew there was nothing more I could do than show the world the paperwork and pray that the experts would help explain and demonstrate these wonders to the public. My biggest challenge was to find that help. That was one thing I always prayed for: that people would come forward to help White Arrow. I prayed they would listen to him and help him.

He put his hand on my head and said, 'Believe in my father, Little One, for his children love him and so they will help.' Yes, I thought. I kept forgetting that I was not alone, and I knew in my heart that everything would work out. We would save the trees.

'We're nearly there,' said Hala. Five minutes later we pulled up outside the Virgin Mary's tree. Hala bought the tickets and we entered the courtyard. My stomach was turning yet again. Although Mary had been there at other times, I could not take it for granted that she would always be there. I just prayed that she was now. White Arrow had told me to return here, and now my mind was racing, wondering what she was to say.

There she was, at the far side of the trees in the middle of the courtyard. Since starting this journey I had witnessed many things, each a miracle, but what I was about to witness was the biggest and the most holy of all of them. As I walked towards her I remembered to walk around the dead tree in the centre three and a half times. Mary stayed where she was as I walked. When I had finished, I stood in front of her. Val and Hala were talking to the keepers of the trees. My mind was only on Mary and her words.

I started to say I was sorry and tried to explain why, but she put her hand up and started to speak. As she did so I heard Hala shouting, 'Ann! Look! Look!' I carried on looking at the Virgin Mary when Hala pulled my hand. 'Ann, look!' she cried.

As I turned, I saw she was pointing at the bottom of the tree. I saw what I first thought was a long weed. I am not a gardener, and because my mind was on the Virgin Mary I did not digest why they were all so excited. 'Ann, don't you see it? Don't you see? It's a baby tree growing!' (*See* figure 34.1.)

Never had they seen a miracle like this. That is what they were calling it: *a miracle*. I stared at the tree. The Virgin Mary had said in January that if I touched the dead tree a new one would grow here. And it had. Mary had shown the world her miracle, for all to see. She had shown what her son had been trying to tell us: that the tree was sacred. Her son had been trying to tell the world of the dangers that lay ahead of us if we failed to recultivate the rainforest. Now the Virgin Mary had brought the tree back to life in her own way. For the world, she grew a tree for us, showing her love and caring for us all.

My tears were of joy and happiness inside. White Arrow had

Figure 34.1 The newly grown tree at Matariyah

brought miracles, though they were yet to be validated and accepted by the experts and the public. But here in front of me stood a miracle that all could see with their own eyes. We did not have to wait for some distinguished person to say, 'This is real and true.' How could a new tree grow after 2,000 years, unless it was God's doing? Like his son, he had sent the Virgin Mary to help humanity.

I turned and looked at Mary. I had been told to come to receive a message from her, to give to humankind. I thought White Arrow had meant she was going to say something, but instead she had brought me to show the world the baby tree, which would save our future on Earth – that was the message. 'Thank you, God. Thank you, White Arrow. Thank you, aliens, thank you . . . But most of all, Virgin Mary, I thank you.' I touched the leaf of the tree, moved by the wonder of it all.

I turned and walked back to the Virgin Mary and stood in front of her. She spoke quietly. 'There are many miracles to come. Some you must keep to yourself until the right time. The tree is one of the first of many. I thank you for believing in what you have seen and heard. I shall work with you from now on. We are the father, the son, and I am the mother. We will travel together.' Mary told me to thank Hala – she blessed her future children. She thanked Val for being my right hand on this journey.

Suddenly, she was holding a necklace of thorns. She leaned forward and put them around my neck. 'These are of Jesus Christ. Now you will carry this, but you understand why you have to.' Yes, I knew, for my journey would be hard. 'The tree will grow. For this we thank you for everything. Now you know why you did not see the child. The child is with you.' She was referring to my first visit to Egypt. 'The seed was put in you. You are the mother now.'

She asked for forgiveness, for her part in not giving the full story – the father and the son had to speak first. 'You will follow the path of Jesus. This tree will grow, and in thousands of years' time the story of the tree will be heard of by many. You understand?'

As she said that, a small child, a living boy-child, was standing by the baby tree. Hala spoke to him and asked him his name. 'Mohammed,' he replied.

The Virgin Mary spoke. 'I have brought the child, like the kitten, for birth.' The child and his religion were important to the Virgin Mary. She was saying that this miracle was for all religions, not one. In the Christian faith the miracle involved Jesus and Mary. In

Egypt, it involved Mohammed. Yet this was all one, for this was of one God. As White Arrow had said once, 'I am known by many names.'

'Your journey starts now. Here it is finished.' Mary was saying my Egyptian saga was over. 'The tree will be looked after. Now you follow the footsteps of Jesus Christ.' I knew she had finished now.

She bent down and pointed to a stone. 'Take the stone,' she said. I picked it up and put it safely away, thanking her. I turned to White Arrow. I did not know what to say. I was in shock about the tree. I so wanted the world to know of its existence.

'Patience, Little One. The world will know in time,' he said. He looked at the small tree. 'This is the symbol of life. The new tree represents all the rainforests that are to regrow. This is the first tree of the new rainforests.'

Hala spoke to me. 'I have just heard a story from the keeper here. They had decided to cut the baby tree and grow it in another spot, where it would have more room, but the tree regrew again!'

I looked at White Arrow. 'Take the message to the world,' he said, pointing to the small tree. 'The tree will keep growing, for it has a message. My father, through my mother, grew the tree to tell the world that the world must stop the destruction of the rainforests. For the tree is humanity's saviour. The tree will keep all people living. As the tree saved me, so it will save you all.'

I slowly left the courtyard, knowing that my journey was almost complete. Would I ever return? I knew I would one day – I wanted to remember all the wonders I had seen and the memories of the Virgin Mary. But as for White Arrow's journey, I knew this one was completed. Now I would have to return home and give it to the world.

Whoever reads this book is part of this journey, for it is not just Ann Walker who follows the footsteps of White Arrow. It is each and every one of us. By partaking of this journey, you and I can help God, the son and the mother Mary by helping them achieve the saving of us all.

The rest of the day we spent with Hala's family. It was good to rest, but I still wanted to finish what White Arrow had asked me to do. 'Before you tell the world, you must tell Egypt first, for they safeguarded the secrets until this time, and I wish to thank them.' I had promised him I would do this, and I meant to keep my word.

That night, before I went to sleep, Eagle said to me, 'Tomorrow, you will see someone from the government. You will present the book as it is. You will not show pictures until you receive a letter from them. You have done well.

'Now we can save the Earth. Much work is yet to be done. We will start tomorrow. White Arrow will be shown. Trust us, for we are here to help White Arrow. I have finished. Tomorrow, let White Arrow speak. I will see you tomorrow night.'

Then I saw Bear. Both of them, all through this Egypt trip, had never left White Arrow's side. I thanked God for them all, for without them none of this would be possible. I put the pen down, then fell asleep.

· 35 ·

The Hall of Records

It was day six of our Egyptian visit, 27 July 1994. As I sat with my head against the pillow, I gazed at the case containing all the paperwork, and then looked away. I had come to realize what White Arrow had meant some time before when he had said that two men, Sheban and Hakim, had the writings of Jesus Christ. I had thought he meant they had paperwork from Jesus. What he actually meant was that they would confirm that I already had the paperwork myself, and that they could explain what it all meant.

These were the remaining pages; they held many messages for the world in a pre-Latin language. They contained messages from the beginning of time and, when the Hall of Records is opened, scientists and experts will find the same information inside as was written on those remaining pages. I had still more at home and I knew I had more to draw. White Arrow, through my hand, had recorded information concerning the beginning of time and the early roots of humanity – the true Bible.

I shut my eyes, wondering what the true and full story was behind the Hall of Records. I had not had time to ask Hakim for the story. The only person who really knew it was White Arrow – I would have to wait for him to let me know. What I did know was that there *were* writings hidden in the Hall of Records. Then there was the Stone of the Plough – a stone from another planet. To-gether, the writings and the stone would prove to the world how the history of man on our planet began.

Looking back at the case, I remembered what White Arrow had said a year before: 'Little One, I want you to write the true Bible.' At the time I thought he was joking. But here, in front of me, was that true Bible, written in symbol form, not in my language. I had not only written about my journey with him to Egypt, but I had written a new Bible as well.

'White Arrow, you are going to cause a big problem!' I said. Clearly, some people would not appreciate this material.

'The truth must be known, to save the Earth,' he said quietly.

'I know, White Arrow, and I will write whatever you want me to, but . . .' I turned over. What was the use? It had to be done. All of us have a right to know the truth, and I had no right to hold it back from anyone.

Eagle appeared. 'Today, White Arrow will be with you,' she said. I was now beginning to realize what she meant by that. White Arrow was usually around me, but the statement 'he will be with you' meant that I would be him. His spirit would be within me. 'Let him talk. We will be with you at the meeting.'

I wondered if I would actually be able to meet anyone from the Egyptian government. I had promised White Arrow I would not tell anyone outside Egypt about our findings until I had told the Egyptians first, and I meant to keep my promise.

Eagle left. Val and I got ready to meet Fergany in the hotel lobby. We had to wait for Hala's phone call. She was waiting to meet an Egyptian official and was also trying to make contact with the Minister of Culture. I was lucky to have these people help me. Hala and her family had tried so hard to help White Arrow.

I am nobody special; what government official would want to meet me, an ordinary housewife? It was a bit incongruous. Yet I had to get someone in a sufficiently high position to talk to me, for White Arrow's sake. I prayed that a miracle would happen. To White Arrow it did not seem to matter exactly who it was that I saw, as long as he could thank the Egyptian people through the government. It was his way. He respected the prerogative of the Egyptians.

I was a bundle of nerves. I knew that once I had managed to see a senior official in the government I would have completed the journey to Egypt. Moreover – and this had more personal signifi-cance – I would not have let White Arrow down. We sat having coffee all morning, biding time and chatting. At 11am I needed to call Tony, so I left the others and went to our room. After speaking to him I was getting up to go back to join the others, when Eagle spoke. 'By 2 o'clock this afternoon it will be over.'

'What will be over, Eagle?'.

She carried on, ignoring my question. 'Have something to eat now, for you won't have time later. Also, do another copy of the translations.'

I could have kicked myself! I had only one set. How could I give that one away? Hakim would not have time to do another copy for me – I was leaving first thing in the morning. Thank God Eagle had told me! I rushed down to Val. 'We must go up and do an extra copy of the translations, in case I do get a meeting with someone. We only have the one copy!' So Val and I wrote out an extra copy, then we went and had an early lunch. I did not know what Eagle was up to, but I had learned through experience that it was a wise person who followed her advice.

We had just finished our meal when Hala phoned. 'Ann, I've been talking to the government official. He says you must have credentials as to what you do before he can see you. I have been speaking to him for 40 minutes.' Well, this was the way officials operated. People like me cannot waste their time; one cannot just turn up without credentials. 'He will see you in a week if you can get everything together,' she continued. 'Stay another week, Ann.'

'I can't, Hala,' I replied. 'I can't afford it, and my husband and children will miss me too much. I don't have the time. Never mind,' I said. At least I had tried for White Arrow, and that was the point.

'I will come over at 2pm, Ann,' said Hala.

Of course I felt disappointed, but I had tried. Maybe it would work next time I came to Egypt. Fergany put his hand on my shoulder. 'Ann, come with me to see the government minister.' Fergany had spoken about him before, but because Hala was the one who was taking care of the matter I had not really asked Fergany about this man. But now I was anxious to help White Arrow.

'This man is very important, Ann,' said Fergany. 'If anyone knows, he will understand what you are talking about. Let us go and see him now. I know he will see you. I have spoken about you to him.'

'All right, Fergany, let's go.' What did I have to lose? The disappointment turned to excitement. Maybe he could help? As long as I told someone from the government . . .

Grabbing the translations, I left Val waiting for Hala and went with Fergany. We took a taxi to the minister's office, located next to the pyramids. Within five minutes of arriving, we were walking into his office. It was quite large, and behind the ample desk was a man in his 40s or 50s, speaking on the telephone. I sat waiting for him to finish his call, with Fergany opposite me. I knew White Arrow was with me, but I was still nervous. I had to convey White Arrow's information. I had promised him I would inform someone from the government about our findings.

The man put the phone down and turned to Fergany. They spoke to each other in their own language, then he turned to me. 'Yes, can I help you?' he asked.

I explained why I was in Egypt. I told him I knew where the Hall of Records was. He raised his eyebrows. I gave him Hakim's translations and a copy of the report from the book *Little One*, concerning global warming and the rainforests. I had been speaking only a few minutes when the phone rang. He picked it up and spoke for a few seconds. While still on the phone, he said to me, 'Will you go on television for me?' I was taken aback, but I said yes. He spoke again to the person on the phone and put the receiver down.

'You can go now to the television studios. This will be all right?'

'Fine,' I replied.

'Now, Mrs Walker, what would you like from me?'

'Just a letter stating that I have given you the information about the Hall of Records, before I pass over the information about the secrets of all the tombs. It is White Arrow's wish.' I had already explained that I worked for White Arrow.

The minister leaned back, took out a sheet of headed notepaper and wrote, 'Ann Walker tells the truth of the Hall of Records.'

All of this took ten minutes. As I left his office I felt good – at least I had kept my promise to White Arrow. It did not matter to me if the minister believed me or not, although I certainly hoped he did! I had told him what I needed to tell him, and that had completed my journey to Egypt. The rest was over to him. I had kept my promise to White Arrow. I went to the television studios that afternoon and spent an hour there. The interview went well and they told me they would let me know when it was to be broadcast. I thanked the producer and left.

That night, lying in bed, I wondered why this man had put me on television. Did he believe me? What had White Arrow said that had convinced him? Had Fergany staked his reputation on this? I am not a politician, nor a scientist, but somehow this man seemed to believe what I had said. I was grateful I had completed part of the journey.

I looked at White Arrow. He was sitting on the bed. 'The journey has been hard, but you have done well. I thank you for your faith. Tomorrow you return to your family. Sleep well. Egypt now knows I have returned.'

This was the end of my journey. I had the secrets and was willing to share them with the world, but it had to be left to the people who know how to open the tombs. I knew I would have to face people who would not believe in all this. Yet I could do no more than pray that someone would help in opening the tombs, for therein lay the true story of the beginning of human life on Earth. In the tombs they would find evidence that White Arrow speaks the truth. Thus the world could be saved. For then, and only then, will the people of the Earth realize that the trees must be saved.

White Arrow spoke. 'You have found the Stone of the Plough.' I looked at him, wondering what he meant. 'The Stone of the Plough is a spacecraft. This is the Hall of Records where man started life.' I looked at him in amazement. 'Buried deep between the Sphinx and the Giza pyramids is a spacecraft which has been there for millions of years.'

I was overjoyed that I had at last found the meaning of the Stone of the Plough. White Arrow helped me understand that the Hall of Records is from another planet which had encountered a similar problem, and that planet could not be saved. In the spacecraft would be answers to some of our problems – problems they had also encountered on their planet. This would make it possible to save our own world.

In *Little One*, Zipper had mentioned another race who had been warned of a disaster like ours – now I knew he had meant another race from another planet. But the people did not listen, and so the planet was destroyed. Some of their people made it to Earth. Between the Great Sphinx and the Giza pyramids the evidence of this has lain hidden, to be opened only if and when our Earth came close to being destroyed itself. Opening the Hall of Records would make the people of the Earth realize what was happening and would cause us to set about saving this planet.

The only person who knows how to open the Hall of Records is White Arrow. I pray no one will stop it being opened. I pray that the Egyptians will open this and the other reliquaries in the name of humanity. In Egypt they have another name for the Hall of Records: it is called the Hall of the Future. Yet this hall also represents the beginning of human history on Earth, when humans from another world first set foot on our Earth. These humans were the ones from whom we are descended.

In this book there have been miracles that only God and his son could have sent. To me the greatest was the Virgin Mary's miracle, the sprouting of the dead tree. It was an appeal to humanity: 'Please help White Arrow save the rainforests.'

I turned to White Arrow. 'People will want to know more details about the Hall of Records.'

'I know, Little One, and I will say this. Long ago a planet like yours existed in your galaxy. They had knowledge beyond mankind's on Earth but, like you on Earth, they forgot that their planet needed help. By the time they realized they needed help, it was too late. Like people on Earth now, they were sent help, but they chose to ignore the pleas of my father. I know this to be true, for I was the one my father sent. My tears were of great sadness, for they chose not to listen. So the planet was destroyed.

'Some spacecraft made it to the planet Earth, and so life began. At Giza one of these ships landed and was hidden deep in the Earth. These people looked to the sky towards their home – they built the Great Pyramids at Giza, aligned towards the stars where the planet was. The Giza pyramids are a monument to a planet which was home to millions of people. Just like your world, this lovely planet Earth.

'Inside the spacecraft are records of their planet. That is why I have chosen to open the entrances to the spacecraft. That is why it is called the Hall of Records. The pyramids can show mankind the information it needs. The information can save man from the same kind of destruction that now faces it.'

'What if the government of Egypt will not listen to me, White Arrow?'

'This I say. Man *must* open the Hall of Records, for therein is to be found the truth I have spoken of. There are people who know of the Hall of Records and the spacecraft – it has been passed down over the centuries that the Hall of Records exists. The Egyptian government knows. Man has looked for the entrances over the centuries. Now I bring mankind the key to open them, to save your planet.

'Let Giza be a reminder to all mankind. It is, I say, a monument to the people who died. The pyramids were built in the shape of the spacecraft, pointing to the home they left behind, destroyed by their follies. Do not let it come to pass that there is another monument erected on another planet, pointing to where our Earth used to be, due to our own folly.'

Later in 1994, Hakim sent a fax to explain what the Hall of Records was. These stories had been passed down over the centuries amongst the tribal people. It confirmed what White Arrow had said, and more. These are his words:

> I have chosen certain subjects of the Giza area, on the Hall of Records. This first-light matrix pyramid contains records concerning humanity's pre-Earth existence, its arrival on the planet and its initial experiences within this physical world. It also contains the Merkabah light vehicle used by the intelligences of Molona, the planet that once existed between Mars and Jupiter, destroyed about 17 million years ago, now the asteroid belt.
>
> A number of its citizens escaped to Earth in the Merkabah and became humanity's earliest teachers. Records from that planet's history and accomplishments are also found within the pyramid. Also from 50,000 BC to 28,000 BC the Giza and Saqqara areas were abandoned and neglected. After the cataclysms of 28,000 BC, however, influxes of foreign peoples entered into the land of prehistoric Egypt and each added their own new elements.
>
> Beginning about 20,000 BC various spiritual masters from Atlantis, escaping the growing material corruption of their civilization, came to Egypt as culture-bearers and raised the standards of its people to the status of a civilization in its own right.
>
> Manetho and other later chroniclers recorded this as the Age of the Gods. In the Hermetic treatise *Virgin of the World*, the deities of Egypt were described as once having been rulers who came from afar and ended barbarism among the prehistoric Egyptians.
>
> According to the *Ed Fu Building Texts*, they redesigned the physical structures at Giza into a single sanctuary dedicated to the god PN or Eternal One. At that time the Nile flowed to the very foot of the plateau and it was called the Island of the Egg of Creation.
>
> The sanctuary stood in a field of reeds and was shaped like a lotus flower surrounded by protective radionic Djed columns that produced extremely low frequency energy. The PN sanctuary also incorporated the Hry H'w or face of the original Sphinx, and it covered over the entranceway leading into the BW-Hmn, the Place of Deep Underground Construction – the primordial Hall of Records.
>
> So my friend! I'll try to make the long story short, to teach, not to preach. Yours, Hakim.

Hakim said that only White Arrow would know the true Atlantis and only I could go to him. Turning to White Arrow, I asked him, 'What and where is Atlantis, White Arrow?'

'It is the planet I have spoken of, mankind's original home, which has become known as a legend – the Legend of Atlantis.'

The fax dropped out of my hands. Yes, I was in shock. Man had not started with Adam and Eve, or descended from the apes. Human life had come from another planet. My heart raced. I had been brought up to believe one thing and now that belief was destroyed. There had been writings about the beginning of time, which had been stored in the Library of Alexandria. But in the 7th century the library was destroyed, and with it the records. So there was now only one record which has laid hidden below Giza for millions of years. Now that humanity was in a position to destroy the Earth, the beginning of time would have to be brought to the surface.

I have now come to the end of my journey in Egypt. All the facts lie between these covers.

White Arrow has, since then, grown even closer to me. Half of the time it is difficult to know who is speaking, him or me. It leaves people confused, and I understand their confusion. I am Ann Walker, and when they speak to me, the answers they receive seem to come from me. Yet they often come from White Arrow. White Arrow I am not – I am a normal housewife with a family, who allows White Arrow to enter me. I will not stop White Arrow's work, for it is for the safety and benefit of mankind. Yet it often leaves me confused!

'White Arrow, people will think that I have *chosen* to be you because they only see Ann Walker.'

'Little One, do not fear. To these people I say this. I will speak through Ann Walker at all times on her journey – this I have said before. This has to be the way. If humanity will look beyond her, they will see it is *I*, the White Arrow, the Messenger. I need to use you, Little One, and I appreciate that you are afraid of those who might not wish to believe, but there are many on Earth who will know that I do indeed work through you, for they will see the difference. The children who believe in my father will know.

'The world must be saved, and I have proved and will prove the genuineness of the miracles of my father. Often I have said that man will not want you here. What I meant was that some people will not want to acknowledge that their beliefs differ from what I have presented. This is their choice. However, I would like mankind to join together as one force to save the Earth.

'It will be a struggle for you. My father has told you the road will not be easy, and you have found this. The road will become harder, but your faith in my father will come through, for you think of the living. Do not be afraid, Little One: allow me to talk to my people, for those who listen will surely know within their hearts that I am who I am.'

Sometimes I privately wish I could come off this path – not because of any lack of love for the father, for White Arrow and the aliens, but because of people and what I anticipate their reactions will be. It is difficult to express how I feel, and to share my fears with others. I just wish we could all realize and accept that God has sent his son to save us once again. Whatever has been written, we must all remember that our trees need saving, that the comet will come.

As I sit and write this, two and a half years have gone by since I first knew of the comet on 7 January 1992. Forty-seven years is all we have left before that stellar fragment or comet comes, so we have to start repairing the rainforests now in order to restore the planet. That is all White Arrow asks, nothing more. Yet two years and ten months have passed, and I am still wondering if mankind will listen to him. Are they going to worry about who Ann Walker is or what authority she has to convey this message? Are they going to waste time trying to prove everything is a lie?

Someone said to me not long ago, 'Ann, you are angry.' White Arrow replied through me, 'One must realize the difference between anger and compassion, for it is the compassion within me that makes me seem angry.'

I do not want to fail White Arrow or you, the reader, but I am human and I need your help. I need you not to judge me as a person, but as a helper of God. All of you are helpers of God. Please do help White Arrow. Let him speak, as he has spoken before.

People will say, 'Why doesn't he come in person? Why pick you?' So many questions! I do not know, nor do I ask, for it is not my place to ask such questions of the Son of God or of his father. I just do what I am asked to do – and that is to write his words and broadcast them. While there is life in my body I will do that, for like all of you I love God and his son.

I have two more journeys to make for White Arrow – two more journeys that I *know* of, at least! I wonder what lies ahead? I know I must not fail him, yet I do have trepidations about what waits at the end of it. I know I must complete this next journey, whatever it takes. I know that if I do this, the world can be saved.

But my energy is fading. The journey is lonely and hard, and yet, with the love of White Arrow and his friends, I know I will make it. But it is not I alone who will make it, for this and every journey I have made is *your* journey. Each and every one of you has been a part of it, for it is humanity's journey.

White Arrow stood in front of me, and I prayed that the people of the world would help him and make his ends attainable. He is the saviour of humanity and the planet. He has come to help us save ourselves. We are the same, you and I – deep down, we believe in God in his many appearances, and we all love our Earth. With hands and hearts joined together, let us all bring about a happy ending, together, as one.

Let us stand together and say: 'This is our Earth. This is our children's inheritance. "Thy Will be done on Earth, as it is in Heaven." ' Let us prove to our father, with thanks and mercy, that mankind is of the nature of goodness.

White Arrow took me back to where the small tree grows in Cairo. His mother was at his side, pointing to the new tree. 'This I give to the world,' he said quietly. 'To you and to everyone, I give the boundless love of my father. Help me to help you save your beloved Earth.' NEINGH S/T PULTY – 'Virgin of the Holy Tree'.

I watched as he looked up. I saw his lips slightly moving, his eyes dark blue, his head tilted back, facing heaven. I knew he was silently praying to his father. In the peace and tranquillity of that prayer I knew that, with our hearts open, we would all hear that prayer, in time.

Then, slowly, my heart cried, for a tear emerged from his eye, slowly rolling down his cheek. He turned to me and said, 'No, Little One. The tears are not tears of unhappiness. The tears are my children's tears, that I have come to take from them.'

His hand touched his cheek. With his finger he lifted the tear. 'Take my tear to the world, Little One. Show them that even the Son of God cries. For the Son of God is one of them, a human. Show them they do not have to fear me, for I come in love.'

He held his hands out. In his hands were the cup of him, the bread of him and, behind him, the Holy Cross. 'I am of my father.

These I bring to give to the world. I give everything, but please help me to help you save the trees.'

Again, his head was bent back. I heard him say, from deep in his heart, 'Our father, who art in heaven . . .'

Appendix 1: Interpretation of Illustrations by Adrian Gilbert

Figure 2.1 (page 11)

This picture shows a pyramid with snakes running down its side and the sun behind it. To the left are various stars – a group of three above one, and another set labelled 'R', 'S', 'M' and 'P'.

These stars (or planets) I believe represent the planet Mars and the stars Rigel (in Orion), Sirius (Canis Major) and Procyon (Canis Minor). The pyramid with the snakes must represent the Pyramid of Quetzalcoatl at Chichen Itza in Yucatan, Mexico. On the days of the equinoxes (22 March and 22 September) the afternoon sun strikes this pyramid in such a way that it casts shadows down the balustrades, looking like serpents moving down the pyramid. The indication seems to be that we are looking at an equinoctial date.

Using SKYGLOBE I find that the best fit for these stars is the spring equinox of 1993. On this day the stars rose at Mexico City in such a way that we had Rigel, Mars and Sirius above the horizon and Procyon below. This was the date when Rudolf Gantenbrink, a German robotics engineer, made his historic discovery of a small 'door' at the end of the southern star-shaft of the Queen's Chamber in the Great Pyramid, Giza (see *The Orion Mystery* by Robert Bauval and Adrian Gilbert, 1994).

Figure 2.2 (page 12)

This picture seems to represent the end of the southern shaft in the Queen's Chamber of the Great Pyramid. In March 1993, Gantenbrink sent a small robot, UPUAUT 2, up this shaft and took a photograph of a little door at its end. It looks just like this.

The codes 'North, South, East and West' indicate that direction is important. However, the order of the names around the drawing indicates that these are not intended to be cardinal directions – they do not fit. Rather, I think, it draws attention to the orientation of the drawing itself. In fact this shaft faces south, and at one time it aligned on the culmination point of Sirius, the 'Arrow Star'.

Bauval and I believe there may be a secret chamber behind this door and that it could conceal something of great interest. Meanwhile, its discovery and the way it has been announced to the world caused great offence to the Egyptians. They have closed the chamber and forbidden Gantenbrink to carry on his exploration or to open the door.

Figure 2.3 (page 13)

This picture shows the pyramids of Giza and a curved line for the horizon. A line runs from the central pyramid to the one on the left, and then up to some stars. These lines are labelled 'Light'. Rising over the curved horizon are various stars and star groups, some connected by lines and others on their own. There is a caption: 'When the two are in line we will be ready.' Where the stars are rising is labelled 'North', whilst where some more stars are 'rising' (?) on the right of the picture is labelled 'East'.

Now, to make some sense of this one needs to know certain things. The first is that around the summer solstice the sun rises at its most northerly point on the horizon. At Giza this corresponds to a line which runs through certain satellite pyramids to the pyramid of Chephren (the central one of the three large pyramids). This, I believe, is what is being hinted at with the labels 'Light' on the lines. They are saying: 'This will occur around the summer solstice.'

The pattern can be elaborated further when it is realized that the figure on the right is not really rising in the east but in the north. The picture has somehow got itself mirror-imaged. It then becomes clear that the left-hand constellation of stars is Orion, and the right-hand one (which really should be to the left of the first) is Ursa Major, the Great Bear.

Rising above Orion are four stars (or planets) divided into a group of three, with one below.

The entire configuration of planets and stars in fact occurs at Giza on 1 July 1996. On this day, at sunrise, Orion will come over the eastern horizon with a line of Mars, Venus and the star Aldebaran (in Taurus) above it. Below them and to the right of Orion will be Mercury – three and one. In the north, the Great Bear constellation will be rising, with the star Dubhe over the horizon. It is important to realize that at the latitude of Giza, not all of the Great Bear is circumpolar – some of it sets below the horizon.

Figure 2.4 (page 14)

This picture shows the sky at Giza. It seems to show three constellations linked by lines to an object on the horizon which Ann Walker has felt to be important. She has written: 'I feel it lights up the sky. Is it the moon or something else . . . ?'

Looking at the diagram I recognize three constellations, though not quite as we usually draw them. On the left is Cassiopeia, normally drawn as a 'W'. In the centre is the square, 'bucket' portion of the Little Bear (Ursa Minor). On the right, drawn as an arrow, is the Great Bear (Ursa Major). I believe the body rising over the horizon is indeed the moon. Below it is seen a symbol representing, I think, the sun below the horizon. This configuration fits best with the New Moon on 2 March 1995. On that day something is presumably to happen. Could it be the opening of Gantenbrink's door in the Great Pyramid?

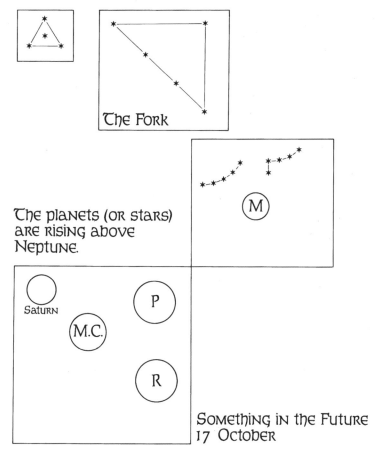

Figure Appendix.1 The trident of Neptune

Figure Appendix.1

Neptune is both a planet and the Roman god of the sea, whose weapon was a trident or three-pronged fork. It seems we are being directed to look for a fork shape of planets (or stars) rising out of Neptune.

The diagrams show a line of planets (or stars) with one out to the side. This theme is developed and made more concrete as the squares go on. The largest square shows a central circle with the captions 'M.C.'. I believe this to represent Mercury. Above it is a circle labelled Saturn and below it one marked either 'sun' or 'R', and to the side is a circle marked 'P'. This I believe represents Pluto.

Applying SKYGLOBE to the problem we find that there was such an arrangement on 4 December 1994. On this day, in the morning, the planets rose above Neptune in a three-pronged fork, with Mercury at its crossing-point.

What is also interesting is that as the day goes on, so the fork can be extended back to Saturn, and there comes a point where all the planets plus the sun and moon are above the horizon – a sort of meeting of the gods. This does not happen very often. On this day Ann Walker visited Adrian Gilbert in Dorset, to talk to him about the decoding of these diagrams!

Appendix 2: Philippine Reef and Rainforest Project

The Philippine Islands is one of the many areas of rainforest around the world that is under threat.

If tropical forests are the lungs of the earth Philippine Reef and Rainforest Project is a breath of fresh air.

The Philippine Reef and Rainforest Project (PRRP) isn't just sitting talking about saving tropical forests – it is actually doing it. With PRRP you can become a 'Founder Owner' of the tropical paradise island of Danjugan, one of the few islands in the area which still has its original tropical forests literally teeming with wildlife and surrounded by a beautiful coral reef which is in urgent need of protection. The PRRP gives everyone an opportunity to 'do their bit' to save the island from destruction by purchasing a Green Share in the island. It costs as little as £25 – so it doesn't cost the earth to take positive action.

Phone (0)1986 874422 for a free information pack or write to: Philippine Reef and Rainforest Project, Blyth House, Bridge Street, Halesworth, Suffolk, IP19 8AB, UK, fax number (0)1986 874425, E-mail: jabwwlct@gn.apc.org.

Your local libraries and administrative centres house information and addresses for other organizations devoted to saving rainforests, like the one above. You can write to these groups with a donation or letter of support – both will help. Above all, contact your heads of state. These are the people whom the scientists report to and they are more than aware of the problem. These are also the people who at the moment have the power to influence and stop deforestation.

Please help me to help White Arrow by writing to the King, Queen, President or Prime Minister of your country. Below you will find addresses for points of contact in the United States of America. The USA has the power to do something now by cutting Third World debts and encouraging for some of them means of income other than the lethal but easy chopping down of a tree.

Mr Alan Greenspan
Chairman of The World Bank
1818 H. Street North West
Washington DC 20433

US Botanical Gardens
245 First Street South West
Washington DC 20024

President William Clinton
The White House
1600 Pennsylvania Avenue
Washington DC 20500

We have to work to save the great rainforests of the world.

Our dead never forget the beautiful world that gave them being.
They still love its winding rivers, its great mountains and its seques-
tered vales.

Chief Seattle's speech to George Washington 1854

Please do whatever you can, wherever you are in the world. Help me to
help White Arrow to help us to help ourselves. Deforestation of the
earth's surface must be stopped. WE HAVE TO SAVE THE TREES.